The Occult Philosophy in the Elizabethan Age

'She has raised questions which will occupy scholars for decades to come.... It is a very great book. A crowning achievement, one might say.'

Christopher Hill

'Among those who have explored the intellectual world of the sixteenth century, no one can rival Frances Yates. Wherever she looks, she illuminates.... No one has done more than she to recreate, from unexpected material, the intellectual life of past ages.'

Hugh Trevor-Roper

Routledge Classics includes

Theodor Adorno

Martin Buber

Jonathan Culler

Jacques Derrida

Émile Durkheim

Terry Eagleton

Albert Einstein

Marc Ferro

Michel Foucault

Sigmund Freud

Erich Fromm

F.A. Hayek

Christopher Hill

Fredric Jameson

Carl Gustav Jung

Carl Kerényi

Frank Kermode

Jacques Lacan

Georges Lefebvre

Claude Lévi-Strauss

Konrad Lorenz

Alasdair MacIntyre

Marshall McLuhan

Bronislaw Malinowski

Marcel Mauss

Maurice Merleau-Ponty

Mary Midgley

Iris Murdoch

Eric Partridge

Jean Piaget

Karl Popper

Kathleen Raine

I.A. Richards

W.H.R. Rivers

Jean-Paul Sartre

Roger Scruton

Adrian Stokes

D.T. Suzuki

A.J.P. Taylor

Max Weber

Simone Weil

G. Wilson Knight

Ludwig Wittgenstein

Frances Yates

For a complete list of titles visit www.routledgeclassics.com

Frances
Yates

The Occult Philosophy
in the Elizabethan Age

London and New York

First published 1979
by Routledge & Kegan Paul
Reprinted as volume VII of
The Selected Works of Frances Yates 1999

First published in Routledge Classics 2001
by Routledge
11 New Fetter Lane, London EC4P 4EE
29 West 35th Street, New York, NY 10001

Reprinted 2001, 2003

Routledge is an imprint of the Taylor & Francis Group

Typeset in Joanna by RefineCatch Limited, Bungay, Suffolk
Printed and bound in Great Britain by
TJ International Ltd, Padstow, Cornwall

British Library Cataloguing in Publication Data
A catalogue record for this book is available from the British Library

Library of Congress Cataloging in Publication Data
A catalog record for this book has been applied for

ISBN 0–415–25409–4

CONTENTS

PART II The Occult Philosophy in the Elizabethan Age

PART III The Occult Philosophy and Rosicrucianism and Puritanism. The Return of the Jews to England

ILLUSTRATIONS

PLATES (*between pp. 116–17*)

FIGURE

PREFACE

This book has been difficult to write. It was necessary to find an order for the exposition, and, as soon as I began to work on it, about 1975, it became clear that there must be a first part on the history of Christian Cabala, as introduction to the study of the occult philosophy in the Elizabethan age. When this was achieved, the later parts of the book expanded in new directions, some of them quite unexpected by myself. The result is, I hope, a readable exposition of certain trends and movements hitherto quite unexplored in relation to the Elizabethan age, its philosophy, and its poetry. It is only a first attempt at tackling a problem which will take years of further work and thought to solve.

I began to write drafts for chapters of the book in 1975, continuing through 1976 to 1978. The oldest part of the book, that is to say the point on which I first began to work and think, is the chapter on George Chapman's *Shadow of Night* and the inspired melancholy, as depicted in Dürer's famous *Melencolia I* engraving. The thought that Dürer's imagery might help to solve the Chapman mystery came to me in 1949 when I was asked by Fritz Saxl to assist with the preparation of the new edition of *Saturn and Melancholy* by Klibansky, Saxl and Panofsky. In this way, I became familiar with the arguments and illustrations of this book long before it was published in 1964. Saxl suggested that I should write something on Elizabethan melancholy for inclusion in the book. This essay became much too long and detailed for incorporation in the book and it has remained in my files unpublished, though I used part of it as the basis of an (unpublished) lecture on 'Chapman and Melancholy' given in the symposium on Chapman organised by Donald Gordon at Reading University in 1952. Though very different from the argument on Dürer and Chapman developed in the present book, this early lecture, for me, links the present work with the period of my early Warburgian studies under the original members of the Warburg Institute, Saxl and his group. It is my hope that the new approach to Saturn and Melancholy through the Hermetic–Cabalist tradition which is attempted in this book may perhaps eventually help to connect the early Warburgian studies with those of later scholars connected with the Institute.

In January 1977 I gave a lecture to the Society for Italian Studies on 'Elizabethan Neoplatonism Reconsidered: Spenser and Francesco Giorgi'. This lecture was published by the Society for circulation among members only. With some alterations and revisions, it forms the basis of the chapter on 'Spenser's Neoplatonism and the Occult Philosophy: John Dee and *The Faerie Queene*'. I am indebted to the Secretary of the Society for permission to reprint it. Apart from this one chapter, the whole of this book is newly written. No other part of it has been printed elsewhere.

This book obviously owes a very great debt of gratitude to the work of Gershom Scholem, without which it could not have been written. The influence of the late Chaim Wirszubski was very important. There were useful discussions with Raphael

Loewe. David Goldstein made valuable corrections. Conversations which I had with Isaiah Schachar not long before his death, though not directly about my work, were subtly relevant. In the summer of 1976, Daniel Banes called and left with me his extraordinary edition of *The Merchant of Venice*, an event which I record here with gratitude.

My friends and colleagues of the Warburg Institute have, as always, been my support, but I want here to emphasise strongly that the responsibility for the book, and for its daring arguments, rests upon myself alone. Other friends to whom I am deeply grateful are Sheila McIlwraith who encouraged me in a dark hour and gave valuable advice about the revision of the typescript, and Joanna Harvey Ross whose support has enabled me to carry on in the face of considerable difficulties.

For assistance in assembling the material for the illustrations, I am indebted to Jennifer Montague and Elizabeth McGrath. For their kind permission to reproduce works of art and printed material in their collections I am indebted to the Librarian of the British Library; the Warburg Institute; the Deputy Keeper of the Department of Prints and Manuscripts, British Museum; the National Monuments Record; The National Gallery of Scotland; and the Curator of the Staatliche Kunsthalle, Karlsruhe. The Index was compiled by Oula Jones.

INTRODUCTION

This book must begin with the statement that, like all my other books, it is a strictly historical study. It is not an enquiry into 'the occult' in general, which I am certainly not qualified to undertake. It is about what was known as 'the occult philosophy' in the Renaissance. This philosophy, or outlook, was compounded of Hermeticism as revived by Marsilio Ficino, to which Pico della Mirandola added a Christianised version of Jewish Cabala. These two trends, associated together, form what I call 'the occult philosophy', which was the title which Henry Cornelius Agrippa gave to his highly influential handbook on the subject.

There has been a tendency in modern studies to concentrate on the Hermetic side of the occult philosophy, a tendency to which I may myself have contributed in my other books. Yet I have always insisted that the philosophy, or the movement, should be called 'Hermetic–Cabalist', not solely 'Hermetic', and I devoted a chapter in my book *Giordano Bruno and the Hermetic Tradition* to an attempt to expound Pico's addition of Jewish Cabala, in a Christianised form, to Ficino's Hermeticism. The

Cabalist side is fundamental because it was in touch throughout the period with the living tradition of Jewish Cabala, and, through its Christianisation, it exercised a most powerful influence on the history of religion. If I were to try to formulate my intention in the present book in a title I would have to fabricate a phrase like 'The Hermetic Philosophy in the Elizabethan Age particularly in its relation to Christian Cabala'. Obviously this would be impossibly clumsy, yet the unfolding of the argument will show that it is 'the occult philosophy' on its Christian Cabalist side, or as Christian Cabala, with which I am particularly concerned. I hope that I may be forgiven for attempting a subject so difficult, and one for which I do not have the complete qualifications, for I am not a Hebrew scholar.

The modern scholar who by his remarkable work initiated the serious study of the history of Cabala is Gershom Scholem whose great book, *Major Trends in Jewish Mysticism*, first published in English in 1941, revealed to the world the extraordinary wealth and importance of this neglected area of the history of thought and religion. All modern accounts of Cabala or references to it, including those in the present book, are based on Scholem's work which is one of the outstanding scholarly achievements of our age. Scholem's work has hardly yet been integrated into general history. It remains a specialist study of a Jewish tradition by a first-class Hebrew scholar; yet it should also be a revelation for all historians.

What is Cabala? The word means 'tradition'. It was believed that when God gave the Law to Moses he gave also a second revelation as to the secret meaning of the Law. This esoteric tradition was said to have been passed down the ages orally by initiates. It was a mysticism and a cult but rooted in the text of the Scriptures, in the Hebrew language, the holy language in which God had spoken to man. Out of Cabalist studies of the Hebrew text there developed a theosophical mystique, nourished on elaborate search for hidden meanings in the Scriptures, and on elaborate manipulation of the Hebrew alphabet. Cabala was basically a method of religious contemplation which could, rather easily, pass into a kind of religious magic, though such a use of it was actually a degradation of its higher purposes.

Scholem has shown how Cabala developed in the Middle Ages in Spain as a theosophical system based on the 'Sephiroth', intermediaries or emanations of the divine, and using techniques for manipulating the letters of the Hebrew alphabet for purposes of mystical contemplation. In lucid and powerful analyses, Scholem has given the non-Hebraist some idea of the main systems of Spanish Cabala and of its literature, of which the famous Zohar was only one item, and of the main scholars influential in the stages of its historical development.

In 1492 that development was interrupted by a vast historical tragedy, the expulsion of the Jews from Spain. The centres of Jewish life and culture, forcibly expelled from their main medieval home in Spain, moved with the exiles to other lands, to Italy, France, Germany, Turkey; some came to England in the reign of Henry VII. With them went the Cabala in forms intensified by suffering and exile.

Christian Cabala was founded by Pico della Mirandola in Florence, shortly before the Expulsion of 1492. He learned the techniques from Spanish Jews but interpreted them in a Christian direction, for he believed that Cabala confirmed the truth of Christianity. Moreover, in associating Cabala with Hermeticism, he introduced Hermetic magic into the system. 'Christian Cabala' thus differs basically from Jewish Cabala in its Christian use of Cabalist techniques and in its amalgamation of Hermeticism and Hermetic magic into the system. Yet there were basic affinities between the Hebrew type of gnosis, supposedly descending from Moses, and the Hermetic gnosis supposedly descending from its Egyptian founder, Hermes Trismegistus.

The pioneer book on Christian Cabala was that by J. L. Blau, *The Christian Interpretation of the Cabala in the Renaissance* (1944). The

French scholar, François Secret, has accumulated a very large volume of research on documents of Christian Cabala, and in his book *Les Kabbalistes Chrétiens de la Renaissance* (1964) he brings together a wealth of material which impresses on the reader the tremendous ramifications of this subject, how little it has been explored, and how fundamental it is for any deep understanding of the Renaissance.

Certainly it is fundamental for the so-called Neoplatonism of the Renaissance, the movement inaugurated in the Medici circle in Florence by Marsilio Ficino and Pico della Mirandola in the late fifteenth century. Through the infiltration of Spanish Cabala into this circle, it is possible to see in Pico the pioneer figure in the gradual integration of modern Jewish influences into European culture which was intensified by the Expulsion.

The magical side of the Hermetic-Cabalist core of Renaissance Neoplatonism, and its influence on the Renaissance conception of man as magus, has been explored in modern scholarship. The Cabalist side gave powerful support to the whole movement. Through the intensive cult of angels, Cabala reaches up into religious spheres and cannot be avoided in approaches to the history of religion. The enthusiasm for Cabala and for its revelations of new spiritual depths in the Scriptures was one of the factors leading towards Reformation. Christian Cabala may be said to belong to Renaissance studies through its integration with Neoplatonism, and it belongs to Reformation studies through its influence on Reformation movements, both Protestant and Catholic.

Moreover, this was the side of Renaissance Neoplatonism which developed and expanded most strikingly after the time of Ficino and Pico. Probably through the influence of exiled Jews of the Expulsion, the interest in Cabala increased enormously in the later years of the fifteenth century and throughout the sixteenth century. The Cabalist influence on Renaissance Neoplatonism increased accordingly, and tended to affect the movement in a more intensively religious direction, and more particularly in the direction of the idea of religious reform.

If one were to look for Renaissance Neoplatonism at its most intense one would find it in the *De arte cabalistica* of Johannes Reuchlin published in 1517. Reuchlin had acquired his interest in Cabala in Italy and was a disciple of Pico. His first Cabalistic work was his *De verbo mirifico* (1494). His *De arte cabalistica* is the first systematic treatise on the subject by a non-Jew, and it is by a German. Cabala has moved to the north, and is beginning its connection with the German Reformation. And, within its predominantly Cabalist framework, Reuchlin's book is also Renaissance Neoplatonism, full of quotations from Plato and the Neoplatonists, and from Ficino, imbued also with 'Hermes Trismegistus' and *prisca theologia*. Renaissance Neoplatonism takes a new turn with Reuchlin, a turn towards reformation and the north, and with greatly increased emphasis on Cabala.

In Italy, Cabala was fervently adopted by enthusiasts for Catholic reform, for example by the Hebrew scholar, Cardinal Egidius of Viterbo. One of the most famous of the Italian Cabalists was Francesco Giorgi, the Franciscan friar, who was imbued with Renaissance Neoplatonism and all its Hermetic adjuncts, and above all with Christian Cabala, re-enforced by Franciscan mysticism. The attractive figure of the Cabalist Friar of Venice presents the tradition in a new aspect. Though Giorgi would not have existed without Ficino and Pico, yet he is very different from them and belongs definitely to a later age.

And the gentle Franciscan friar may seem very different from his contemporary, Henry Cornelius Agrippa, by whom the magical side was so much emphasised. Yet the angelic thought-structure within which Agrippa operates is really the same as that which supports Giorgi's mysticism, and Agrippa, too, can be called a Renaissance Neoplatonist, and a Christian Cabalist deeply interested in religious reform. In the later sixteenth-century reaction against Renaissance occultism and its reforming sympathies, Agrippa was to become the scapegoat of the whole movement, hounded as a black magician.

The student of the influence of Renaissance Neoplatonism at a time, say, in the late sixteenth century, or more than a hundred years after the original Ficino–Pico movement, needs to take into account these later developments. He needs also to consider whether the country in which he is studying the movement was northern or southern and to what extent it was influenced by reformation. Take, for example, Elizabethan England. It would surely not be wise to assume that this northern country, in which a certain type of Reformation had been established, absorbed its Renaissance Neoplatonism direct from the original Ficino–Pico movement of a hundred years earlier, without taking into account what had happened to that movement in the century since its inception. Yet this is what, on the whole, has been done. There has been no consistent attempt at unravelling 'Elizabethan Neoplatonism' as a historical phenomenon.

So far as the history of thought is concerned, the Elizabethan age is still basically unexplained. At both ends it is mysterious, both in where it came from and what became of it. It cannot be explained as medieval survival, nor can it be explained in terms of 'Italian Renaissance'. Take, for example, the poet Edmund Spenser's 'Neoplatonism'. What is it exactly? The movement of the present book will be towards suggesting that it is Christian Cabalist Neoplatonism, adapted to the expression of a northern poetic reformation. And how was it that John Dee, the philosopher of the Elizabethan age, could base himself on Agrippa's occult angelology whilst at the same time believing himself to be the ardent supporter of a widespread Christian reform? The answer surely is that Dee believed himself to be, like Giorgi and Agrippa, a Christian Cabalist.

The present book which makes a rash attempt at exploring these problems will not be a perfect structure. It will be a temporary, even a makeshift, edifice, which later architects with better equipment will no doubt revise and alter. Nevertheless, even a temporary structure is better than no structure at all.

The plan of the book is roughly as follows.

The first part is an abbreviated and superficial history of the occult philosophy, using only a few key figures. I begin with Ramon Lull as an example of Christian Cabala in Spain before the Expulsion. Then I travel from Pico della Mirandola to Reuchlin, Giorgi, Agrippa, and Dürer; the first part ends with some account of the reactions against Renaissance occult philosophy. The second part is on the Elizabethan age in which the reader will have been prepared (I hope) to see connections with the general history in the first part. I have already mentioned the alarming idea of interpreting Spenser's Neoplatonism as really Hermetic-Cabalist Neoplatonism. Another alarming feature will be the approach to Marlowe's *Faustus* as the reflection of the contemporary witch-hunts against Agrippa. And Chapman's *Shadow of Night* will be seen as a Düreresque vision of inspired melancholy, based on Agrippa, and, in a sense, a reply to Marlowe's terrors. Through these and other studies the Elizabethan age may begin to appear as profoundly influenced by the later movements of the occult philosophy, now threatened by the terrible witch-hunting of the repression. We are not in happy days when Christian Cabala seemed the solution of all religious problems, but in the age of the witch-hunts in which the Renaissance perished amid the nervous breakdowns of a Faust, a Hamlet, or a Lear.

The last chapters attempt to connect Elizabethan occult philosophy with Rosicrucianism, with Puritanism, and with the preparation for the return of the Jews to England.

Part I

The Occult Philosophy in
Renaissance and Reformation

1

MEDIEVAL CHRISTIAN CABALA: THE ART OF RAMON LULL

In the illustration shown in Plate 1,[1] four men are seen sitting under a neat row of trees, neatly labelled. In the background is a rich countryside: in the foreground a refreshing stream flows from a fountain. The illustration is taken from an engraving in the eighteenth-century edition of the works of Ramon Lull, which is based on medieval tradition of Lull illustration. The lady whose horse wades in the stream is Intelligence; severe intellectual work is going on. The men so calmly seated in these pleasant surroundings are doing the Lullian Art.

In the lifetime of the Catalan philosopher and mystic, Ramon Lull (1232–c. 1316), the Iberian peninsula was the home of three great religious and philosophical traditions. Dominant was Christianity and the Catholic Church, but a large part of the country was still under the rule of the Moslem Arabs; and it was in Spain that the Jews of the Middle Ages had their strongest centre. In the world of Ramon Lull, the brilliant civilisation of the Spanish Moslems, with its mysticism, philosophy, art, and science, was close at hand; the Spanish Jews had intensively developed their philosophy, their science and medicine, and their mysticism, or Cabala. To Lull, the Catholic Christian, occurred the generous idea that an Art, based on principles which all three religious traditions held in common, would serve to bind all three together on a common philosophical, scientific, and mystical basis. The men under the trees in the picture represent a Gentile or pagan; a Jew; a Saracen or Moslem; and a Christian. The representatives of the three religions have been found by the Gentile doing the Lullian Art together, and perceiving their unity in the fountain of life or mystical truth.

The scientific principle held in common by Christians, Moslems, and Jews, and on which Lull based his Art, was the theory of the elements.[2] It is unnecessary to enter here into the historical origins of the elemental theory which was held by scientific men in Lull's period as a universally valid assumption about nature. The theory assumed that everything in the natural world is composed of four elements—earth, water, air, fire. To these corresponded the elemental qualities—cold, moist, dry, hot. These formed different compounds, or different concords and contrasts, which could be exactly classified or graded. The elemental theory had its prolongation into the world of the stars, for the seven planets and the twelve signs of the zodiac were held to have either predominantly cold, moist, dry, or hot influences. Though these elemental characteristics of the stars, and their connection with terrestrial elements, were derived from the teachings of astrology, the elemental theory was not in itself astrological, but might more properly be called an astral science.

The use of the Lullian Art as astral science can be studied in Lull's *Tractatus de astronomia* (1297) in which he works out a theory and practice of astral medicine through calculating, by the Art, the grading of elemental qualities. This treatise is preceded by a diatribe 'against astrology', from which Lull scholars of the past used to deduce (without reading the treatise) that Lull had discarded the astrological world view. Careful reading of the treatise reveals that it describes an astral medicine, based on belief in elemental qualities in the seven planets and the twelve signs, and their connection with terrestrial elements. This is a scientific use of a universally held theory of astral correspondences. It is not astrology in the sense of horoscope-making with its assumption of astrological determinism which Lull is 'against'. In fact it is a kind of scientific escape from such determinism. In almost exactly the same way, two hundred years later, Pico della Mirandola was to pronounce himself 'against astrology',[3] meaning that he was against astrological determinism whilst accepting those astral correspondences which underlie 'Renaissance Neoplatonism' as he and Ficino understood it.

The religious principle upon which Lull based his Art which was held by all three religious traditions, was the importance which Christian, Moslem, and Jew attached to the Divine Names or Attributes. The Attributes, or, as Lull prefers to call them, the Dignities of God on which the Art is based are *Bonitos* (Goodness), *Magnitudo* (Greatness), *Eternitas* (Eternity), *Potestas* (Power), *Sapientia* (Wisdom), *Voluntas* (Will), *Virtus* (Virtue or Strength), *Veritas* (Truth), *Gloria* (Glory). Religious Moslems, Jews, Christians, would all agree that God is good, great, eternal, powerful, wise, and so on. These Divine Dignities or Names, combined with elemental theory, gave Lull what he believed to be a universal religious and scientific basis for an Art so infallible that it could work on all levels of creation. And further – and this was its chief importance in Lull's eyes – it was an Art which could prove the truth of the Christian Trinity to Moslems and Jews.

An extraordinary feature of Lullism is that it assigns a letter-notation to notions so exalted and abstract as the names, attributes, or dignities of God. The series of nine dignities, *Bonitas, Magnitudo*, and so on, listed above, become in the Art the nine letters BCDEFGHIK; the unmentioned A is the ineffable absolute. These letters Lull places on revolving concentric wheels, thus obtaining all possible combinations of them. And since the Goodness, Greatness, and so on of God are manifest on all levels of creation, he can ascend and descend with the figures of the Art throughout the universe, finding B to K and their relationships on every level. He finds them in the supercelestial sphere, on the level of the angels; in the celestial sphere, on the level of the stars; in man, on the human level; and below man, in animals, plants, and all the material creation. On these levels, the elemental theory comes into play; ABCD as the four elements works in conjunction with BCDEFGHIK. This relationship continues right up the ladder of creation to the stars, since there are forms of the elements in the stars. Above the stars, in the angelic sphere, the system is purified of all materiality; there are no contrasts and contraries as in the lower spheres; at this height all the contraries coincide, and the whole Art is seen to converge in proof that the highest divine essence is a Three.

This bald outline, though it may give some idea of the Art, is highly misleading in its simplicity. For the Art in its workings is immensely complex. It may have forms based on more than nine dignities. Its combinations of letter-notations almost suggest a kind of algebra. There is a kind of geometry involved, for the Art uses three figures, the triangle, the circle, and the square. The artist in moving up and down the levels of creation applies these figures on each level. The geometry is symbolical; the triangle symbolises the divine; the circle stands for the heavens (by which Lull always means the seven planets and the twelve signs of the zodiac); the square symbolises the four elements.

The Aristotelian categories play a part in the Art which is said to work by a 'natural' logic, but the dominant philosophy is a kind of Platonism. Lull belongs into the tradition of medieval Christian Platonism, based primarily on Augustine; the Lullian dignities can nearly all be found listed as divine attributes in Augustine's works. Like all medieval Platonists, Lull is also strongly influenced by the work on the celestial hierarchies of angels by Pseudo-Dionysius. The nearest parallel to his association of dignities or attributes with the elements is to be found in the *De divisione naturae* of the early Christian Platonist, John Scotus Erigena.[4] Lull's dignities have the creative capacity of Scotus's primordial causes. Moslem forms of Platonic, or Neoplatonic, mysticism had also reached him. Yet perhaps the strongest influence on the formation of the Art was that of the Jewish Cabala.

It was in medieval Spain that Cabala reached a high point of development,[5] and that climax coincides with the appearance of Lullism. The Zohar was written in Spain in about 1275. It was in 1274 that Lull had the vision on Mount Randa in which the two primary figures of the Art were revealed to him. There are many points of contact or resemblance between Cabalism and Lullism.

Spanish Cabala has as its bases the doctrine of the ten Sephiroth and the doctrine of the twenty-two letters of the Hebrew alphabet. The Sephiroth, as defined by G. Scholem, are 'the ten names most common to God and in their entirety they form his one great Name'.[6] The Sephiroth derive from the nameless 'en-soph'; their names are *Gloria, Sapientia, Veritas, Bonitas, Potestas, Virtus, Eternitas, Splendor, Fundamentum*. The parallel with the nine Lullian *Dignitates Dei* derived from a nameless A is striking.

The twenty-two letters of the Hebrew alphabet also contain, for the Cabalist, the Name or Names, of God. They are the creative language of God and in contemplating them the Cabalist is contemplating both God himself and his creation. The thirteenth-century Spanish Jew, Abraham Abulafia,[7] developed a complex technique of meditation through combining Hebrew letters in endless series of permutations and combinations.

Thus the two salient characteristics of the Lullian Art, its basis in the Names or Dignities, and its techniques of letter combination, are both also characteristics of Cabala. Yet there are profound differences, above all the basic fact that the Names in

Cabala are in Hebrew, the letters which it combines are Hebrew letters; in the Lullian Art the Names are in Latin and the letters it combines are the ordinary letters of the Latin alphabet. Lullism may be said to be a Cabalist type of method but used without Hebrew. It is thus debarred from those insights into the linguistic mysteries which the Cabalist believed to be hidden in the Hebrew Scriptures.

Nevertheless, if it is possible to speak of a Christian Cabalist method used without Hebrew, then it may be claimed that Lullism is the medieval form of Christian Cabala.[8] Certainly it is like later Christian Cabala in its missionary aim, its aim of proving the Trinity to Moslems and Jews and thereby converting them to Christianity.

The rigorous method of the Lullian Art is deployed against a background suffused in poetic and romantic charm, the world of medieval Spain. The Lullian hermit wanders through allegorical forests,[9] the trees of which symbolise all the subjects of the Art, neatly categorised and arranged for the Lullist to use in his operations. These operations have not only scientific but also moral value through the use of analogy and allegory which permeates the Art. Thus the concords and contrasts of the elements are allegorised on the 'moral' trees of the Art as concords and contrasts between virtues and vices. The Lullian artist as Lull saw him had not only mastered a universal science; he had learned an ethical and contemplative method through which he might mount on the ladder of creation to the highest heights. Not only that, he was also a poet singing mystical love songs with all the charm of a troubadour; and a knight instructed in astral science and ethics in relation to the code of chivalry.[10]

As the inventor of a method which was to have an immense influence throughout Europe for centuries, Lull is an extremely important figure. Lullism is a precursor of scientific method. Lullian astral medicine developed into Pseudo-Lullian alchemy.

The great figures of Renaissance Neoplatonism include Lullism in their interests, and naturally so since Lullism was the precursor of their ways of thinking.

And from the point of view of history of religion and of religious toleration, surely we admire Lull's vision in taking advantage of the unique concentration of Christian, Moslem, and Jewish traditions in his world for putting forward a common ground between them in an Art, which, though it envisaged conversion rather than toleration, was certainly, in its efforts at understanding, vastly superior to the methods to be used later in Spain for the establishment of religious unity.

The glorious reign of Ferdinand and Isabella (1474–1504) saw the union of the kingdoms of Aragon and Castile through their marriage, and the rapid advance in power of the unified kingdom through their energetic government. Determined on establishing total religious unity within the Iberian peninsula, the two Catholic sovereigns initiated the war against the Moors which ended triumphantly with the conquest of Granada in 1492. In the same year, 1492, the Jews were expelled from Spain; in 1505 the conquered Moors were also expelled. Thus two whole populations, embodying two great civilisations, were cut adrift from their homeland to wander as exiles. Through the tightening up of the Inquisition in Spain, particularly severe against Jews and Moors, return to what had been their native land for so many centuries was impossible. Spain, like France after the Revocation of the Edict of Nantes, became and remained 'toute Catholique'.

Thus, as so often, Europe took a wrong turning and wasted the spiritual resources which might have been used constructively. For of all the countries of Europe, Spain was the best placed for making a liberal approach to the three great closely related religions. Ramon Lull had realised this in his peculiar way when he strove to construct a method based on Divine Names and elemental theory. Though, for him, the Art was not a construction but a revelation from on high shown to him in the vision on Mount Randa.

The old view of the origins of the so-called Renaissance held that the fall of Constantinople to the Turks in 1453 was a starting-point. Recent generations of scholars have weakened that view, through exploration of many other influences and particularly through demonstrating the importance of surviving medieval traditions in the so-called Renaissance. Yet there remains a good deal to be said for the old view, for, after all, it was the Greek refugees from Byzantium who spread the knowledge of Greek in Europe; and it was from Byzantium that the Greek manuscripts of works of Plato and the Neoplatonists, and of 'Hermes Tris-megistus' and other *prisci theologi*, reached Florence to form that rich and confused strain of 'Renaissance Neoplatonism' with its Hermetic core which we associate with Marsilio Ficino.

Another date which has not been so much stressed but which is equally, perhaps more, important, is 1492, the date of the expulsion of the Jews from Spain. Many of them went to Italy and spread there a new interest in the Hebrew language and an enthusiasm for the Jewish mystical tradition, or Cabala. This came to the mystically-minded as a new insight into the meaning of Christianity. Christian Cabala was founded by Ficino's friend and associate Pico della Mirandola.

It was in 1486 that Pico went to Rome with his nine hundred theses, prominent among which were the Cabalist theses. The Cabalist theses were fundamental for Pico's great aim of the concordance of all religious philosophies. Pico's advocacy of Christian Cabala marked a turning-point in the history of the Judaeo-Christian tradition in its modern form. It came at the same time as one of its darkest tragedies. It was in the years immediately before the Expulsion, when the persecutions of the Jews in Spain were mounting in intensity, that Pico della Mirandola adopted Christian Cabala into the Italian Renaissance.

2

THE OCCULT PHILOSOPHY IN THE ITALIAN RENAISSANCE: PICO DELLA MIRANDOLA

Giovanni Pico della Mirandola (1463–94) belonged to the brilliant circle around the Medici court in Florence which included another famous philosopher, Marsilio Ficino. Ficino and Pico were founders and propagators of the movement loosely known as Renaissance Neoplatonism. This movement was stimulated by the works of Plato and the Neoplatonists newly revealed to the West through the Greek manuscripts brought to Florence from Byzantium after the fall of Constantinople. Renaissance Neoplatonism was a rich amalgam of genuinely Platonic teachings with Neoplatonism and with other late antique philosophical occultisms. Prominent among the texts of this type which attracted Pico and Ficino was the *Corpus Hermeticum*, supposedly by 'Hermes Trismegistus', a mythical Egyptian sage whom the Florentines believed to represent an ancient wisdom which was the remote source of Plato himself.[1] 'Hermes Trismegistus' was believed to have lived at about the same time as Moses, or even before Moses, hence the Hermetic texts had a sanctity almost equal to that of Genesis, supposedly written by Moses.

Into this atmosphere of Florentine Neoplatonism, with its Hermetic core, it was not difficult to assimilate Cabala,[2] which was believed to be an ancient wisdom tradition descending from Moses, and which in fact, has gnostic elements which the Renaissance scholar could assimilate to the Hermetic type of gnosticism.

Marsilio Ficino does not use Cabala or Cabalistic methods in his Neoplatonic theology, philosophy, or magic. It was Pico who introduced Cabala into the Renaissance synthesis. And, like Ramon Lull, it was as a Christian that Pico valued Cabala. He believed that the Hebrew texts and teachings could enlarge understanding of Christianity through their revelation of a current of Hebrew mysticism of such great antiquity and sanctity. More than that, Pico believed that Cabala could confirm the truth of Christianity. In this belief he was followed by the many schools of Christian Cabalists who were to succeed him, who all looked back to Pico della Mirandola as the founder or first great exponent of Christian Cabala.[3]

Though Ramon Lull had not used Hebrew in his Art, it is a striking fact that Pico della Mirandola recognised, and stated, that Lullism is a Cabalist method. When discussing the *ars combinandi* of the Spanish–Jewish Cabalist, Abraham Abulafia, Pico says that this is like the *ars Raymundi* that is, the Art of Ramon Lull.[4] Pico thus recognised Lull as a Cabalist and had no doubt understood Lull's use of his Art to demonstrate the truth of the Trinity. Pico had a yet more potent argument, based on Cabalist manipulation of letters and names, through which he believed it possible to prove that Jesus is the name of the Messiah.

Pico's account of Cabala is contained in the seventy-two Cabalist *Conclusions*[5] which he introduces as 'confirming the Christian religion from the foundations of Hebrew wisdom'.

These Cabalist Conclusions are brief statements, often no more than one sentence. They form part of the nine hundred theses which Pico took with him to Rome in 1486 and which he offered to prove in public debate to be all reconcilable with one another. Other Conclusions were on magic, drawn from Hermetic sources; others were from Platonic and Neoplatonic texts; from Orphic hymns and Chaldaean oracles; and from many other sources. The great debate never took place, though the nine hundred theses were published. Considerable orthodox disapproval was aroused by Pico's bold statements and in 1487 he published an apology for his views. Included in this apology was the Oration on the Dignity of Man with which the debate was to have opened.

This, then, is the setting of the Cabalist Conclusions. They formed part of the nine hundred theses in which Pico set forth his synthesis of all philosophies, which was the inspiration of the speech on the Dignity of Man, famous as the proclamation or manifesto of the Renaissance view of man and his position in the world.

Modern scholarship has familiarised students of the Renaissance with the fact that Renaissance Neoplatonism had a Hermetic, or magical, core, and that the Renaissance adoption of Cabala could also involve 'practical Cabala', a form of magic. The Renaissance magus, whose 'Dignity' is described in Pico's speech, is a lofty figure, endowed with powers of operating on the world. This side of Renaissance 'Magia' and 'Cabala' has been discussed by many scholars. What perhaps has still not been sufficiently emphasised or understood is the fact that this was also a religious movement, and that it was a movement believed to be compatible with Christianity. What made possible such an interpretation of a system of thought which included so many disparate elements was, above all, Christian Cabala.

As we have seen, the Hebrew Cabalists believed that their

teachings went right back to Moses through a secret doctrine which had been handed down through initiates. And since, for Pico, Cabala confirmed the truth of Christianity, he believed it to be a Hebrew–Christian source of ancient wisdom which corroborated not only Christianity, but the Gentile ancient wisdoms which he admired, particularly the writings of 'Hermes Trismegistus'. Thus Christian Cabala is really a key-stone in the edifice of Renaissance thought on its 'occult' side through which it has most important connections with the history of religion in the period.

The kind of Cabala which Pico expounds in his seventy-two Cabalist Conclusions is a simplified version of Spanish Cabala. This fact alone is sufficient to indicate that this powerful influence on the Italian thinkers came from Spanish Jews, and was brought about through the disturbances in Spain which uprooted Spanish Jewry and led to the Expulsion of 1492. Though Pico's Cabalist Conclusions were formulated by 1486, some years before the actual date of the Expulsion, there seems little doubt that his instructors were Spanish Jews. Chief among them was the mysterious character known as Flavius Mithridates who provided Pico with Cabalist manuscripts.[6] Pico certainly knew Hebrew fairly well, but would have been dependent on Jewish experts for interpreting these difficult sources. And it would seem that Flavius Mithridates encouraged Pico in the Christian interpretation of Cabala, even to the point of inserting into the texts interpolations of his own pointing in a Christian direction.[7] What can have been Flavius's motive in thus encouraging and directing Pico towards his momentous adoption of Cabala into Christianity, as he understood it, remains a problem, and one which awaits further investigation by the Hebrew experts.

Amongst the momentous Cabalist Conclusions in which Pico states his belief that Cabala confirms Christianity is the seventh Conclusion which affirms that:

> No Hebrew Cabalist can deny that the name IESU, if we interpret it on Cabalist principles, signifies the Son of God.

It is however in the fourteenth Cabalist Conclusion[8] that Pico states most clearly his argument that Cabala confirms the truth of Christianity. Briefly the argument is that the name 'Jesus' is the Tetragrammaton, the ineffable name Yahweh, the four-lettered (in Hebrew letters) name of God but with a medial S (sin) inserted. The meaning implied, and as expanded by later Christian Cabalists (notably by Reuchlin in the De verbo mirifico) (Plate 2) is that the S in the Name of Jesus makes audible the ineffable Name (composed only of vowel sounds) and signifies the Incarnation, the Word made flesh or made audible. This, to our minds, most strange argument was not new but had a patristic and medieval tradition behind it and can be found in the works of St Jerome and of Nicholas of Cusa.[9] But it was brought into great prominence by Pico in the Cabalist Conclusions and was firmly lodged in the later Christian Cabalist tradition descending from him. Depending on elaborate manipulations of the Hebrew alphabet, the argument seemed amazingly convincing to adepts in such studies and many Jews were converted on these lines. Since Cabala confirms the truth of Christianity, it followed for Pico and his followers that Cabalist methods and techniques of religious meditation can and should be adopted by Christians. Hence a door was opened for the acceptance by Christians of Cabalist occult philosophy.

As he explains in his Apology of 1487, Pico divides Cabala into two main branches (as did the Spanish Cabalists). One is the ars combinandi, the art of combining Hebrew letters, which Pico thought rather similar to the Art of Ramon Lull. The other is 'a way of capturing the powers of superior things', or the powers of spirits and angels.[10] Pico carefully warns that this kind of Cabala is good and holy, attaching itself to angels and to good and holy powers, and that it has nothing to do with bad practices through which demons and devils are attracted. If the Cabalist mystic is not himself holy and pure, he may run into spiritual dangers. This warning, and this fear, were always present to the Christian Cabalist who knew that in attempting to scale the heights he might fall into the depths.

Pico is basically a mystic, deeply attracted by the hope held out of communicating through Cabala with God and holy spirits. In the eleventh Cabalist Conclusion he describes a trance in which the soul is separated from the body and is communicating with God through the archangels. These operations of pure Cabala are done in the intellectual part of the soul and can be so intense as to result in the death of the body ('this kiss of death')[11]

Pico envisages a mystical ascent through the spheres of the universe to a mystical Nothing beyond them. In the forty-eighth Cabalist Conclusion he sets out the order of the Sephiroth of Cabala in their relation to spheres of the cosmos.[12] The names of the ten Sephiroth are listed, from 'Kether' to 'Malkuth', and opposite them are listed the ten spheres of the universe, from *primum mobile* through the seven planets, to the elements. This cosmic-theosophic system is the ladder through which mystical meditation leads the adept into profound intuitions as to the nature of God and the universe. The magical element in it derives from the power of the divine names; with them are associated names of angels. Pico does not actually list these with the Sephiroth, though he refers in other Cabalist Conclusions to invoking Raphael, Gabriel, Michael. The invoking, or conjuring, of angels forms an intrinsic part of the system, difficult to define, on the borderline of religious contemplation and magic.

This inadequate sketch must suffice to indicate that Pico did in fact know something of Cabala, which was Christianised for him by his belief that Cabala proved that Jesus is the name of the Messiah.

Pico absorbs the Ficinian Neoplatonism, with its Hermetic

core, into his concordance of all religions and philosophies. In fact Pico associates the Hermetic magic with Cabala, for he states that no magical operation is of any value without Cabala.[13] In this way he believes that he both strengthens the Ficinian magic and makes it safe, protected from diabolical influences by holy powers.

Thus Christian Cabala lies at the heart of the Italian Renaissance on its occult side. For, as Scholem puts it when discussing Cabalistic principles and Platonic ideas, this current of Hebrew mysticism undoubtedly suited the spiritual temperament of the circle of Marsilio Ficino and Pico della Mirandola.[14]

The kind of Cabala which influenced Pico and which, in a Christianised form, he introduced into the Italian Renaissance, was Cabala as it had developed in Spain before and up to the time of the Expulsion. As Scholem has shown, after the Expulsion, a new type of Cabala developed, deeply intent on Messianic hopes and using the spiritual techniques more specifically in this direction than the Spanish Cabalists had done. The new type of Cabala is known as the Lurianic Cabala, through the name of its founder, Isaac Luria. Lurianic Cabala developed with ever-growing intensity throughout the sixteenth, and early seventeenth centuries, culminating in the messianic figure of Sabbatai Sevi,[15] after whose failure in 1665 it took other forms.

The movement of Christian Cabala founded by Pico was, of course, quite distinct from Jewish Cabala which was developing intensely throughout the years when Christian Cabala was influential, though there were points of contact between the two, particularly when Christian Cabalists tried to convert Jews, as often happened, and was indeed one of the main aims of Christian Cabala (as it had been of Lullism).

It is to be expected that the influence of Christian Cabala would be important for the history of religion, for it was, in effect, intrinsically bound up with the Judaeo–Christian tradition, an attempt by Christians to use sources of spiritual power newly discovered by them through their discovery of Cabala.

And an aspect of this story which seems not to have been sufficiently emphasised is that, through Pico's introduction of Christian Cabala, a contemporary and modern Jewish movement affected the development of the European mind and soul. This was surely something new, a significant emergence from the Middle Ages.

3

THE OCCULT PHILOSOPHY IN THE REFORMATION: JOHANNES REUCHLIN

Johannes Reuchlin[1] (1455–1522), also known by his humanist name of Capnion, was one of the greatest scholars of the German Renaissance, equally proficient in Latin, Greek, and Hebrew learning. As a young man he travelled in Italy. He tells Pope Leo X in the dedication of the *De arte cabalistica* how he had met Pico della Mirandola and his circle of learned men who were bringing ancient truth to light. It was certainly Pico's work which inspired Reuchlin, and he came to Italy to learn Hebrew and to profit from the wealth of Hebrew literature now circulating in Italy. Reuchlin's first Cabalist work, the *De verbo mirifico*, was published in Germany in 1494, two years after the Expulsion.

The work is in the form of a conversation between a Greek, Sidonius; a Jew, Baruchias; and a Christian, Capnion, or Reuchlin himself. The Jew is characterised as of a sad countenance and placed under the sign of Saturn,[2] an allusion to Saturn as the star of the Jewish religion, and to melancholy as the Saturnian humour. He praises Cabala as a divine science which has come down by tradition among the Jews; and he praises the Hebrew language, in which God speaks to the angels, and in which the true name, or names, of God and of the angels are expressed. There are frequent mentions of Jerome. Jerome was the Hebrew expert among the Christian fathers and knew arguments associating the name of Jesus with the Tetragrammaton which were afterwards used by the Christian Cabalists.[3] He was a kind of patron saint of Cabalists and often appears, as here, in the literature of Christian Cabala.

Reuchlin quotes Pico's Cabalist Conclusions. He repeats the names of the Sephiroth in Hebrew, and shows great interest in the Hebrew names of angels, and how to summon them. In the third book, Capnion, the Christian, speaks and gives the Cabalist proof that Jesus is the name of the Messiah, being the Tetragrammaton with an S inserted (Plate 2).[4] Though the argument had been given by Pico, Reuchlin's little book on the Wonder-Working Word was a potent force in the spread of Christian Cabala.

In a recent article, Charles Zika emphasises that Reuchlin in his De verbo mirifico is deeply concerned with the 'wonder-working' power of Hebrew language as studied in Cabala, and wishes to increase the power of Renaissance philosophy through emphasis on its magical core, and particularly through emphasis on Cabala. Reuchlin belongs to the world of pre-Reform, the time immediately before the outbreak of the Reformation. In that time, scholastic philosophy seemed, to many serious persons, dead, barren, outworn, and irrelevant. The humanist cultural programme which Erasmians were putting in its place seemed insufficient to Reuchlin. For him, culture was not enough. He needed in place of scholasticism another philosophy, a philosophy which would not be empty but would have power. He found this in Neoplatonism with its core of operative magic. But he knew that many people feared operative magic as possibly diabolical. For him, Cabalist magic did away with this fear for it was concerned with holy forces, with angels, with the sacred names of God. The demonic powers of ancient magic were cleansed of evil, made safe through the angels who cast out demons. Hence (suggests Zika) the concentration on angel-summoning in Reuchlin's system.

This is an important observation, though it should be added that Pico in his Magical Conclusions had also emphasised that Magia must always be associated with Cabala in order to be both powerful and safe.[5] And Pico had argued that Christian Cabala, the corner-stone of which was that Cabala proved the divinity of Christ, had sanctified the system and made it possible for Christians to immerse themselves in Hermetic-Cabalist Neoplatonism as a religious philosophy.

In 1517, twenty-three years after the De verbo mirifico of 1494, Reuchlin published his second major Cabalistic work, the De arte cabalistica. In the interval between the two works many more Cabalistic texts than those known to Pico and to the early Reuchlin had become available, and new schools of Christian Cabala had grown up, particularly in Italy. François Secret points out that Reuchlin in the De arte cabalistica shows knowledge of numerous Cabalist works of which he had only known by hearsay, or not at all, in the De verbo mirifico.[6]

The De arte cabafistica is the first full treatise on Cabala by a non-Jew. It is written in Latin, though with many Hebrew quotations. It was the fullest exposition hitherto available to European scholars, outside the actual Jewish tradition, of Cabalist theory and practice, with examination of Hebrew letter-manipulations and other main Cabalist theories and techniques. Reuchlin devotes much attention to the Names, and particularly to the Name of Jesus as that of the Messiah. The De arte cabalistica was to become the bible of the Christian Cabalists.

Like the De verbo mirifico, the De arte cabalistica is in the form of a conversation between three speakers. The representative of Greek thought is now Philolaus, a Pythagorean. At an inn in Frankfurt he meets Marranus, a Moslem; and Simon ben Eliezer, a Cabalist. The presence of the Pythagorean as a speaker is significant for it brings out the importance of number. Pico in his Mathematical Conclusions had stated that 'By number a way may be had for the investigation and understanding of everything possible to be known.'[7] In his mind the Mathematical Conclusions supported the Cabalist Conclusions. The letters of the Hebrew alphabet have numerical values; the names of God and the names of angels can be expressed numerically. In its way, Cabala encouraged a numerological approach to the world (for the Hebrew alphabet was believed to contain the world being the creative word by which the world was made). Abraham Abulafia would translate into numbers his meditations on the combinations of Hebrew letters.[8] Cabala could transform into a kind of mystical mathematics. Hence the representative of Pythagoras has an important place in the dialogue De arte cabalistica, and Reuchlin was sometimes called 'Pythagoras Reborn'.[9]

Some years before the publication of the De arte cabalistica a fierce movement of antisemitism, instigated by a converted Jew called Johann Pfefferkorn, had broken out around Reuchlin. It was the usual kind of virulent attack on Jewish religion and character, directed particularly against the books of the Jews which it was proposed to confiscate and burn. The attack was not, ostensibly, primarily against Cabalist books, but against Hebrew prayer-books and Talmudic treatises.

Pfefferkorn's antisemitism is chiefly remembered because of the brilliant satire on monkish ignorance, intolerance, and immorality which it aroused. This was the famous collection of Epistolae obscurorum virorum[10] which appeared anonymously around 1516–17. The letters of the 'obscure men' violently attack Reuchlin and the Jews, but the imaginary authors, supposedly monks and scholastics, betray their vulgarity and ignorance in every line. Hence the attack was turned against the attackers, and this extremely clever satire covered the reactionaries with ridicule, protected Reuchlin, and helped to prevent the confiscation of the books of the Jews.

The *Letters of the Obscure Men* were written by German humanists. They showed that public opinion had now been educated to a point which made a reactionary antisemitic movement such as that initiated by Pfefferkorn appear ridiculous. And they have tremendous historical importance because they herald Luther. For it was in 1517 that Luther nailed his theses to the door of the church in Wittenberg and the German Reformation began.

In the *De arte cabalistica*, published when the attack on him was at its height, Reuchlin refers to his enemies. It is reasonable to suppose that Reuchlin's Christian Cabala and the importance which he attached to Cabalist literature of the Jews had no small share in arousing the wave of antisemitism led by Pfefferkorn. Moreover, some of the satire in the *Letters of the Obscure Men* makes it clear that Reuchlin's 'Gabala' was an object of the attack on him.

One of the obscure men enquires what 'Gabala' may mean.[11] He has heard that Johannes Reuchlin has written a book called 'Gabala' but he cannot find this word in any dictionary. The obscure man has discussed the theology of the book with some divines at a carouse at which they all drank deep (this is normal satire on the obscure men who are usually represented as fuddled as well as ignorant). The book, moreover, adds the obscure man, contains sayings of Pythagoras who was a necromancer, and necromancy is an unlawful art.

Here at the very beginning of the spread of Christian Cabala one can already detect the ominous sound of a nascent witch-hunt against it.

Reuchlin's controversy with Pfefferkorn became famous all over Europe.[12] Reuchlin was hailed as a hero of the New Learning, victimised by reactionaries. The importance of Cabala in

Pico della Mirandola's synthesis, the fame of which spread with Neoplatonism, showed that Christian Cabala was a most necessary element at the heart of the New Learning; and that the new Hebrew studies were as vital for the Renaissance scholar as the new Greek studies. Erasmus, hero of the Greek revival, is as much an object of fear to the obscure men in their profound ignorance – one of them asks what that book called 'New Testament' can be – as is Reuchlin and his 'Gabala'.

Reuchlin was famed both as a Greek scholar and as a Hebrew scholar; he represented the New Learning as it had spread in Germany. The attack on him was a reactionary attack on the New Learning. The reply to it was the satire of the *Letters of the Obscure Men* which foreshadowed Luther's attack on the reactionaries, which opened the Reformation.

Thus the Reuchlin case is involved with the beginnings of the Reformation, yet Reuchlin's stand is different from that of Luther. Reuchlin is a scholar, seeking, like Pico, a mystical synthesis of the religious problem. Luther is the blunt reformer, carrying an evangelical message to the people. Yet there was, as we have seen, a reform programme of a kind inherent in Christian Cabala for it aimed at substituting a more 'powerful' Christian philosophy for scholasticism. This was a difficult aim and difficult to define. It is still difficult to define. Perhaps that accounts for the neglect, until recent years, of the study of Christian Cabala as an important force behind Renaissance and Reformation.

4

THE CABALIST FRIAR OF VENICE: FRANCESCO GIORGI

Francesco Giorgi,[1] or Zorzi, of Venice (1466–1540) entered the Franciscan Order probably in early life, though there is little documentary evidence about his early years. His main published works were the *De harmonia mundi*,[2] first edition in 1525 (Plate 8), and the *Problemata*, 1536. These show clearly enough the influence upon him of the Florentine Neoplatonic movement. Giorgi's Cabalism, though primarily inspired by Pico, had been enriched by the new waves of Hebrew studies of which Venice, with its renowned Jewish community was an important centre. Giorgi's outlook, as compared with that of Ficino and Pico, has an added Christian intensity, through his Franciscan training. And, like Reuchlin, he can draw upon richer sources of Hebrew religious literature than were available to Pico. Cabalist writings had flooded into Venice and other parts of Italy through the expulsion of the Jews from Spain in 1492.

That Giorgi was a Christian Cabalist is a statement which means, not merely that he was influenced in a vague way by the

Cabalist literature, but that he believed that Cabala could prove, or rather had already proved, the truth of Christianity. As a Hebrew scholar he could follow the processes whereby the manipulation of Hebrew letters in the Name of God was believed to demonstrate that Jesus is the name of the Messiah (Plate 3).[3] To Giorgi this seemed a revelation of the utmost religious and Christian importance. And, like Pico, he could see the many connections and correspondences between the Hebrew gnostic system and the teachings of the supposed 'Hermes Trismegistus', which were also given a Christian interpretation. These influences were completely integrated into Giorgi's Neoplatonism in which was included the whole tradition of Pythagoro-Platonic numerology, of world and human harmony, even of Vitruvian theory of architecture,[4] which, for Giorgi, had a religious significance connected with the Temple of Solomon.[5]

With Giorgi we are in a stream of Cabalist influence contemporary with that which was inspiring Reuchlin and the German humanists. In Italy, the Christian Cabalist movement had as one of its outstanding figures Cardinal Egidius of Viterbo.[6] Collecting and studying the greatly increased range of Cabalist manuscripts now circulating in Italy, the Cardinal and the scholars connected with him were deeply interested in movements for religious reform. In these early years of the sixteenth century the Christian Cabalist was full of hope, believing that he held a new key to the mysteries of his religion.

Giorgi grafts the Cabalist influence onto the traditions of his order. He develops that correlation between Hebrew and Christian angelic systems, already present in Pico, to a high degree of intensity. For Giorgi, with his Franciscan optimism, the angels are close indeed, and Cabala has brought them closer. He accepts the connections between angelic hierarchies and planetary spheres, and rises up happily through the stars to the angels, hearing all the way those harmonies on each level of the creation imparted by the Creator to his universe, founded on number and numerical laws of proportion. The secret of Giorgi's universe was number, for it was built, so he believed, by its Architect as a perfectly proportioned Temple, in accordance with unalterable laws of cosmic geometry.

The Friar was attached to the Franciscan convent of San Francesco della Vigna in Venice, for which a new church was planned. The foundation stone had been laid in August 1534 when difference of opinion arose concerning the proportions of the plan. The Doge decreed that Francesco Giorgi should be consulted. Giorgi's memorandum concerning this plan is printed in Rudolf Wittkower's book, *Architectural Principles in the Age of Humanism*.[7]

Wittkower points out that Giorgi's plan for San Francesco della Vigna was the practical application of the harmonies of macrocosm and microcosm which he expounded in his *De harmonia mundi*. Three other people were consulted about the plan; a painter, Titian; an architect, Serlio; and a humanist, Fortunio Spira.

Giorgi's *De harmonia mundi* was not the work of a fantastic eccentric. It belonged to the centre of Renaissance thought at its most productive.

In addition to his researches into the harmony of the world, the Friar played a part in active life. As a member of the patrician family of Zorzi, he had contacts with Venetian government circles and was entrusted with missions of some delicacy, particularly at the time of the invasion of the peninsula by the Emperor Charles V, and the Sack of Rome in 1527.

At this time of crisis in the European situation, the King of England loomed up, demanding a divorce from his wife, Catherine of Aragon, the Emperor's aunt. It comes as something of a shock to the English reader, immersed in the abstruse Neoplatonic Cabalism of the *De harmonia mundi* of 1525, to learn that four years later the Friar of Venice was deep in business concerning the divorce of our King Henry, the affair which began the tale of Henry VIII and his wives and led to the English break with Rome.[8]

Towards the end of 1529, an Englishman, Richard Croke, came to Venice on a secret mission, which seems to have been the idea of Thomas Cranmer, future Archbishop of Canterbury. Cranmer proposed to the King that he should consult canonist lawyers and leading Jewish rabbis as to the legality of the proposed divorce. The advice of the rabbis was required because different views as to the legality of marriage with a brother's widow can be found in different books of the Old Testament. (It will be remembered that Henry questioned the legality of his marriage to Catherine on the ground that she was his brother's widow.) In Leviticus[9] marriage between a man and his brother's widow is prohibited. In Deuteronomy,[10] on the contrary, it is prescribed if the former union has been without issue. Which was the right view according to expert canonist opinion and in Jewish law? Richard Croke came to Venice to gather views about this, and he consulted the leading theologian of Venice, expert in Hebrew studies and in touch with Jewish scholars – Francesco Giorgi.

Giorgi enthusiastically assisted Croke, taking trouble to procure books and documents bearing on the case. The fact of this mission, and of the important part played by Giorgi in it, is well known. There are letters from Henry VIII himself thanking Giorgi for his valuable assistance. It is not quite obvious why 'the King's cause' attracted the Friar of Venice. Was it his zeal for religious unity which made him anxious to avoid a schism? Or was it the Venetian spirit of independence, cultivating a rapprochement with England as antidote to Hapsburg domination? Nor is it at all clear (to me at any rate) why Henry VIII's English advisers thought it important to send a mission to Venice to consult Venetian Jews, and Giorgi, the Cabalist theologian, about the divorce. This is all the more strange when one remembers that Jews were not allowed in England at that time.[11]

The very great influence of Giorgi's *De harmonia mundi* in Elizabethan England, which will be studied in later chapters, may have some distant historical root in Giorgi's support of Henry VIII's divorce. Queen Elizabeth I might have been favourably disposed towards the philosophy of Francesco Giorgi if she knew that the Friar of Venice had supported her father's divorce, to which she owed her own existence. Giorgi's work was in the library of John Dee, the philosopher of the Elizabethan age, and was, as will be suggested later, a powerful influence underlying the Elizabethan Renaissance.

The *De harmonia mundi* was also a strong influence in the French Renaissance. A French translation of Giorgi's immensely long work was published in 1578, with the title *L'Harmonie du monde*. The translator was one of the three La Boderie brothers, all Hebrew scholars and involved in the intense activity in Hebrew studies then going on in France.[12]

Giorgi's work is thus an extremely important channel for the transmission of Christian Cabala. Curiously enough, though the influence of Giorgi is to some extent recognised, the Cabalist side of his thought tends to be overlooked. Written in Latin (or in French in the French translation) modern readers tend to read it solely as a Platonist's version of universal harmony, ignoring the long Hebrew quotations and the importance of the Christian Cabalist arguments both for the author and for his contemporary readers.

An architect makes a plan or model of a building, says Guy Le Fèvre de la Boderie in the dedication to a friend of his translation of Giorgi's book,[13] which he says is the model of the universe. Thus the reader taking up this large French volume was immediately confronted with the Architect of the Universe. A discourse, added by Guy's brother Nicolas,[14] emphasises the importance of Giorgi's work for the understanding of the Scriptures. This book lifts us up to the highest, or anagogical, meaning of the Scriptures, revealing to us that Centre which is everywhere and its circumference nowhere, echoing the thought (ultimately Hermetic in origin)[15] associated with Nicholas of Cusa. He speaks of the Christian angelic hierarchies, emphasising their concordance with Cabalist angelic and sephirothic schemes. He speaks of the 'number, measure, and weight' governing the creation, and of the Temple of Solomon. Those who understand how to 'pythagorise' and 'philosophise' by mathematics, will, he says, understand the architectural allusion. He speaks of the Unity from which all things proceed by four ways, arithmetic, geometric, harmonic, and musical. He refers to Cabalist methods of meditation by Combination, Notericum, Gematria, and ends with a mystical disquisition on the body of Christ, and with a hymn by 'Mercurius Trismegistus', 'Let us praise the One and the All'.

A figure (Plate 4) accompanying this discourse illustrates numerical relationships between the three worlds, and gives numerical values of the Hebrew letters shown on it in an attempt at presenting in diagrammatic form the Cabalist–Hermetic Neoplatonism as taught by Francesco Giorgi.

The word One, or *Monas*, falls constantly from Giorgi's pen, usually accompanied by a cluster of names of the authorities from whom he derives this concept. As Vasoli puts it, Giorgi wishes to be the carrier of a wisdom capable of including Hermes Trismegistus, Orpheus, Francis of Assisi, Plato and the Cabalists, Plotinus and Augustine, in the common understanding of the *arcana mundi* and of the spiritual destiny of man in the return to the inaccessible One.[16]

The seeker after the *Monas* may retreat, he says, into negative theology and the *docta ignorantia*, or he may seek to follow the divine *Monas* in its expansion into the three worlds.[17]

The supercelestial world is the world of the intelligences or angels. In Giorgi's Christian Cabala, as already emphasised, the angelic hierarchies of Pseudo-Dionysius are connected with the Sephiroth of Cabala. These highest influences pour down through the stars, and by the stars Giorgi means the seven planets and the twelve signs of the zodiac. In Giorgi's system, as with Pico, the system is not astrological in the sense of judicial astrology in which man is conditioned by his horoscope, some of the influences in which might be bad, for example a bad influence of Saturn. In this system, as with Lull and Pico, all the celestial influences are good, and it is only a bad reception of them which can make them bad or unfortunate. There is thus free-will in the system, free-will to make a good, not a bad, use of the stars. The planets are linked to the angelic hierarchies and the Sephiroth. Thus the planetary influences pour down on man purified by the Christian angels and the Cabalist Sephiroth. Though all are equally good they are placed in a descending order of importance matched to the order of the hierarchies.[18]

Thus there are no bad or unfortunate planets. On the contrary, Saturn, unfortunate and bad in normal astrological theory is placed highest in the list. Being the outermost or highest planet in the cosmic order, he is nearest to the divine source of being and therefore associated with the loftiest contemplations. 'Saturnians' are not those poor and unfortunate characters of traditional astrology but inspired students and contemplators of highest truths.[19] They are placed with the Thrones, the next after the Cherubim of the angelic hierarchies. Similarly, Mars, notorious for his bad or angry influence, becomes force or strength of character and is placed with the hierarchy of the Virtues.

Ethically, this means that the virtues and vices take on an astral colouring. That is to say, the aptitudes associated with the planets will become virtues in the person who develops the influence in a good way; if he receives them in a bad way, they will be vices.[20]

In the third or elemental world the divine, angelic, and stellar influences percolate down into the terrestrial world, and govern the movements and combinations of the elements, all of which are in themselves good. The obvious affinities of this type of thought with the alchemical outlook are not specifically developed by Giorgi but are implied throughout his work.

The amalgam of Platonism, Hermeticism, Cabalism, astral cosmology and ethics is given a strongly Christian direction in the last book of the *De harmonia mundi* which presents an elaborate Christological doctrine, infused with Franciscan Christian mysticism, luxuriantly presented in terms of the allegories of the Song of Solomon. Giorgi's Cabalism is nowhere more apparent than in his Christianity, for he heavily emphasises those arguments through which Cabala was said to prove that Jesus is the name of the Messiah.[21] Giorgi has pages and pages on the Name, the Cabalist arguments about which were evidently extremely congenial to his ecstatic temperament.

One result of Christian Cabala is that in practice it tends towards evangelicalism. The Gospel story is proven, hence there can be intense concentration on it. In this way, Christian Cabala supports the simple Gospel narrative. Giorgi, in fact, recounts the life of Christ with intensive mystical concentration. Thus in a curious way Christian Cabala could support evangelical reform; there is even a kind of Erasmianism implicit in Giorgi's outlook.

Though moving in new directions, there is really nothing in Giorgi's Christian Cabala which is not already implicit in Pico. His intensive development of the system towards number is a continuation of Reuchlin. The effort to achieve a 'powerful' philosophy to accompany and interpret Christianity is the effort of Christian Cabala from the start. What is striking in Giorgi is his intensive development of a Franciscan temperament towards the Cabalist–Christian mystique. Above all, Giorgi has a poetic gift,[22] through which his exposé of his complex doctrines has a lyrical quality. Giorgi was a favourite Christian Cabalist with poets.

In 1536, eleven years after the publication of the *De harmonia mundi*, Giorgi published his *In Scripturam Sacram Problemata*. This work, though couched in a seemingly scholastic form, repeats all the arguments of the Harmony of the World, developing even more strongly the magical and esoteric implications of the earlier work. Giorgi now believes in an imminent fulfilment of prophecy to correct the evils of the age in which, instead of that *concordia* which Pico had promised, there was an increase of religious *discordia*. The three problems on invocation of Divine Names are highly magical, and Giorgi seems to think of miraculous and magical powers as ultimately the same.

The question of Giorgi and magic is a difficult one. In a sense, he is a Pichian magus, interpreting Pico's preaching on the Dignity of Man as the dignity of the religious man, or the saint. He provides material for the practice of both natural and Cabalist magic. He collects and lists the flowers, minerals, animals, and so on, associated with each planet, as used in natural magic. And he expounds the manipulation of Hebrew letters as used in Cabalist magic. Yet it is difficult to decide whether Giorgi was actually a practising magus, or rather a holy man of (so to speak) magical sanctity. The rule which the careful scholarship of D. P. Walker has laid down for testing the degree of magic in an author, namely to ask what was his attitude to the magical 'god-making' passage in the Hermetic *Asclepius*,[23] gives a rather indistinct answer in the case of Giorgi. He mentions the 'god-making' passage, and apparently with slight disapproval.[24] One feels that he is deprecating it but without dismissing it. On the whole, one is inclined to the conclusion that Giorgi is a kind of magician, though a very, very white one, very ascetic and holy, with the magical core of his teaching so wrapped in folds of Franciscan piety and mysticism that it would be hardly visible to an earnest follower who might well wonder whether this was the outlook of a miracle-working saint, rather than that of a magus.

Reuchlin had demanded a 'powerful' Christian philosophy, a 'wonder-working' Word. Such a philosophy implies magic, but

Reuchlin believed that a magical philosophy could be made safe, guarded from demonic dangers, by the use of Cabala. Giorgi takes such a philosophy a step further by concentrating so heavily on the Pseudo-Dionysian hierarchies of angels. If Christian angels guard the processes of the magus, surely he cannot go wrong, surely he will be an angelic, not a demonic, character. Yet Christian Cabala did not escape suspicion, and Giorgi's works were to be condemned, as we shall see.

The longest account of Giorgi and his works given by a modern scholar is that by Cesare Vasoli. At the end of his essay, Vasoli suggests a comparison with Rosicrucianism, citing the vast work on world and human harmony by Robert Fludd, the Rosicrucian, as perhaps a close parallel to Giorgi, though written a century later.[25] Certainly Fludd was heavily influenced by Giorgi[26] and the thought that the Giorgi type of Christian Cabala may be a source of Rosicrucianism is suggestive. It may be a suggestion which will turn out to be historically satisfying since, as we shall see, Giorgi's *De harmonia mundi* was a dominant philosophy in the Elizabethan age, and so likely to have been passed on, perhaps by subterranean routes, to Robert Fludd and the Jacobean age.

5

THE OCCULT PHILOSOPHY
AND MAGIC: HENRY
CORNELIUS AGRIPPA

The reputation of Henry Cornelius Agrippa (1486–1535) has
been a survival from the witch-hunts of the sixteenth and seventeenth centuries in which he figured prominently as a prince of
black magicians and sorcerers. The black magician of the ages of
superstition became, in enlightened times, the absurd charlatan
unworthy of serious attention. The same process occurred in the
case of John Dee with the same result, that a figure of great
historical importance disappeared in clouds of nineteenth-
century ridicule, from which the scholarship of the twentieth
century has slowly begun to rescue him. In the case of Agrippa,
his *De occulta philosophia* is now seen as the indispensable handbook of Renaissance 'Magia' and 'Cabala', combining the natural
magic of Ficino with the Cabalist magic of Pico in one conveni-
ent compendium, and, as such, playing a very important part in
the spread of Renaissance Neoplatonism with its magical core.[1]

Charles Nauert's book on Agrippa[2] has placed the study of his life and works on a scholarly footing, and the learned articles of Paola Zambelli[3] have added new and important material. The magician begins now to appear as something of an Erasmian evangelical, combining pre-Reformation humanism with an attempt to provide a 'powerful' philosophy to accompany evangelical reform. In this attempt, Agrippa was undoubtedly inspired by Reuchlin's Christian Cabala. In fact, Agrippa's *De occulta philosophia* can be classed as Christian Cabala for it leads up, in the third book on the supercelestial world, to the presentation of the Name of Jesus as now all-powerful,[4] containing all the power of the Tetragrammaton, 'as is confirmed by Hebrews and Cabalists skilled in the Divine Names'. He is quoting from Pico's Cabalist Conclusions. Christian Cabala is leading to a kind of evangelicalism, supported by the occult philosophy. His attempt to combine what he believes to be Erasmian evangelicalism[5] with a magically powerful philosophy makes of Agrippa a reformer of a strange and interesting kind.

The picture of Agrippa now emerging is thus strangely unlike the sorcerer with his black dog hunted in the witch-crazes, and serving later as the image of the nineteenth-century idea of the necromancer. In what follows I shall attempt to outline, though briefly and inadequately, Agrippa's life and work from the new points of view.

Agrippa's interest in the occult seems to date from his earliest years at Cologne;[6] he says that one of the first texts he studied on these subjects was the *Speculum* of Albertus Magnus, also a native of Cologne. The pattern of his life as a constant traveller, mysteriously in touch with groups of people in different places, is perceptible from the start. Nauert has suggested that he and his associates formed some kind of secret society.[7] Paola Zambelli is also of the opinion that he may have been the centre of secret societies.[8] Such affiliations are always difficult to prove; nevertheless the groups of people always ready to receive and support

Agrippa in his constant travels do suggest that there may have been some kind of organisation. The groups would seem to have been concerned with alchemy, and with the investigation of Hermetic, Neoplatonic and Cabalist literature. Quite early in his life, Agrippa is reported to have been lecturing on Reuchlin.[9]

In 1509–10, Agrippa was in Germany, visiting the learned abbot Trithemius, and it was at about this time that he wrote the first version of the *De occulta philosophia.*'[10] The manuscript of this version exists.[11] It is dedicated to Trithemius, who was undoubtedly an important influence on Agrippa's studies.

At this significant time in his career, when his ideas were already sufficiently formulated for him to be writing the first version of the *De occulta philosophia*, Agrippa's mysterious travels took him to England.

In 1510, in which year a dedication proves that Agrippa was in England,[12] Henry VIII had recently ascended the throne. Erasmus was in England, and the early humanist movement around Thomas More and John Colet was spreading. Agrippa was probably only in London for a few months; we do not know whether he met Erasmus there, but he was certainly in contact with John Colet, for we hear of him studying the Epistles of St Paul with Colet.[13] A link between Agrippa and Colet may well have been Cabala, in which Colet was certainly interested. The study of Pauline epistles with Colet, shows, according to Nauert, that Agrippa was early exposed to the Biblical Christianity which characterised Colet and the Erasmian reform movement generally. Nauert suggests that there was probably a direct connection between Agrippa's biblical studies in London and his enthusiasm for occult studies, with 'cabalistic exegetical methods serving as the link between them'.[14]

In about 1511, Agrippa went to Italy, thus gaining the Italian experience which was so important for the northern humanist. A few years earlier, in 1506–9, Erasmus had visited Italy for the first time, and it is interesting to compare the two visits.[15] When he went to Italy, Erasmus had been in full possession of Italian humanist scholarship and had been using it for years; on his Italian visit he saw it in action in its latest form in the Venetian circle of Aldus Manutius. Similarly, Agrippa on his first visit to Italy was in full possession of the Renaissance Magia and Cabala, stemming from Ficino and Pico, and had been using them for years. Yet the Italian visit was very important for Agrippa, as it was for Erasmus, and for the same reason, namely that he was able to meet and assimilate the tradition which he already knew, as it had been further developing in Italy. For Erasmus this was the tradition of classical scholarship, now personified in Aldus and the Aldine press. For Agrippa, it was the tradition of occult philosophy, as it had developed in Italy in recent years, that he was bent on assimilating during this visit.

Agrippa in Italy studied the Hermetic tradition and Cabala with scholars who regarded themselves as heirs of Ficino and Pico. He came in contact with Cardinal Egidius of Viterbo and with Agostino Ricci, a converted Jew, who were interested in the Catholic reform movement and were using the influences of Christian Cabala in that direction.[16] And Agrippa was also briefly in contact with Francesco Giorgi,[17] the Christian Cabalist Friar of Venice. All these Italian Cabalists were using Cabalist books and manuscripts now available in much larger quantities in Italy and being eagerly studied by scholars.

Thus the German Cabalist reformer made contact with Italian Christian Cabalists. Francesco Giorgi's ideas, though apparently less extreme than those of Agrippa, are actually pretty close to them, though softened by a gentler Italian colouring.

The never-stationary Agrippa next appears in the northern city of Metz where the growing influence of Luther was causing turmoil. As Nauert puts it, Agrippa in Metz has moved from the exciting and vital culture of Renaissance Italy to the exciting and vital culture of northern Europe on the eve of the Reformation.[18] Agrippa and his friends closely followed the writings of Luther.

Some of these friends afterwards became Lutheran Protestants. From Metz, Agrippa moved to Geneva where he had occultist friends. Some historians of the origins of Protestantism in Geneva have regarded Agrippa and his circle of the early 1520s 'as the seed-bed of the reformed faith'.[19]

In 1524, Agrippa went to France where he had many friends. Here he published, in 1526, one of his two famous books, the *De vanitate scientiarum*. This book argues that all man's knowledge is vain, all sciences empty, including the occult sciences. His other famous book, the *De occulta philosophia*, the handbook of Renaissance occult sciences, was already written in its first form, but was not published until 1533. Why Agrippa published first a book on the vanity of the sciences, including the occult sciences, whilst reserving for future publication his already written book on the occult sciences, is one of the many problems of his life and work.

In France[20] he had contacts with French doctors (he was versed in medicine), humanists, scientists, alchemists, Lullists (Lullism was one of his specialities) and the like. This world of early French humanism must have been congenial to Agrippa. Under strong Erasmian influence, the new learning was making great strides; ideas about religious reform were moving; and there were powerful Hermetic influences at work. The great French scholar and Hermeticist, Lefèvre d'Etaples, was in contact with Agrippa, and Rabelais mentions 'Herr Trippa'.[21]

In 1528 Agrippa was in Antwerp, getting his books printed, including the *De occulta philosophia* (1533), and a re-issue of the *De vanitate*. The publication of his books increased his fame. The imperial ambassador to the English court wrote to him that all learned men in London were praising his *De vanitate* and his *De occulta philosophia*, and urged him to take up the defence of Queen Catherine of Aragon, repudiated as his wife by the king, Henry VIII.[22] It was said that Queen Catherine herself had wanted to have Agrippa to defend her.[23] However, he refrained from involving himself in this controversy, unlike Francesco Giorgi, who, as we have seen, became much involved in it on the king's side. Judging by Giorgi's experience it was perhaps as a Hebrew scholar that Agrippa's advice would have been sought, for the problem necessitated appeal to Jewish law on divorce.

At about this time there is evidence of contact between Erasmus and Agrippa. Erasmus wrote to Agrippa, asking him to advise a student of the occult whom he (Erasmus) was not able to satisfy, adding that the De vanitate had caused Agrippa's name to be very well-known, though he has heard that the book is rather daring. Agrippa replied eagerly, protesting that he was an Erasmian and obedient to the Church, and asking for Erasmus's opinion of the De vanitate. Erasmus did not reply until 1533, when he praised the book but warned Agrippa to be careful, urging him not to involve him (Erasmus) in his controversies because he already had enough ill-will against him.[24]

Though Erasmus had at first encouraged Reuchlin, whom he admired as a scholar, his views on Cabala later hardened into a strong aversion for 'Judaising' studies, an aversion not untinged with antisemitism. Erasmus particularly disliked the attempt of the occult philosophy to increase the magic in Christian ceremonies as a way to strengthen religion through the 'more powerful' philosophy.[25] This is really the theme of the third book of Agrippa's De occulta philosophia which is on 'ceremonial magic'. The aim of the occult philosophy of reform through increasing the power of 'ceremonial magic' was diametrically opposed to reform through the Erasmian kind of 'Christian philosophy'. Yet it is possible that Agrippa himself, and perhaps some of his followers, may not have quite clearly grasped the basic difference between Agrippan and Erasmian ideas of reform.

Erasmus, Luther, Agrippa, exhibit different facets of the spiritual force which was breaking down the past and ushering in the future.

AGRIPPA'S WORKS (1): DE VANITATE SCIENTIARUM[26]

In this striking work, Agrippa surveys all human intellectual effort and decides that all is empty, all man's learning is of no account, nothing can be certainly known about anything. Like the preacher in Ecclesiastes, from which he quotes, Agrippa decides that all is vanity of vanities and there is nothing new under the sun. Was he then a total sceptic? He has been treated as such by some modern scholars, but this is a mistake. Agrippa was not a sceptic, as more attentive reading of his work clearly reveals.

The first chapter begins in an atmosphere of Hermetic 'Egyptianism' with reference to 'Theut' and 'Thamus' evoking the Hermetic dialogue on Egyptian mysteries.[27] It then states the book's theme of the uncertainty of all man's learning. The list of vain sciences includes, grammar, poetry, the art of memory, dialectic, Lullism, arithmetic, music, geometry, cosmography, architecture, astronomy, magic, Cabala, physics, metaphysics, ethics, monkish superstition, medicine, alchemy, jurisprudence. These selected titles indicate the curious scope of the work. It is not only against occult sciences, such as magic, Cabala, alchemy. It is against the sciences of number, arithmetic, geometry, architecture, astronomy. It is against physics and metaphysics and the intellectual framework of the scholastic tradition. And there is an indication in 'monkish superstition' that the author is writing at a time when the storms of Reformation are beginning to blow.

The following chapters demolish the sciences in detail, a process in which Agrippa shows a great deal of knowledge of all this range of learning. He dwells much on magic and its divisions. There is a natural magic and a mathematical magic. There is a bad magic which calls on bad demons; there is a good magic which calls on angels through Cabala. There is a natural philosophy which discusses questions such as Can there be a plurality of worlds? and What is the soul? This leads on to metaphysics and moral philosophy. By the time he reaches the one hundredth chapter, Agrippa would appear to a sixteenth-century reader to have covered practically everything. All is vain, save one thing only, namely the Word of God in the Scriptures through which we may come to know Jesus Christ. The title of the one hundredth chapter is *De verbo Dei*.

Agrippa is not an atheist; he is an evangelical. He frequently refers to the Epistles of St Paul, and from one of these the title of his sermon could have been taken: 'I am determined to know nothing among you save Christ Jesus.'[28] Agrippa's evangelical convictions come out, not only in the impressive statements in the hundredth chapter, but incidentally throughout the work. In chapter 54 it is stated that only Christ can teach moral philosophy; this is an evangelical reaction against scholasticism. In chapter 97 on scholastic theology it is stated that, though formerly taught by good men, this subject has now degenerated into sophisms and is to be superseded. In the chapter on images (chapter 25) the use of images in the Church is criticised; we are to learn the truth not from these but from the Scriptures, which prohibit idolatry. All these asides throughout the book breathe the spirit of reform, the spirit of Erasmian evangelical reform. The statements of the hundredth chapter are but a summing up of this theme.

There is no other key to knowledge, says this chapter, but the Word of God. The writer of Ecclesiastes was right when he said that all learning is vanity. We must confess our ignorance and think of ourselves as asses. Then follows Agrippa's famous Praise of the Ass. Christ entered Jerusalem upon an ass. Apuleius in *The Golden Ass* tells how his hero was not initiated into the mysteries of Isis until he had become an ass.[29] These Christian and Hermetic–Egyptian examples of holy ignorance sum up Agrippa's theme of the insufficiency of worldly learning. This theme is basically mystical, to be found in medieval mystical writings such as *The Cloud of Unknowing* which describes the negative mystical experience. And Agrippa no doubt had in mind the great philosophical statement of the theme in Nicolas of Cusa's work On learned ignorance. But the closest analogue to Agrippa's De vanitate is much nearer to him in time and belongs precisely to the movement of Erasmian evangelicalism. It is, in fact, a work by Erasmus himself, the famous Praise of Folly. Agrippa's Encomium Asini is a counterpart of the Encomium Moriae by his great contemporary.

Erasmus wrote his Praise of Folly (Encomium Moriae)[30] when he was living in the household of Thomas More in London during that momentous visit to England from 1508 to 1513. It will be remembered that Agrippa was in London in 1510 and in contact with a member of the More circle, John Colet. There is no evidence that Agrippa met Erasmus on that visit, or knew that he was writing The Praise of Folly, but we have seen that in later years Agrippa was particularly anxious to have Erasmus's views on his own De vanitate, perhaps because he hoped that Erasmus might see a kinship between Vanity and Folly. At any rate, it is very instructive to compare the two works.

Erasmus's Folly is a woman who laughs at all the sciences, at Grammar, Rhetoric, Mathematics, Astronomy, Physics; she passes them all by; the ideas and figures and arguments of the philosophers all seem to her absurd. Though she is mainly concerned with exposing the emptiness of orthodox learning, she also mentions some occult sciences, magic and alchemy, as vain. Her distrust of learning is closely associated with her pre-Reform attitudes. She mocks at pardoners and indulgences, at the sermons of monks and friars. The Erasmian wit is very fully deployed in this brilliant work which had an immense vogue as the expression of irritation against the old order of things and the longing for reform. Folly quotes Ecclesiastes on vanity of vanities, all is vanity. She quotes St Paul on science which puffs up pride. The Christian religion, she says, is a doctrine of simplicity, and the man absorbed in the love of heavenly things can look a fool.

The moral is very close to that of Agrippa's *De vanitate*. After surveying all the sciences, Folly finds security only in the Gospel. In both books, the attack on the vanity of learning is also a satire on the vanity of monkish learning. Erasmus has much less than Agrippa on the vanity of the occult sciences, but he does include them. And Agrippa is not only concerned with the vanity of occult sciences but also with the emptiness of scholastic learning. The conclusion of both is that only in the simplicity of the Gospel is security.

The parallel was noted by Philip Sidney who remarks in his *Defence of Poetry*:

> Agrippa will be as merry in showing the vanity of science as Erasmus was in the defending of folly. Neither shall any man or matter escape some touch of these smiling railers. . . . But for Erasmus and Agrippa, they had another foundation than the superficial part would promise.[31]

I suppose that this 'other foundation' would be the Gospel, alone exempt from scepticism according to both Erasmus and Agrippa.

Erasmus did not throw away his classical and patristic scholarship nor discontinue his life-work as a humanist scholar because of the *Praise of Folly*. Nor did Agrippa abandon the occult sciences because of his praise of the Ass. On the contrary a few years after the publication of the *De vanitate* he published *De occulta philosophia*, his full-scale positive treatment of the occult philosophy.

AGRIPPA'S WORK (2): DE OCCULTA PHILOSOPHIA[32]

I have made efforts in other books[33] to present in some moderately lucid form the contents of this strange work, and I must now make the attempt again.

In the first two chapters, Agrippa lays down the outline. The universe is divided into three worlds, the elemental world, the celestial world, the intellectual world. Each world receives influences from the one above it; so that the virtue of the Creator descends through the angels in the intellectual world, to the stars in the celestial world, and thence to the elements and all things composed of them in the terrestrial world. In accordance with this outlook, Agrippa's work is divided into three books. The first book is about natural magic, or magic in the elemental world; it teaches how to arrange substances in accordance with the occult sympathies between them, so as to effect operations in natural magic. The second book is about celestial magic, or how to attract and use influences of the stars. Agrippa calls this kind of magic mathematical magic because its operations depend on number. The third book is about ceremonial magic or magic directed towards the supercelestial world of angelic spirits, beyond which is the One opifex or the creator himself.

Agrippa is summarising the disciplines of Renaissance magic; the Hermetic magic taught by Ficino, and the Cabalist magic introduced by Pico della Mirandola.

As was discovered by D. P. Walker, Ficino's magic was ultimately based on that taught by the supposed Egyptian sage, Hermes Trismegistus, whom Ficino believed to be a contemporary of Moses and a prophet of Christianity. Ficino describes his magic in his book *De vita coelitus comparanda*, the most popular and widely read of all his works. It is based very largely, as Walker showed, on the *Asclepius*, supposedly by Hermes Trismegistus, which describes how the Egyptians attracted celestial influences into the statues of their gods.[34]

Ficino describes how to attract influences of the planets, by using arrangements of substances, by incantations, and by talismans inscribed with the images of the planets and supposed to contain, or attract, their virtues. It is the Ficinian magic which Agrippa teaches in his first book, though he teaches it in a much bolder way. Ficino was nervous of the magic; he was anxious to keep his magic 'natural', concerned only with elemental substances in their relations to the stars and avoiding the 'star demons', the spirits connected with the stars. It was really not possible to teach astral magic whilst avoiding the star demons, as Agrippa saw and boldly accepted the challenge.

Agrippa's second book is on celestial magic, dealing with the stars, not only through their influences on the elements, but ascending to the 'middle' celestial world to grapple with them. This involves number and the celestial magic becomes a mathematical magic. He states the necessity of mathematical disciplines for mathematical magic. The magical statues of the *Asclepius* depended, he says, on number. Miraculous effects can be obtained with geometry and optics. Pythagoras taught the prime importance of number, and physics has a mathematical basis. Ficino had not discussed mathematical magic (he would have avoided it because of his avoidance of star demons), but for Agrippa 'mathematical magic' held a profound attraction.

In the third book, Agrippa boldly advances into the intellectual and angelic world, and sets out schemes for reaching angels and spirits through Cabalist magic. This depends on manipulation of Hebrew letters, which have numerical values, so this again is a kind of mathematical magic though aiming much higher. This book deals with the ceremonies of religions; it is a religious magic, and the magus who reaches this point in his studies has gone far beyond natural magic and mathematical magic. He has drawn close to the Creator himself and knows how to call upon the Names of God.

Agrippa certainly believes himself to be a Christian Cabalist, for the third book leads up to the Name of Jesus as the final mystery. Pico had said in his Cabalist Conclusions that the only name with which the Cabalist can now operate is the Name of Jesus. Agrippa repeats this, word for word.[35] The famous magician undoubtedly believed that, like Pico della Mirandola, he could qualify as a Christian Cabalist.

In fact, I believe that Agrippa's aim is precisely that of providing the technical procedures for acquiring the more powerful and 'wonder-working' philosophy which Reuchlin had called for, a philosophy ostensibly Neoplatonic but including a magical Hermetic–Cabalist core. Constantly on Agrippa's lips in the *De occulta philosophia* are the names of Plato, Plotinus, Proclus, and other Neoplatonists, and, of course, 'Hermes Trismegistus'. He is expounding in matter-of-fact text-book terms the 'wonder-working' Neoplatonism which Reuchlin had desired to encourage in place of dry and barren scholasticism as the philosophy to accompany Christianity.

If one re-reads the *De occulta philosophia* attentively one will notice that in each of the three worlds Agrippa brings in Hebrew names and formulae. This happens in the exposition of magic in the elemental world and in the celestial world, as well as in the supercelestial world where Cabala naturally belongs. Agrippa probably believes that he is both strengthening natural magic and celestial magic by bringing them into contact with powerful Hebrew magic, and also purifying these magics, making them safe by associating them with holy Cabalist influences. Like Reuchlin (and Pico) by associating all the magics with holy influences he makes them safe. He makes sure that only good and holy angelic influences are invoked, and that the star-demons are made harmless through their help. Agrippa's occult philosophy is intended to be a very white magic. In fact it is really a religion, claiming access to the highest powers, and Christian since it accepts the name of Jesus as the chief of the wonder-working Names.

As already suggested, Agrippa's outlook seems very close indeed to that of Francesco Giorgi, though in the *De harmonia mundi* Giorgi is slightly more cautious (he is much bolder in the *Problemata*). His Franciscan affiliations would no doubt have made him seem less alarming than Agrippa, the strange wanderer with no religious home.

The function of Cabala as Agrippa saw it was not only to provide the highest 'supercelestial' magic, but to guarantee the safety of the operator against demons at all levels. The fear of demons had haunted Ficino, but Cabala eliminates this fear. It is an insurance against demons, a guarantee that bold attempts after unlimited knowledge and power will not lead to damnation.

Though the genuine Hebrew Cabalist might be shocked by Agrippa's interpretation of Cabala solely as white magic, yet this interpretation served a purpose in fortifying man for intellectual and spiritual endeavour.

6

THE OCCULT PHILOSOPHY AND MELANCHOLY: DÜRER AND AGRIPPA

The famous German artist, Albrecht Dürer, was born in 1471 and died in 1528. He was thus a contemporary of Erasmus, Luther, and Agrippa: five years younger than Erasmus; twelve years older than Luther; fifteen years older than Agrippa.

Always a deeply religious man, Dürer's spiritual power was early shown in the remarkable Apocalypse illustrations. After his second visit to Italy (1505–7) his style changed, for he had absorbed the Italian art theory based on harmony of macrocosm and microcosm, understood in subtle geometrical terms, on the proportions of the human body as related to laws governing the cosmos, as laid down by the Architect of the Universe. Dürer became the chief northern exponent of this theory,[1] in which proportion is a link between man and the universe, expressed through proportion in architecture as laid down by Vitruvius, and in all the arts. It is the foundation of beauty, of aesthetic satisfaction. In this theory, geometry was the primary mathematical science, on which beauty in architecture, painting, music, must be based. With his intense vision, Dürer penetrated to the religious core of this theory; with his brilliant mind he seized its mathematical basis; with his artist's hand he executed designs of profound religious meaning with faultless geometrical precision. Dürer saw art as power, and the root of aesthetic power was in number.

In 1519 and the following years, Dürer went through a spiritual crisis because he had come into contact with Luther and the stirrings of Reformation.[2] In October 1517, Luther had nailed his theses to the door of the Wittenberg church. Always anxious about abuses in Church and Papacy, as is apparent in the Apocalypse illustrations, Dürer was deeply impressed by Luther and his movement. He became a Lutheran Protestant. An entry in Dürer's diary is a moving apostrophe to Erasmus to come over openly to the side of Luther and Reform.[3]

> Oh Erasmus of Rotterdam, why dost thou not come forward? Look, what can the unjust tyranny of worldly force and the power of darkness avail? Hear, thou knight of Christ, ride forward by the side of the Lord Christ, protect truth, attain the martyr's crown. Thou art but an old little man; I have heard that thou givest thyself two more years in which thou wilt be fit to accomplish something. Use these well for the benefit of the Gospel and of the true Christian faith.

Erasmus did not take the step which Dürer is urging, yet Dürer and Erasmus are close, the one the great classical scholar, the other the great artist and art-theorist. Both are deeply concerned with the religious problems of the age, though the one became a Protestant and the other did not.

And what of Dürer and Agrippa? What was the reaction of Dürer to the author of the *Occult Philosophy*? The scholarly labours of Raymond Klibansky, Erwin Panofsky, and Fritz Saxl have proved that one of the most compelling of Dürer's engravings, the *Melencolia I* (1514), is based on a passage in Agrippa's *De occulta philosophia*.

The interpretation of this engraving as a representation of 'inspired melancholy' was first put forward in a study in German by Panofsky and Saxl published in 1923. It was again discussed by Panofsky in his book on Dürer in 1945. It is fully expounded in the work *Saturn and Melancholy* by Klibansky, Panofsky, and Saxl published in 1964[4] which is a mine of detailed information and rich scholarship about the humours and their representation in art. Through Klibansky's learned discussion of the four humours in ancient and medieval psychology; through Saxl's survey of the pictorial types of the humours; through Panofsky's analysis of the engraving in terms of Renaissance iconography, a view of Dürer's *Melencolia I* was built up in which all these strands were used for the interpretation of the extraordinary, dark-faced, figure, absorbed in profound meditation, and surrounded by a strange medley of objects (Plate 5).

According to the Galenic psychology, dominant through the Middle Ages, the four humours or temperaments into which all men could be classified were the sanguine, the choleric, the phlegmatic, and the melancholic. Sanguine people were active, hopeful, successful, outward-looking; they made good rulers and men of affairs. Choleric people were irritable, inclined to fighting. Phlegmatic people were tranquil, somewhat lethargic. Melancholy people were sad, poor, unsuccessful, condemned to the most servile and despised occupations.

The theory locked man's psychology into the cosmos, for the four humours correspond to four elements and four planets, as follows:

> Sanguine – Air – Jupiter
> Choleric – Fire – Mars

Phlegmatic – Water – Moon
Melancholy – Earth – Saturn

The theory was bound up with astrology. If Saturn dominated in a horoscope, the person concerned would be inclined to melancholy; if Jupiter, the outlook would be more hopeful, and so on.

The most unfortunate and the most hateful of all the four humours was Saturn–Melancholy. The melancholic was dark in complexion, with black hair and a black face – the *facies nigra* or livid hue induced by the black bile of the melancholy complexion. His typical physical pose, expressive of his sadness and depression, was to rest his head on his hand. Even his 'gifts', or characteristic occupations, were not attractive. He was good at measuring, numbering, counting – at measuring land and counting money – but what low and earthy occupations were these compared with the splendid gifts of the sanguine Jupiter man, or the grace and loveliness of those born under Venus!

Dürer's Melancholy has the livid hue, the swarthy complexion, the 'black face' of the type, and she supports her pensive head on her hand in the characteristic pose.[5] She holds compasses for measuring and numbering. Beside her is the purse, for counting money. Around her are tools, such as an artisan might use. Obviously she is a melancholic, characterised by the physical type, pose, and occupations of the old, bad, melancholy, but she seems also to express some more lofty and intellectual type of endeavour. She is not actually doing anything, just sitting and thinking. What do those geometrical forms mean, and why does a ladder rise heavenward behind the polyhedron?

There was a line of thought through which Saturn and the melancholy temperament might be 'revalued', raised from being the lowest of the four to become the highest, the humour of great men, great thinkers, prophets and religious seers. To be melancholy was a sign of genius; the 'gifts' of Saturn, the numbering and measuring studies attributed to the melancholic, were to be cultivated as the highest kind of learning which brought man nearest to the divine. This radical change in the attitude to melancholy had results in affecting a change in the direction of men's minds and studies.

This change was brought about through the influence of a text the authorship of which was ascribed to Aristotle but which is more safely described as Pseudo-Aristotelian.[6] The thirtieth of the *Problemata physica* in this Pseudo-Aristotelian treatise discusses melancholy as the humour of heroes and great men. The argument is very detailed and medical but the main point is that the heroic frenzy, or madness, or *furor*, which according to Plato is the source of all inspiration, when combined with the black bile of the melancholy temperament produces great men; it is the temperament of genius. All outstanding men have been melancholics, heroes, like Hercules, philosophers, like Empedocles, Plato, and practically all the poets.

The theories of Pseudo-Aristotle on melancholy were not unknown in the Middle Ages, but in the Renaissance they attracted general attention. Assimilated into Neoplatonism through the Platonic theory of the *furores*, the notion of the melancholy hero whose genius is akin to madness became familiar to the European mind.

Ficino knew the Pseudo-Aristotelian theory and mentioned it in the *De triplici vita*,[7] the work in which he sets forth his astral magic. Addressing students who were thought to suffer from melancholy through solitariness and concentration on their studies, he advises that the Saturnian or melancholic man should not avoid the deep study to which he is prone by temperament but should take care to temper the Saturnian severity with Jovial and Venereal influences. The ingenuity of Klibansky-Saxl-Panofsky has proved that Dürer's engraving shows knowledge of Ficinian theory for they demonstrate that the square on the wall behind the melancholy figure, containing an arrangement of

numbers, is a magic square of Jupiter, calculated to draw down
Jupiter influences through its numerical arrangement. Thus the
severe influence of Saturn and his inspired melancholy is being
tempered in the engraving with Jupiter influences, as Ficino
advised.

Dürer's immediate source for the inspired melancholy was,
however, not Ficino, but Agrippa's *De occulta philosophia*. The date
of the engraving is 1514, that is nearly twenty years before the
publication of the printed version of Agrippa's work in 1533. It
is therefore assumed that Dürer must have used the manuscript
version of 1510 which was circulated in many copies and was
certainly available in the circles in which Dürer moved.[8] In *Saturn
and Melancholy* the passage as it is in the manuscript version is
translated into English. The following is an abridged quotation
from it :[9]

> The *humor melancholicus*, when it takes fire and glows, gen-
> erates the frenzy (*furor*) which leads us to wisdom and revela-
> tion, especially when it is combined with a heavenly influence,
> above all with that of Saturn. . . . Therefore Aristotle says in the
> *Problemata* that through melancholy some men have become
> divine beings, foretelling the future like Sybils. . . . while others
> have become poets . . . and he says further that all men who
> have been distinguished in any branch of knowledge have
> generally been melancholics.
>
> Moreover, this *humor melancholicus* has such power that they
> say it attracts certain demons into our bodies, through whose
> presence and activity men fall into ecstacies and pronounce
> many wonderful things . . . This occurs in three different forms
> corresponding to the threefold capacity of our soul, namely the
> imagination (*imaginatio*), the rational (*ratio*), and the mental
> (*mens*). For when set free by the *humor melancholicus*, the soul
> is fully concentrated in the *imagination*, and it immediately
> becomes a habitation for the lower demons, from whom it

often receives wonderful instruction in the manual arts; thus we see a quite unskilled man suddenly become a painter or an architect, or a quite outstanding master in another art of some kind; if the demons of this species reveal the future to us, they show us matters related to natural catastrophes and disasters, for instance approaching storms, earthquakes, cloud-bursts, or threats of plague famine and devastation. . . . But when the soul is fully concentrated in the *reason*, it becomes the home of the middle demons; thereby it attains knowledge of natural and human things; thus we see a man suddenly become a philosopher, a physician, or an orator; and of future events they show us what concerns the overthrow of kingdoms and the return of epochs, prophesying in the same way that the Sybil prophesied to the Romans. . . . But when the soul soars completely to the *intellect* it becomes the home of the higher demons, from whom it learns the secrets of divine matters, as for instance the law of God, the angelic hierarchy, and that which pertains to the knowledge of eternal things and the soul's salvation; of future events they show us for instance approaching prodigies, wonders, a prophet to come, or the emergence of a new religion, just as the Sybil prophesied Jesus Christ long before lie appeared.

This remarkable classification immediately accounts for the curious fact that the title of Dürer's engraving is *Melencolia I*. It must be one of a series, the first of the series described by Agrippa, concerned with imagination, and the inspiration of painters, architects, and masters in other arts. In fact we see in the engraving the tools, the geometric figures, alluding to the traditional 'occupations of Saturn', his skills in number and measurement, but transmuted in the atmosphere of inspired melancholy to becoming the instruments of inspired artistic genius. The only actual figure in the engraving is the *putto*, and he appears to hold an engraver's tool.[10]

It will be noted, and the authors of *Saturn and Melancholy* have of course drawn attention to this,[11] that the classification of the three kinds of melancholy seems to recall the design of the *De occulta philosophia* as a whole, in which the author rises through three worlds in the three books. Where then are 'Melencolia II' and 'Melencolia III'? The engraving which we have cannot be the whole answer to the problem of inspired melancholy, as Dürer saw it.

The book *Saturn and Melancholy* proves with immense learning the concern of Dürer's engraving with the melancholy humour in its inspired form, and it points to Agrippa's work as a basic source for Dürer's thought on the subject. Yet, after all the brilliance and learning assembled in the book, Panofsky's actual interpretation of the engraving comes as something of a disappointment and an anticlimax.

Panofsky believes that the engraving represents the frustration of the inspired genius.[12] He points to the wings of 'Melencolia', large powerful wings which she is not using as she sits inactive. For Panofsky the wings are the aspirations of genius, folded and useless, and this frustrated state is the cause of the melancholy. The engraving reflects, thinks Panofsky, the suffering condition of creative genius, unable to express its visions, hampered by its material conditions, lapsing into melancholy inactivity because of the sense of failure and inadequacy. Panofsky wishes to move Dürer's image in a modern, or perhaps a nineteenth-century, direction, expressive of the sense of suffering and failure of the creative artist. Melancholy is surrounded by the tools of her art, but she is not using them. She does not unfold her wings but sits inactive, unable to mount. Even the emaciated and half-starved dog in the engraving is drawn into this depressed atmosphere of failure, melancholy of frustrated genius.

I venture to disagree with this romantic interpretation which does not take into account the outlook of the 'occult philosophy', with which Dürer must surely be concerned, if he is influenced by Agrippa. As now generally realised, the occult philosophy from Pico onwards and as formulated by Agrippa included the Hermetic and magical thought of Ficinian Neoplatonism, adding to this the Cabalist magic introduced by Pico. The book *Saturn and Melancholy* does not deal with either of these two basic categories. Though there is much on Dürer's debt to Ficino's *De vita*, this work is treated predominantly for its treatment of melancholy and without reference to its general importance as a text for spiritual magic, as defined by D. P. Walker.[13] Walker's discoveries about the Hermetic influence in *De vita* had not yet been published when Panofsky was contributing to *Saturn and Melancholy*. Hence all that side of the occult philosophy is insufficiently covered.

Still more unfortunate is the total omission of Agrippa's Cabalism. This is deliberately omitted because the authors of *Saturn and Melancholy* believed that there is no Cabala in the 1510 version of the *De occulta philosophia* which Dürer used.[14] This is not really the case. On the contrary, Charles Zika is able to argue that there is more Cabalist influence in the 1510 manuscript than in the later printed version of Agrippa's book, and that he is already presenting, in the 1510 manuscript, that synthesis of magic and religion, through Cabala, which Pico had adumbrated and which Reuchlin carried further.[15] The Reuchlin synthesis as expounded in *De verbo mirifico* would have been fully accessible to Dürer, and was probably the main inspiration of his engravings, together with his knowledge of the unpublished version of *De occulta philosophia*. It was the exciting thought of a religion made stronger by Hermetic and Cabalist magic which reached Dürer through the influence of Reuchlin and Agrippa in his environment.

I therefore believe that the approach to the Dürer engraving needs to be re-assessed in terms of our new understanding of Renaissance thought on its occult side. I put forward the following remarks as a beginning of an attempted interpretation of the

Dürer engraving which would be in line with the Agrippa occult philosophy.

In the previous chapter, the part played by Cabala in Agrippa's *De occulta philosophia* was emphasised, not only in the supercelestial world of the angelic hierarchies and religious mysteries, but also through all three worlds as a guarantee of safety, that the magic described was a white magic guided by good and angelic forces which ensured protection from evil powers. The three stages of inspired melancholy described by Agrippa would seem to be much in need of such protection since the inspiration is definitely said to be of a demonic nature. Dürer's Melancholia with her angel's wings may express exactly the Agrippan combination of Magia and Cabala. Surrounded by Saturnian allusions and Saturnian occupations, she magically invokes the inspiring influence of the highest of the planets, and is protected from harm by the angel of Saturn. Her angelic character is suggested not only by her angel wings but also by the ladder behind her, leading, not to the top of the building but generally upwards into the sky, Jacob's ladder on which the angels ascend and descend.

Dürer's Melancholy is not in a state of depressed inactivity. She is in an intense visionary trance, a state guaranteed against demonic intervention by angelic guidance. She is not only inspired by Saturn as the powerful star-demon, but also by the angel of Saturn, a spirit with wings like the wings of Time.

The starved dog is an important key to the meaning. This hound, in my opinion, is not yet another indication of a depressed mood of failure. It represents, I believe, the bodily senses, starved and under severe control in this first stage of inspiration, in which the inactivity is not representative of failure but of an intense inner vision. The Saturnian melancholic has 'taken leave of the senses' and is soaring in worlds beyond worlds in a state of visionary trance. The only sense which is alive and waking is the artist's hand, the hand of the *putto* recording the vision with his engraving tool – the hand of Dürer himself recording his psychology of inspiration in this marvellous engraving.

The classic moralisation of the senses as hunting dogs is that given by Natalis Comes in his interpretation of the Actaeon fable,[16] where Actaeon's dogs are the senses. The melancholy temperament was supposed to subdue the senses. A theorist on the humours defines Melancholy as 'the sweet sleep of the senses'.[17] Or we may turn to John Milton who gave in Il *Penseroso* the supreme poetic expression of the theory of inspired melancholy. 'Divinest Melancholy', whose black face hides a saintly visage too bright for human sense, is accompanied by 'spare diet', and in her soaring visions she escapes from the senses:

> Or let my lamp at midnight hour
> Be seen in some high lonely tower,
> Where I may oft outwatch the Bear,
> With thrice great Hermes, or unsphere
> The spirit of Plato to unfold
> What worlds or what vast regions hold
> The Immortal mind *that hath forsook*
> *Her mansion in this fleshly nook*;
> And of those demons that are found
> In fire, air, flood, or underground,
> Whose power hath a true consent
> With planet or with element.

Milton's melancholy inspiration is also demonic, but a white ascetic magic (the starved dog of the senses), and connecting with higher realms of prophecy and angelic hierarchies. His Melancholy brings with her

> Him that yon soars on golden wing,
> Guiding the fiery wheeled throne
> The Cherub Contemplation.

Dürer's *Melencolia I* represented the first of Agrippa's series, the inspired artistic melancholy. There was also a stage relating to prophetic inspiration, and a stage in which the inspired intellect rose to the understanding of divine matters. All three are included in Milton's Melancholy, the saintly dark figure who seems to descend from Reuchlin via Agrippa. And all three may be intimated in Dürer's *Melencolia I* through the angelic wings which he gives to his black-faced figure.

In the same year, 1514, in which he engraved the *Melencolia I* Dürer produced his famous engraving of *St Jerome in his Study* (Plate 6). In his book on Dürer, Panofsky suggests, that Dürer must have thought of the *St Jerome* as a kind of counterpart to the *Melencolia I*, since he was in the habit of giving these two engravings together to his friends. No less than six copies were disposed of as pairs, while only one copy of the *Melencolia I* was given away singly.[18]

Gazing at the two engravings side by side, as Dürer intended us to do, it is clear that there is an intended parallel between them. The holy man is seated at his desk profoundly absorbed in his inspired writing. His cell is described by Panofsky as a 'place of enchanted beatitude', informed with geometrical truth. The construction of space in this engraving 'is impeccably correct from a mathematical point of view. . . . Everything in this informal and unpretentious room is subject to a mathematical principle. The apparently indelible impression of order and security which is the very signature of Dürer's "St Jerome" can be accounted for by the fact that the position of the objects freely distributed about the room . . . is firmly determined by perspective construction.'[19]

Panofsky contrasts this with the disorder surrounding *Melencolia I*, the unhappy tragic genius in her frustrated despair. This, I believe, erroneous interpretation of *Melencolia I* prevents us from realising that Dürer may be representing different stages of inspired vision. In *Melencolia I* the inspired imagination of the artist is on a lower rung of the ladder of vision than is Jerome in his ordered surroundings. Jerome might be on the third grade of the Agrippan classification of inspired melancholy, in which *mens* 'learns the secrets of divine matters, as for instance the law of God, the angelic hierarchy, and that which pertains to the knowledge of eternal things'.

In fact I would suggest that the *St Jerome* may actually be *Melencolia III*. At this stage the *mens* sees into all truth, including the divine truth of geometry, obscurely and confusedly distinguished by *imaginatio* in *Melencolia I*.

The revaluation of the melancholy humour, and the theory of inspired melancholy derived from it, would appear on the surface to have no necessary connection with Cabala, either Jewish or Christian. Apart from the fact that Agrippa included his exposition of the theory of inspired melancholy, and its stages, in his *De occulta philosophia*, it is not easy to see why melancholy was so closely associated with the occult philosophy. Yet there is no doubt that it was so associated. The inspired melancholy undoubtedly belongs into the atmosphere of Renaissance occult philosophy.

This is why it has been important to attempt some re-interpretation of the most famous representation of melancholy, Dürer's *Melencolia I*. The tentative re-interpretation of the engraving which I have here outlined as the representation of an inspired trance in which the visionary is protected from demonic dangers by holy angelic presences would bring it into line with Christian Cabala as understood by Pico, Reuchlin, and Agrippa.

Some years after the appearance of Dürer's engraving (which is dated I 5 14) Lucas Cranach painted a group of pictures which are obviously influenced by Dürer's imagery. In these Cranach compositions (Plate 7) a woman, obviously derivative from Dürer's Melancholy sits at the right of a picture lost in a trance whilst putti play with a wakeful dog.[20] The woman is not transported by holy visions; her melancholy is not protected by Christian Cabala from demonic powers. On the contrary, she is a witch; above her in the sky rides a witches' sabbath; the trance of the witch's melancholy implies that she is absent worshipping the devil at the sabbath.

It is revealing to compare the sleeping dog of the senses in Dürer's ascetic vision with the evil, wakeful dog and putti of the Cranach picture. Making a wrong use of magic, without purity of intention, unprotected by holy angels, the melancholy witch has taken a wrong turning and has fallen into the power of Satan. Inspired melancholy has become witchcraft; the serious putto of the Dürer engraving has become a riot of sensual putti; the sleeping dog of the senses has become evilly awake. Christian Cabalists always warned of the danger which Cranach illustrates by turning the imagery of Dürer's melancholy in the direction of witchcraft.

The new interpretation of Dürer's *Melencolia I*, and the comparison of Dürer's inspired melancholy with Cranach's melancholy witch, introduce the problem of whether there may have been a connection between the witch scares of the later sixteenth century and the cultivation of the inspired melancholy in Renaissance occult philosophy.

7

REACTIONS AGAINST THE OCCULT PHILOSOPHY: THE WITCH CRAZE

It has been said that for Cardinal Egidius of Viterbo the discovery of the Cabala by the Christians of his own day marked a great turning-point which affected all humanity. It was a 'cause and symptom of the spiritual unity of mankind' which Egidius hoped to see soon accomplished.[1] This vision lay behind the efforts of the early Christian Cabalists. It was behind that unification of all philosophies and religions sought by Pico della Mirandola and behind the hopes of Reuchlin for a more powerful and wonder-working philosophy. It aroused opposition from the start. It is unnecessary to remind here of the story of Pico's difficulties with the orthodox, or of Reuchlin's troubles with the 'obscure men'. The opposition was always there but in the earlier years of the sixteenth century the hopes of the enthusiasts remained high. The Christian Cabalist movement belonged with the general advance into new fields of learning and experience.

Its enemies were not in the ascendant. But as the century moved on into darker years, the orthodox opposition to Renaissance occult philosophy hardened, a development comparable to the hardening of opinion against Erasmus and all that he stood for. The hopes for unity had not materialised; Reformation and Catholic reaction had increased disunity. The Council of Trent intensified the lines of opposition, and in the later sixteenth century the happy visions of a Franciscan Cabalist, such as Francesco Giorgi, could not go unchallenged by the censors.

The history of Giorgi's reputation[2] reflects the changing times. We have seen that the work of the Cabalist Franciscan on universal harmony lay at the heart of fundamental Renaissance movements, whether religious, philosophical or artistic. Towards the end of the century, both the *De harmonia mundi* and the more overtly magical *Problemata* appear in lists of works either prohibited or awaiting correction. Giorgi's books belonged to the latter class, not entirely prohibited but in need of severe expurgation. Cesare Vasoli has said that it is difficult to find in any Italian library today a copy of the *De harmonia* which does not show on many pages the black ink of the censor.[3]

The only copy of the Latin edition of the *De harmonia* in the British Library[4] shows very plainly the black ink of the censor. It is a copy of the 1525 edition originally in the Royal Library (the binding is of the reign of George III). The censor has written on the title-page that the work abounds in the arguments of the Platonists and Cabalists (*abundat hoc opus Platonicorum et Cabbalistarum placitis*) and is therefore to be read with caution (*caute legendum*) (Plate 8). Not content with this warning on the title-page, the censor has scored through and through many pages of the text (Plate 9).

The problems which the work of Francesco Giorgi presented to the censor have been discussed by Antonio Rotondo. He calls Giorgi's *De harmonia* and *Problemata* the two most disconcerting works of the Italian religious literature of the first half of the sixteenth century. They were not included in the *Index* of 1559 because they had not yet assumed the historic importance of works which raised problems of censorship. In 1583 a censor was finding it embarrassingly difficult to revise or correct Giorgi's works. Yet it was becoming clear that heresies could be drawn out of the works of the Friar of Venice, with their cultural latitudinarianism, their Erasmian tendency, and their Platonic, Hermetic, and Cabalist elements. The problem of censoring Giorgi belonged into the wider problem faced by censorship in Italy, namely the general aim of discouraging the Platonism of the first half of the sixteenth century, with its many associated strands. Giorgi's *De harmonia mundi* was the quintessence of the early sixteenth-century Platonism, and it was really impossible to take out, or suppress, parts of an absolutely coherent whole.

Gradually it became apparent to the Congregation of the Index that the whole of Renaissance Platonism was dangerous, particularly in its combination of Platonism and Cabala. Thus the movement of suppression gained momentum. The discouragement of Giorgi's works was followed by the discouragement of the religious Platonism of Francesco Patrizzi.[5] The philosophy to be used with Catholic orthodoxy was not to be that of Pico, Egidius of Viterbo, Giorgi, or Patrizzi, but a return to a more rigorous type of Aristotelianism, the philosophy from which Cardinal Bellarmine was to censor Giordano Bruno.[6]

The case of Francesco Giorgi is extremely important, and that not only because the *De harmonia mundi* is such a complete statement of the philosophy of universal harmony, with its Hermetic, Cabalist, and Pythagorean associations. It is important for its history which illustrates the Counter-Reformation attempt to suppress the Renaissance. For behind Giorgi was Ficino with his Hermetic Platonisin, and Pico della Mirandola with his introduction of Cabala into the system.

One cannot read the *De harmonia mundi* with 'caution', avoiding the errors of the Platonists and the Cabalists. To do so one would have to forget Ficino and Pico and the Renaissance.

Though Giorgi's work was discouraged by disapproving censorship there does not seem to have been any strong movement of polemic against it. Very different was the case of the later reputation of Henry Cornelius Agrippa.

In the early Renaissance we have caught glimpses of Agrippa as a respected Hebrew scholar, thought of as a possible authority on the divorce of Henry VIII, like Giorgi, or reading the epistles of St Paul with Dean Colet. We have seen that there was a very strong religious and reforming side to Agrippa's thought, as in the case of Giorgi. Agrippa, too, was touched by Erasmian and evangelical influences. And Agrippa's 'occult philosophy' was in many respects closely parallel to that of Giorgi.

Like Giorgi, Agrippa rises through the three worlds, the elemental world, the celestial world, the supercelestial world. Like Giorgi, Agrippa concentrates on number, on proportion in man and the universe using the Vitruvian figures. Like Giorgi, Agrippa rises to the supercelestial world where he is in contact with angels, where the Trinity is proved, whence influences from the angels pour down through the planets, where the Hebrew Names of God are listed, though the Name of Jesus is now the most powerful of all Names. All planetary influences are good since the influences of the celestial hierarchies descend through them. The operator, who is operating a completely white magic, free from demons, is a pious and good Christian Cabalist.

The outlook of the *De occulta philosophia* is almost identically the same in its main outlines as the outlook of the *De harmonia mundi*. It is true that Agrippa appears to give more especially magical advice than Giorgi, but such specifically magical instructions are not absent from Giorgi's work, particularly in the *Problemata*. Agrippan propositions, such as the continuity of the planets with the angels, when found in Giorgi are scratched through by the censor, yet there is no virulent pursuit of Giorgi as a black magician, as there is in the case of Agrippa.

Why did Agrippa in the later sixteenth century have the reputation of being the blackest of black magicians, and conjuror of devils, whilst Giorgi escaped with a censorship which was not very much publicised? I do not know the answer to this question, which needs deep investigation. Possibly Giorgi's mystical Franciscanism provided a cover for his occult philosophy which was a more effective protection for him, a better guarantee of his 'whiteness', than the obscure German wanderer Agrippa, could produce.

At any rate the fact is that Agrippa, though he had some faithful disciples, was not generally believed to be 'white'. The legend propagated by Paolo Giovio of the black dog which was Agrippa's familiar spirit and which jumped into a river at his death was typical of Agrippa's image as the black conjuror of devils. Agrippa's reputation as the 'Archimagus', the personification of evil sorcery, was finally fixed by the Jesuit, Martin del Rio, in his authoritative work on magic.[7]

Agrippa as a Christian Cabalist, using a more 'powerful' philosophy than scholasticism, had failed to convince his critics. Followed by his 'schwarze Pudel' he was to pass into Goethe's Faust,[8] the accepted image of the seeker after unlawful knowledge.

During the rest of this chapter I propose to study, and to compare, the reputations of Giorgi and Agrippa at a certain time in the late Renaissance and in a certain country. The time is around the end of the 1570s and the beginning of the 1580s. The country is France. By choosing a particular historical moment and a particular place for this investigation, I hope to bring out certain issues more clearly than would be possible in a generalised treatment.

In the French Renaissance, the influence of Giorgi was very

strong, one of the channels through which, in sixteenth-century France, Neoplatonism associated with Hermetic and Cabalist influences flowed into thought, art, science, literature, and in countless ways helped to build the foundation of men's thoughts and activities. In my book *The French Academies of the Sixteenth Century* I emphasised that Giorgi's presentation of universal harmony influenced (of course in association with other similar influences) the theories of the Academy of Poetry and Music[9] founded by Antoine de Baïf, one of the group of poets known as the Pléiade of which Ronsard was one. The philosophical theorist of the Academy was Pontus de Tyard upon whose writings the influence of Giorgi is obvious.[10]

In a long poem, called *La Galliade*, all the modern French writers, artists, architects, musicians, poets, are introduced in a philosophical-historical setting, based on Renaissance theories of universal harmony, such as that of Giorgi, adapted to French patriotic and monarchical themes. The author of this poem, published in 1578, was Guy Le Fèvre de la Boderie,[11] an enthusiast for Hebrew and Cabalist studies, and associated as a Hebrew expert with the new Polyglot translation of the Bible, being published at Antwerp by Plantin.

This French Hebrew expert and admirer of the Cabalist Friar of Venice contributed notably to an intensification of interest in Giorgi by publishing in 1578 a French translation of his great work now called *L'Harmonie du monde*. The prefaces by La Boderie and his brothers in this large and impressive volume have been referred to in the study of Giorgi in an earlier chapter.[12] Important as these prefaces are for their statement of Giorgi's philosophy, they are also important as reflecting the Giorgi revival in the late French Renaissance. In 1578, we are no longer in the earlier years of the century when Giorgi's work first appeared; we are in later days when, in Italy, the censorship of Giorgi is beginning. Yet in the La Boderie prefaces the enthusiasm for Christian Cabala is unabated, or rather, seems to have increased.

The readers of the French translation are told of the numero-logical and architectural formulations of universal harmony. An elaborate diagram of the numerological correspondences between the three worlds brings out the complexity of Giorgi's attempt to express the universe in terms of number (Plate 4). The importance of the Temple of Solomon as the great exemplar of architectural numerology is emphasised, and the preface ends with 'Hermes Trismegistus' on the One. This preface is a remarkable statement of Neoplatonic philosophy which em-phasises the Cabalist, Hermetic, and Pythagorean interpretations of the movement.

And, above all, the La Boderie prefaces emphasise the Chris-tian application. This is fully apparent in the text of the transla-tion in which the Cabalist endorsement of Christianity can now be read in French, interspersed with many quotations in Hebrew, as in the original. And that this book is the work of a Christian Cabalist is strongly underlined in the La Boderie prefaces.

The publication of this translation of Giorgi emphasised to the contemporary world of the late French Renaissance the Hebraic and Cabalist side of the Florentine Neoplatonism whence so much of its culture was nourished. And this was still further emphasised through the inclusion in the same volume of a French translation by Nicolas Le Fèvre de la Boderie (brother of Guy) of the *Heptaplus* of Pico della Mirandola. This work of Pico's, first published in 1489, is a commentary on the Genesis account of the Days of Creation.[13] Perhaps it is the work of Pico's in which his profound immersion in Cabalist mysticism and sym-bolism is most apparent. And it is profoundly Christian Cabala, in which the Christian angelic hierarchies are assimilated to the Cabalist Sephiroth and the angelic influences pour down through the planets to the terrestrial world in the manner which Giorgi was afterwards to systematise in the *De harmonia mundi*. In fact, Pico's *Heptaplus* was one of Giorgi's chief sources, as is pointed out by Nicolas Le Fèvre de la Boderie in his preface to the French translation.

Thus the volume as a whole presents Pico as an essentially Christian Cabalist, with Giorgi as his disciple. It is an intensive revival of Christian Cabalism and Christian Hermeticism, as the core of Renaissance Neoplatonism.

We are accustomed to look for reforming influences in connection with Christian Cabala. In this case such views are not clearly stated, but Guy Le Fèvre de la Boderie belonged to the circle of François D'Alençon, brother of the French king, heir to the French throne, and leader of the 'politique' party which sought to soften religious divisions and maintain peace by a policy of religious toleration. The fact that the translator of L'Harmonie du monde was secretary to the 'only brother of the King' is stated on the title-page. The translation is dedicated to one of the few people who are certainly known to have been members of the secret sect known as 'the Family of Love'.[14]

We can therefore perhaps see the politico-religious implications of this Christian Cabalist volume as reflecting, or arousing, 'politique' tolerance, and the softening of animosities of opposite sides in the wars of religion.

It may also be significant that François D'Alençon was soon to become suitor for the hand of Queen Elizabeth I of England and to travel to England to prosecute his suit. Was the Christian Cabalist volume translated by members of his circle a gesture of 'politique' toleration, preparing the way for that visit of a Catholic prince to a Protestant Queen?

In all this intensification of Christian Cabala in France, which was connected with the intensive prosecution of Hebrew studies in the circle of the famous French Cabalist, Guillaume Postel,[15] there is no hint of any disapproval of Giorgi, such as was beginning to be expressed in Catholic circles in Rome. The French Catholic Christian Cabala fully accepted Giorgi at this time; thus the influence of his writings could have passed into England, with the 'politique' prince, D'Alençon, as an approved form of Christian Cabala.

I now turn to the reputation of Henry Cornelius Agrippa in the same period and in France. At the same time, and in the same French courtly circles as those in which the reputation of Giorgi was flourishing, there developed a fierce attack on Agrippa who was presented, not as a pious Christian Cabalist using a rather exceptionally 'powerful' philosophy, but as the blackest of black magicians and sorcerers. This attack on Agrippa was also dangerous for Pico's reputation, as the following analysis will show.

There was published in Paris in 1580, that is two years after the Giorgi–Pico volume, a work which is a devastating and dangerous attack on Pico della Mirandola's use of Cabala. This was the *De la démonomanie des sorciers* by Jean Bodin, a book which has attracted a good deal of attention of late owing to the contemporary interest in witchcraft.[16] For it is a terrific indictment of witchcraft and witches, an enquiry into the whole problem undertaken in an impressively learned fashion, giving many examples of supposed witches, with legal advice as to how they should be tried and punished. Bodin believes intensely in the real existence of witches and in the reality of the witches' sabbath. He is horrified at what he believes to be the increase in the number of witches and takes the stern view, based on Biblical authority, that witches must die. This work had an enormous influence in fomenting the terrible witch craze which raged with such intensity in Europe in the late sixteenth and early seventeenth centuries.

In their fascination with the witchcraft problem, modern readers of this book have tended to lose sight of the fact that it begins with an attack on Renaissance magic, and particularly on Pico della Mirandola and Cornelius Agrippa. This fact was, however, pointed out in 1958 by D. P. Walker in his book *Spiritual and Demonic Magic from Ficino to Campanella*.[17] It is above all for what he regards as his wrong use of Cabala that Bodin attacks Pico. Pico's advice in the Magical and Cabalist Conclusions about marrying earth and heaven by magical procedures, about the use of Cabalist letter-formations in magic, is quoted with horror as the wicked teachings of a magician. Pico's statement that the hymns of Orpheus have as much power for magic as the Psalms of David for Cabala is an abominable attempt to equate pagan incantations for attracting the demon, Pan, with the pure use of the Psalms by a pious Cabalist. In fact, Pico's teaching of the use of Cabala for magic is presented as a most wicked degradation of the true religious meaning and use of Cabala.[18]

And if Pico is a wicked magician, Agrippa is much worse. Bodin's fulminations against the *De occulta philosophia* are alarming. It is an utterly damnable work. The famous black dog was the demon who had inspired his master's evil practices. The wrong use of Cabala by such a sorcerer is compared with the true Cabala, which is a spiritual discipline and a method of Scriptural exegesis used by good and holy men. It draws out deep meaning through allegorical interpretation and leads the devout into holy mysteries.[19]

Bodin was justified in connecting Pico with his strictures on Agrippa, for Pico had said that no magical operation was powerful without Cabala, advice which Agrippa followed in the *De occulta philosophia* in which Hebrew words are used with the magic throughout. The essence of Renaissance 'Magia and Cabala' was that it combined Hermetic processes and traditions with Cabala. The holy Hebrew magic both strengthened the weaker magic, and, still more important, made it safe, ensured that it was using angelic and not demonic powers. Bodin's onslaught on Pico and Agrippa destroys this claim. The use of Cabala as magic is forbidden, and those who have allowed or advised this are no better than wicked magicians, not excluding that great and famous philosopher of the Renaissance, Pico della Mirandola.

The building up of Agrippa as a black magician had been

going on for some time, so readers of Bodin's book might not have been surprised at this presentation of him. But I do not know whether it had ever before been pointed out so succinctly that if you condemn Agrippa you must condemn Pico as well. Yet this is certainly logically the case.

What has made Bodin's book historically so important is his legal and learned presentation of the case against witches, his re-affirmation of the whole legendary apparatus concerning them, presented with impressive authority by a learned magistrate. And the witch scare, the intense belief in the stereotype of the witch, propagated by Bodin, and which had such terrible results in encouraging the wholesale execution of these unfortunate women, is quite clearly associated in Bodin's mind with his campaign against the wrong use of Cabala by Pico and Agrippa. Though it is not actually stated in the *Démonomanie* that it was Pico and Agrippa and their disciples, who, by their wrong use of Cabalist magic, had let out the demons who entered the witches, this seems to me to be implied.

Bodin also attacks fiercely the work of Johann Weyer (*De praestigiis daemonum*, first edition in 1563). Weyer was a disciple of Agrippa. His crime in Bodin's eyes was that he had dared to suggest that witches were not infernal agents, but merely silly and deluded old women, suffering from melancholy.[20] Bodin, intent on maintaining the stereotype of the witch, angrily dismisses this dangerous rationalist interpretation which would have prevented, or reduced, the witch craze if it had gained currency. These mild and heretical views about witches were also those of Agrippa, who once defended a woman accused of being a witch.[21] The so-called black conjuror held merciful and psychologically advanced views about witches. Agrippa is Bodin's *bête noire* not only for teaching the kind of magic which the fierce magistrate believed encouraged the spread of witches, but also for undermining belief in the reality of witches.

Bodin says nothing against Francesco Giorgi in the *Démonomanie*, yet the onslaught on Pico would surely indirectly affect Giorgi, Pico's disciple. Indeed, Bodin's censorship of Pico would affect whole areas of the thought and artistic activity of the contemporary French Renaissance.

The year after the publication of the *Démonomanie* there was produced at the French court a wonderful series of entertainments which were infused with the influence of Renaissance magic. Presumably, for Bodin, the sirens and satyrs of the *Ballet comique de la reine*[22] (produced at court in 1581) would have been classed as demons. In fact, in the propaganda against the king, Henry III, as a sorcerer, which was encouraged by his enemies of the Catholic League, the famous sirens and satyrs of his great court entertainment were used as proof of the king's cult of demons.[23]

Yet Bodin moved close to the French court and was an important member of the circle of François D'Alençon, the very same prince as he to whom La Boderie was secretary. There is an extraordinary discrepancy of outlook revealed here between men who ostensibly belonged to the same circle, the circle of D'Alençon and the 'politiques'. Strangely different in tone and temper from the enthusiastic Christian Cabalism of Giorgi, as presented in La Boderie's French translation of 1578, is Bodin's fierce attack in 1580 on Pico's use of Cabala, his severe condemnation of Christian Cabalists like Pico and Agrippa.

Bodin was in England with D'Alençon during the time of his courtship of Queen Elizabeth I. Bodin's politico-religious attitudes are rather obscure. At one time the noted 'politique' and admirer of Queen Elizabeth I, he later seems to have changed his course and veered in the direction of the Catholic League and the circle of Mary, Queen of Scots.[24] I cannot begin to attempt to untangle here the many problems concerning Bodin's politico-religious views, merely noting that he came to England and could have spread there the attitudes of his *Démonomanie*, attitudes so deeply opposed in temper to the Christian Cabalism of Francesco Giorgi.

Another famous contemporary figure who was in France at the same time as Bodin and who, like him, went thence into England, was Giordano Bruno. Bruno was much influenced by Agrippa's *De occulta philosophia*.[25] In Paris in 1582 he published a book on magic memory, dedicated to Henri III, which contains incantations, quoted from Agrippa,[26] of the kind which Bodin thought most diabolical. Bodin would surely have approved of the burning, in 1600, of Bruno, the dangerous magician.

We thus have in the Paris of these late-sixteenth-century years a situation of mounting excitement and danger. On the one hand, Christian Cabala is revived and strong as shown in the translation of Pico and Giorgi by the La Boderie brothers. On the other hand, Jean Bodin publishes his *Démonomanie*, one of the most influential works in encouraging the witch craze, which is a fierce attack on Pico della Mirandola's use of Cabala, and still more on Agrippa as a black magician.

Since Bodin believed that Pico and Agrippa made a bad use of Cabala, his persecution of witches would be a result of that belief. What has happened is that Bodin breaks down the safeguard. Since Cabala may not now be used, as Pico advised, to ensure that the magic is good and holy, the proliferation of witches from the bad use of Cabala would be the result, and the righteous magistrate must exterminate them, as Scripture commands.

In his important book, *Religion and the Decline of Magic*, Keith Thomas carefully and rightly distinguishes two strands in the witch craze and the reactions to it, the popular and the learned.[27] The village sorcerer following the traditions of popular magic was little touched, he thinks, by the spread of learned magic in the Neoplatonic movement. Though he is undoubtedly right that this distinction between the popular and the learned strands in the Renaissance proliferation of magic must be emphasised, yet there are many unsolved problems in the situation. In the case of Bodin, for example, the learned magistrate arrives at his theoretical condemnation of witches through his disapproval of the learned magic of Pico and Agrippa, yet the unfortunate women whom his intellectual theory of magic leads him to condemn were ordinary village witches, or accused of being such. The case of Bodin causes one to wonder how far the witch craze was a genuinely popular movement, and how far it was a popular movement manipulated and intensified from above.

However, it does not come within the scope of this book to pursue this problem. The magic with which I am concerned is certainly the learned magic of the Renaissance. Bodin's logic cut at the root of Renaissance magic with all its religious and cultural associations, threatened by clouds of witch-hunting. And witch-hunts can always be used against personalities or politico-religious movements which the hunters desire to eliminate, concealing them – even from future historians – within folds of diabolic propaganda.

Part II

The Occult Philosophy in the
Elizabethan Age

INTRODUCTION

The Elizabethan world was populated, not only by tough sea-
men, hard-headed politicians, serious theologians. It was a
world of spirits, good and bad, fairies, demons, witches, ghosts,
conjurors. This fact about the Elizabethans, reflected in their
poetry, is too well known to need elaboration. The epic poem in
which the aspirations of the age found expression evolved
around a 'fairy' queen; one of the most significant figures in the
poem is an enchanter. And the greatest plays of the greatest poet
of the age are suffused in the atmosphere of the occult. Macbeth
meets witches; Hamlet is haunted by the ghost. Was this preoccupation with the occult derived solely from popular traditions or influences? Or did it have some deep-seated connection
with the philosophy of the age?

In other words, was there a philosophy of the occult characteristic of the Renaissance which might still have been operating
with renewed vigour in the Elizabethan Renaissance? The history
of such a philosophy has been the theme of the first part of this
book. The second part, now beginning, connects closely with

the first part, for it will argue that the dominant philosophy of the Elizabethan age was precisely the occult philosophy, with its magic, its melancholy, its aim of penetrating into profound spheres of knowledge and experience, scientific and spiritual, its fear of the dangers of such a quest, and of the fierce opposition which it encountered.

The characteristic philosopher of the Elizabethan age was John Dee whose mathematical preface to the English translation of Euclid (1570) begins with an invocation to 'Divine Plato' and quotes Henry Cornelius Agrippa on the three worlds. Dee's preface is the work of a Renaissance Neoplatonist organically connected with the Hermetic–Cabalist core of the movement, particularly as formulated by the most extreme of its exponents, Agrippa. Dee quotes Pico della Mirandola on number, and follows Pico, Reuchlin, and Agrippa in developing intensely the Pythagorean or mathematical side of the movement. His 'mathematical' preface, and his teaching in general, were immensely influential in stimulating the Elizabethan scientific Renaissance.

As is well known, Dee was not only famous as a mathematician but also famous, or infamous, as a 'conjuror'. How did he manage to reconcile his scientific and occult interests with his earnest claim to be a devout Christian and with his support of the Tudor Reformation? I believe that the answer to this question lies in realising that Dee was a Christian Cabalist, supporting the 'more powerful' philosophy implicit in Neoplatonism as understood by Pico, Reuchlin, Giorgi, Agrippa and as developed in the Renaissance occult tradition.

To view Dee as a Christian Cabalist explains, I believe, what appear to be the curious anomalies in his outlook. It explains how the same man could be a brilliant mathematician and ardent propagator of scientific studies, and a 'conjuror' of angels, whilst fervently believing himself to be an ardent reformed Christian. It explains, too, his mysterious world-wide schemes of a religious nature, his missionary journey to the continent. As a representative of the inspired melancholy with its three stages of insight as expounded by Agrippa, he would see Christian Cabala, the 'more powerful' philosophy which was to supersede scholasticism, as potentially a world-wide movement of reform, to be applied not only in Elizabethan England.

If, after studying the history of the occult philosophy in the Renaissance outlined in the first part of this book, we follow the themes into the life and work of Dee, we may begin to see Dee in his true historical context. He appears as truly a man of the late Renaissance developing Renaissance occult philosophy in scientific directions, involved in the religious and reforming side of the movement, but overtaken by the reaction of the later sixteenth century.

It is important to bear in mind the late date of the Elizabethan Renaissance. It begins to flourish at a time when, on the continent, the reaction against Renaissance Neoplatonism and its associated occultisms was growing greatly in intensity as part of the Counter-Reformation effort to apply a restrictive attitude towards Renaissance Neoplatonism. The building up of Queen Elizabeth I as a Neoplatonic heroine by Spenser was in itself a challenge to the Catholic Counter-Reformation powers and their attitude to Renaissance philosophy.

In the 1590s, when Spenser published his magical poem about a fairy queen and his Neoplatonic hymns in her honour, the continental reaction was in full swing. Their 'Neoplatonism' stamped the Elizabethan philosopher, Dee, and the Elizabethan epic poet, Spenser, as adherents of the occult philosophy which the Catholic reaction, powerfully aided by the Jesuits, was endeavouring to stamp out. Spenser's Neoplatonism is of the Hermetic-Cabalist variety, expressive (so I shall argue) in poetic form of the Dee outlook and the Dee patriotic occultism. I believe that a major influence on Dee and Spenser may have been the work of the Cabalist Friar of Venice, Francesco Giorgi.

This second part of the book opens with an account of John

Dee and his thought, divided into three parts to correspond to the three main periods of Dee's life. I then pass to a re-examination of Spenser's Neoplatonism, as presented in his poetry, endeavouring to bring out the occult influences on *The Faerie Queene*.

Marlowe's *Doctor Faustus* is seen as belonging to the reaction, to the atmosphere of the witch crazes and the attacks on Agrippa. With the assault on occult philosophy in *Faustus* was associated the antisemitism of *The Jew of Malta*. Chapman's *Shadow of Night*, on the contrary, defends the occult philosophy, and, by implica-tion, the Dee–Spenser point of view, through its subtle exposition of the 'Saturnian' inspired melancholy.

Within this framework of the occult philosophy in the Eliza-bethan age and the controversies it aroused, new approaches are made to Shakespeare. *The Merchant of Venice* is believed to allude to the contemporary issue of the conversion of the Jews by Chris-tian Cabala, and to echo the work on universal harmony by the Cabalist Friar of Venice, Francesco Giorgi. Hamlet's melancholy is the inspired melancholy with its prophetic visions. Shake-speare's preoccupation with the occult, with ghosts, witches, fairies, is understood as deriving less from popular tradition than from deep-rooted affinity with the learned occult phil-osophy and its religious implications.

King Lear, written during Dee's third period, the time of his disgrace and poverty, is seen as reflecting Dee himself as an old and broken man, ill-rewarded for having devoted his life to the interests of 'British Monarchy', his occultism alluded to through Tom o' Bedlam's supposed possession by devils.

In *The Tempest*, written after Dee's death and during the period of 'the Elizabethan revival within the Jacobean age', Dee is shadowed through Prospero in this most daring play which presents a good conjuror at a time when conjuring was a dreaded accusation of the propaganda of the reaction.

The theme of this part of the book is thus, in many ways,

novel and challenging. My aim is to try to penetrate into the Elizabethan age and its philosophy as a period of thought which can be identified and its origins assessed.

8

JOHN DEE: CHRISTIAN CABALIST

The subject of John Dee's thought, science, position in the Elizabethan age, is, at the time at which I am writing this, in the melting pot. New factual material is constantly turning up; many scholars are trying to assess his scientific thought; the old prejudices against him as a ludicrous figure still subsist, though very much diminished in force as it becomes more and more apparent that Dee had contacts with nearly everyone of importance in the age, that his missionary journey to Bohemia had enormous repercussions, that, in short, the life and work of John Dee constitute a problem the solution of which is not yet in sight.

Under these circumstances my plan in the present chapter is to avoid, as far as possible, the unsolved problems, and to concentrate on bringing together indications that the label 'Christian Cabalist' might cover his outlook, or the greater part of it. If this can be done at all convincingly a step will have been taken towards the solution of the general problem of Dee, and his place in the history of thought, even though many factual matters are left untouched, and great gaps, awaiting the new synthesis, will have to be evaded.

I believe it to be most important to distinguish carefully between the three periods of Dee's life. I therefore divide this chapter into three parts, corresponding to the three periods.

DEE'S FIRST PERIOD (1558–83): THE LEADER OF THE ELIZABETHAN RENAISSANCE

John Dee (1527–1608),[1] was the son of an official at the court of Henry VIII. He was thus born into the Tudor world at a time immediately before the break with Rome, when the divorce issue was looming. His connections and patrons during the early part of his life were the noblemen whose families had been influential in the Tudor Reformation. He was particularly close to the Dudley family, strong adherents of radical reform. Robert Dudley, afterwards Earl of Leicester and favourite of Queen Elizabeth I, had been Dee's pupil when a child; throughout his life he encouraged Dee and his enterprises. Dee's memories went back to the time of Edward VI and the radical reform of that reign; and he served with zeal the last of the Tudors, Queen Elizabeth I, promoting with enthusiasm the Elizabethan expansion.

He was of Welsh descent, and believed himself to be descended from an ancient British prince, even claiming some relationship to the Tudors and to the queen herself. He associated himself intensely with the Arthurian, mythical, and mystical side of the Elizabethan idea of 'British Empire'.

Among the thousands of books in Dee's library[2] were the writings of the authors with whom we have been concerned. He had a considerable collection of Lullist works. He possessed the works of Pico della Mirandola and of Reuchlin. He owned several copies of Agrippa's *De occulta philosophia*. He had the 1545 edition of the Latin version of Giorgi's *De harmonia mundi*. There is no doubt that he was fully conversant with these works and with many others of similar tendency. Though such works may have formed the core of Dee's library, and filled the centre of his mind, that library and that mind also included a vast wealth of scientific knowledge of all kinds, and of literary and historical material. It was the library of a man of the Renaissance, bent on assimilating the whole realm of knowledge available in his time.

This library was at the disposal of friends and students. Here came courtiers and poets, like Sir Philip Sidney (nephew of the Earl of Leicester), navigators and mathematicians, historians and antiquaries, all learning from Dee's stores.

The manifesto of Dee's movement was his preface to Henry Billingsley's translation of Euclid, which was published in 1570. I have been through this preface from various points of view in other books. It is now available in a facsimile reprint.[3] The following résumé is therefore only the briefest possible outline made from the point of view of this book.

With the opening invocation to 'Divine Plato' we are at once in the world of 'Renaissance Neoplatonism'. The subject of the Preface is the importance of number and of the mathematical sciences, and this is confirmed by quotation from one of Pico della Mirandola's Mathematical Conclusions: 'By number, a way is had, to the searching out and understanding of every thyng, hable to be knowen.' Dee's outlook is that of Renaissance Neoplatonism as interpreted in Pico della Mirandola's synthesis. And Dee's Neoplatonism is associated with Renaissance Cabala, for the outline of the Preface is based on Agrippa's *De occulta philosophia* on the three worlds. Like Agrippa, Dee thinks of the universe as divided into the natural, the celestial, and the super-celestial spheres. The tendency of the movement towards concentration on number as the key to the universe, which is apparent in Agrippa and in Giorgi, and which Reuchlin had accentuated through his emphatic association of Pythagoreanism with Cabala, is carried forward by Dee in a yet more intensely 'mathematical' direction.

Dee's mathematics were applied in the practical sphere through his teaching and advice to navigators, artisans, technicians. He also had a grasp of abstract mathematical theory, particularly the theory of proportion as taught in the work on architecture by the Roman architect, Vitruvius. The Preface contains many quotations from Vitruvius; Dee follows Vitruvius on architecture as the queen of the sciences and the one to which all other mathematical disciplines are related.[4]

Dee's numerical, or numerological, theory is closely related not only to Agrippa's basic statement about number, but also to the more extended treatment of this theme in a Cabalist setting by Francesco Giorgi. Dee does not mention Giorgi in the Preface – the only Cabalist whom he mentions is Agrippa – but he had Giorgi's work in his library and there is no doubt that he had studied the De harmonia mundi carefully. Yet Dee seems to be coming to his subject of proportion in relation to number more through Agrippa and the Germans than through Giorgi and the Italians. Giorgi's architectural symbolism was related to his knowledge of Italian architectural theory. As we have seen he applied the theory of architectural harmony to the plan for a Franciscan church in Venice. Dee, however, refers for the theory of proportion to the German artist and theorist Albrecht Dürer.

It is significant that, at the point in the Preface at which Dee advises the reader to consult Vitruvius on theory of proportion, he also advises him to consult, on the same subject, Agrippa and Dürer.[5] Thus the reader of the Preface would look at the diagrams in the De occulta philosophia on proportion in relation to the human figure, and also at the same diagrams in Dürer's basic Four Books of Human Proportion (Vier Bücher von Menschlicher Proportion, 1528) which transferred to the north the Italian art theory on proportion.

Dee and his readers are coming to theory of proportion through Agrippa, the occult philosopher and Cabalist; he cites the German artist, Dürer, as the exponent of the theory. This is an interesting indication that Dürer's work was known to Dee, and presumably to the English readers whom he is addressing, and it suggests that Dee's artistic theory, which was one form of his concentration on number, came to him through the German Renaissance rather than the Italian, though he would find the same theory in the Italian tradition on which Giorgi depended.

Like Reuchlin, Agrippa, and the Christian Cabalists generally, Dee was intensely aware of the supercelestial world of the angels and divine powers. His studies in number, so successful and factual in what he would think of as the lower spheres, were, for him, primarily important because he believed that they could be extended with even more powerful results into the supercelestial world. In short, as is well known, Dee believed that he had achieved, with his associate Edward Kelley, the power of conjuring angels.[6] In one of the descriptions of his séances with Kelley, Dee speaks of the book of Agrippa as lying open on the table, and there is no doubt that Agrippa was Dee's main guide in such operations. The sensational angel-summoning side of Dee's activities was intimately related to his real success as a mathematician. Like the Christian Cabalists generally, he believed that such daring attempts were safeguarded by Cabala from demonic powers. A pious Christian Cabalist is safe in the knowledge that he is conjuring angels, not demons. This conviction was at the centre of Dee's belief in his angelic guidance, and it explains his pained surprise when alarmed and angry contemporaries persisted in branding him as a wicked conjuror of devils.

The angel-conjuring is not apparent in the Preface, which can be read as a straightforward presentation of the mathematical arts. The underlying assumptions are, however, indicated in the fact that Dee is certainly following Agrippa's outline in the *De occulta philosophia* and that was a work founded on Renaissance Magia and Cabala. Also he hints in the Preface at higher secrets which he is not here revealing, probably the secrets of the angel-magic.

The extremely complex nature of Dee's mind and outlook baffles enquirers, many of whom have begun to become aware of his importance and are impressed by the Preface, but would like to forget the angel-magic. Real progress in the understanding of the past cannot, however, be made on obscurantist lines. The facts about Dee must be faced, and one fact certainly is that this remarkable man was undoubtedly a follower of Cornelius Agrippa and attempted to apply the 'occult philosophy' throughout his life and work.

Another very important aspect of Dee's mind was his belief in alchemy. The studies prosecuted with Kelley included not only the angel-magic, but also, and above all, alchemy. Kelley was an alchemist and was believed, according to some rumours, to have succeeded in effecting transformations and in making gold. Practical Cabala and practical alchemy thus seemed to go together in the Dee–Kelley partnership.

I am faced here with a historical question. What place had there been in the Hermetic–Cabalist tradition, stemming from Ficino and Pico, for the Hermetic science of alchemy? The Ficinian outlook, with its emphasis on astral correspondences, would, one would think, have been a philosophy favourable to application as alchemy. Little has, however, as yet been heard of alchemy as an interest of Ficino or of Pico, and their followers. Yet there is a point at which alchemy does enter this tradition, and that very decidedly, and that is with Cornelius Agrippa.

In Agrippa's mysterious travels he was in contact with alchemists in many different places.[7] Sometimes he is heard of performing alchemical operations in a laboratory; he certainly sought out alchemical books and was deeply interested in the subject. He cannot, surely, have been the only Cabalist to be interested in alchemy. Was there a Cabalist alchemy, or an alchemical Cabala, which represented some new kind of combination of such interests already formed in the time of Agrippa? This is at present an unanswered question. Here I am only concerned to state that some close connection between alchemy, Cabala, and his other interests, existed in Dee's mind.

A curious diagram, to which Dee attached the greatest importance as a statement of his whole philosophy, was the *Monas hieroglyphica* (Plate 10), published in 1564 with a dedication to the Emperor Maximilian II,[8] and an explanatory text which leaves the reader thoroughly bewildered. Dee's *monas* is a combination of the signs of the seven planets, plus the symbol for the zodiacal sign, Aries, representing fire. It must have some astral significance; alchemical operations seem implied through the fire sign; it is also some kind of mathematics or geometry; but above all it is Cabala. It is related to 'the stupendous fabric of the Hebrew letters'. It is a 'Cabalistic grammar'. It can be mathematically, cabalistically, and anagogically explained'.[9] It is a profound secret which Dee wonders whether he has sinned in publishing.

There are no Hebrew letters in the *monas* sign itself, yet one gathers that the parts of the planetary signs of which it is composed were to be manipulated in a manner analogous to the manipulation of Hebrew letters in Cabala. There is also a mathematical process going on, though the mathematical side is not so prominent in the *Monas hieroglyphica* as it is in the *Aphorisms*,[10] a work published by Dee a few years earlier (1558) with which he states that the *Monas hieroglyphica* is closely connected. The *Aphorisms*, in which the *monas* sign appears, would seem to be stating in a more obviously mathematical form the Cabalist meaning of the *Monas hieroglyphica*.

I would suggest that an important source in which to study the mode of thought out of which Dee evolved his *monas* sign is Giorgi's *De harmonia mundi*. Here he would have found numerological theory combined with Cabalist theory as the double key to the universe in a manner which is closely analogous to the double meaning of the *monas*, numerological and Cabalist. Giorgi begins with the One, or the *monas*,[11] out of which, as expounded in the *Timaeus*, the numbers one to twenty-seven proceed to form the universal harmony in both macrocosm and microcosm. Combining Pythagoro–Platonic theory with Cabalist letter-mysticism, Giorgi arrives at his synthesis. Dee's mind would work in a similar way in the *monas*. His composite planetary symbol would imply a composite Cabalist symbol. Behind its planetary cosmology would be the 'tremendous structure' of the Hebrew alphabet.[12]

The *monas* symbol includes a cross. It is a Christian Cabalist symbol, no doubt believed by its creator to have great magical power.

Dee was not only an enthusiast for scientific and mathematical studies, in the strange contexts in which he saw them. He wished to use such studies for the advantage of his countrymen and for the expansion of Elizabethan England. Dee had a politico-religious programme and it was concerned with the imperial destiny of Queen Elizabeth I.

I have discussed in my book, *Astraea. The Imperial Theme in the Sixteenth Century* (1975) the nature of Elizabethan imperialism. It was not only concerned with national expansion in the literal sense, but carried with it the religious associations of the imperial tradition, applying these to Elizabeth as the representative of 'imperial reform', of a purified and reformed religion to be expressed and propagated through a reformed empire, the empire of the Tudors with their mythical 'British' associations. The glorification of the Tudor monarchy as a religious imperial institution rested on the fact that the Tudor reform had dispensed with the Pope and made the monarch supreme in both church and state. This basic political fact was draped in the mystique of 'ancient British monarchy', with its Arthurian associations, represented by the Tudors in their capacity as an ancient British line, of supposed Arthurian descent, returned to power and supporting a pure British Church, defended by a religious chivalry from the evil powers (evil according to this point of view) of Hispano-Papal attempts at universal domination.

Though these ideas were inherent in the Tudor myth, Dee had a great deal to do with enhancing and expanding them. Believing himself to be of ancient British royal descent, he identified completely with the British imperial myth around Elizabeth I and did all in his power to support it.

Dee's views on the British-imperial destiny of Queen Elizabeth I are set out in his *General and rare memorials pertayning to the Perfect art of Navigation* (1577). Expansion of the navy and Elizabethan expansion at sea were connected in his mind with vast ideas concerning the lands to which (in his view) Elizabeth might lay claim through her mythical descent from King Arthur. Dee's 'British imperialism' is bound up with the 'British History' recounted by Geoffrey of Monmouth,[13] based on the myth of the hypothetical descent of British monarchs from Brut, supposedly of Trojan origin, and therefore connecting with Virgil and the Roman imperial myth. Arthur was the supposed descendant of Brut, and was the chief religious and mystical exemplar of sacred British imperial Christianity.

In the *General and rare memorials* there is a complicated print (Plate 11), based on a drawing in Dee's own hand,[14] of Elizabeth sailing in a ship labelled 'Europa', with the moral that Britain is to grow strong at sea, so that through her 'Imperial Monarchy' she may perhaps become the pilot of all Christendom. This 'British Hieroglyphick', as Dee calls the design, should be held in mind at the same time as the *Monas hieroglyphica*, as representing a politico-religious expression of the *monas* in the direction of a 'British imperial' idea.

Much of the material on Dee which I have here resumed is familiar but Dee and his activities may appear in a somewhat new light when viewed in relation to the studies in this book. In what light would this deep student of the sciences of number, this prophetic interpreter of British history, have been seen, both by himself and by his contemporaries?

I suggest that the contemporary role which would exactly fit Dee would be that of the 'inspired melancholic'.[15] According to Agrippa, and as portrayed by Dürer in the famous engraving, the inspired melancholic was a Saturnian, immersed in those sciences of number which could lead their devotees into great depths of insight. Surely Dee's studies were such as to qualify him as a Saturnian, a representative of the Renaissance revaluation of melancholy as the temperament of inspiration. And after the first stage of inspiration, the inspiration coming from immersion in the sciences of number, Agrippa envisages a second stage, a prophetic stage, in which the adept is intent on politico-religious events and prophecies. And finally in the third stage, stage of inspired melancholy, the highest insight into religion and religious changes is revealed.

It may seem suggestive that not only was Dee's programme for the advance of science based on Agrippa on the three worlds in the *De occulta philosophia*, but also that the stages of his prophetic outlook might be clarified from the same source. First Dee as Saturnian melancholic studies the sciences of number; then he gains prophetic insight into British imperial destiny; and finally vast universal religious visions are revealed to him. Yet all the time he was, like Agrippa, a Christian, a Christian Cabalist with leanings towards evangelicalism and Erasmian reform.

It must be remembered that Dee's ideas, which we have to try to piece together from scanty and scattered evidence, would have been known to contemporaries through personal contact with this man, who was ubiquitous in Elizabethan society and whose library was the rendezvous of intellectuals. And there were many works by Dee passing from hand to hand in manuscript which were never published. In his *Discourse Apologetical* (1604), Dee gives a list of his writings, many, indeed most, of which are unknown to us but which may have been available to his contemporaries in manuscript. From that list I select the following titles of lost writings by Dee:

> *Cabala Hebraicae compendiosa tabella, anno* 1562.
> *Reipublicae Britannicae Synopsis, in English, 1565.*
> *De modo Evangelii Iesu Christi publicandi . . . inter infideles, 1581.*
> *The Origins and chiefe points of our auncient British histories.*

Through these lost titles, we catch glimpses of Dee studying Cabala, immersed in his 'British History' researches, and interested in missionary schemes for publishing the Gospel of Jesus Christ to the heathen.

Dee is not a person who can be lightly dismissed as a sorcerer, in accordance with the labels affixed to him in the witch scares. He must have been one of the most fascinating figures of the Elizabethan age, appealing to that brilliant world for his learning, his patriotism, and for the insight associated with Christian Cabala.

DEE'S SECOND PERIOD (1583–9): THE CONTINENTAL MISSION

In 1583, John Dee left England and was abroad for six years, returning in 1589.[16] During these years on the continent Dee appears to have been engaged in some kind of missionary venture which took him to Cracow, in Poland, and eventually to Prague where the occultist emperor Rudolf II, held his court. It is possible, though there is no evidence for this, that when in Prague, Dee was in contact with the Rabbi Loewe, famous Cabalist and magician, who once had an interview with Rudolf (see *The Rosicrucian Enlightenment*, p. 228). Dee stayed for several years in Bohemia with a noble family the members of which were interested in alchemy and other occult sciences. His associate, Edward Kelley, was with him, and together they were fervently pursuing their alchemical experiments and their attempts at angel-summoning with practical Cabala.

To this period belong the séances described in Dee's spiritual diary,[17] with their supposed contacts with the angels Uriel and Gabriel and other spirits. Dee was moving now on the more 'powerful' levels of Christian Cabala through which he hoped to encourage powerful religious movements.

The evidence about Dee's continental mission is somewhat obscure and incomplete. It is referred to thus by a contemporary observer:

> A learned and renowned Englishman whose name was Doctor Dee came to Prague to see the Emperor Rudolf II and was at first well received by him; he predicted that a miraculous reformation would presently come about in the Christian world and would prove the ruin not only of the city of Constantinople but of Rome also. These predictions he did not cease to spread among the populace.[18]

Dee's message appeared to be neither Catholic nor Protestant but an appeal to a vast, undogmatic, reforming movement which drew its spiritual strength from the resources of occult philosophy.

In the context of the late sixteenth century in which movements of this kind abounded, Dee's mission would not have seemed incredible or strange. Enthusiastic missionaries of his type were moving all over Europe in these last years of the century. One such was Giordano Bruno, who preached a mission of universal Hermetic reform, in which there were some Cabalist elements.[19] Bruno was in Prague shortly after Dee; he had been in England preaching his version of Hermetic-Cabalist reform, and was to go on into Italy, where he met the full force of the Counter-Reformation suppression of Renaissance Neoplatonism, and its allied occultisms, and was burned at the stake in

Rome in 1600. Dee was more cautious, and was careful not to venture into Italy.

For Dee's mission, the *Monas hieroglyphica* is probably the most important clue, for it contained in the compressed form of a magic sign the whole of the occult philosophy. And it had reference to contemporary rulers who were to be the politico-religious channels of the movement. The first version of it had been dedicated to the Emperor Maximilian II, Rudolf's father. Dee may have hoped that Rudolf would step into his father's role, and accept the *monas* as his occult imperial sign. In England, Dee had transferred to Queen Elizabeth I the destiny of occult imperial reform, signified by the *monas*.

There is some kind of congruity between the ideas associated with Rudolf and those associated with Elizabeth. As R. J. W. Evans has said: 'Both the unmarried Emperor and the Virgin Queen were widely regarded as figures prophetic of significant change in their own day, as symbols of lost equilibrium when they were dead.'[20] It is perhaps in some such sense of occult imperial destiny linking Elizabeth and Rudolf that the true secret meaning of Dee's continental mission may lie. On the more obvious level it would seem to have been a movement antagonistic to the repressive policies of Counter-Reform, and as such it would have made dangerous enemies.

The emperor did not enthusiastically support Dee, and when he returned to England in 1589 it must have been far from clear to the queen and her advisers whether he had accomplished anything at all, beyond making extremely dangerous enemies.

However he had sown powerful seeds which were to grow to a strange harvest. It has been shown that the so-called 'Rosicrucian manifestos', published in Germany in the early seventeenth century, are heavily influenced by Dee's philosophy, and that one of them contains a version of the *Monas hieroglyphica*.[21] The Rosicrucian manifestos call for a universal reformation of the whole wide world through Magia and Cabala. The mythical

'Christian Red Cross' (Christian Rosencreuz), the opening of whose magical tomb is a signal for the general reformation, may perhaps, in one of his aspects, be a teutonised memory of John Dee and his Christian Cabala, confirming earlier suspicions that 'Christian Cabala' and 'Rosicrucianism' may be synonymous.

DEE'S THIRD PERIOD (1589–1608): DISGRACE AND FAILURE

When Dee returned to England in 1589, he was at first received by the queen, but his old position at the centre of the Elizabethan world was not restored.[22] During his absence, the Armada victory of 1588 had occurred, and this, one would think, might have been seen as the triumph on the seas of the patriotic movement in which Dee had had so large a share. On the other hand, the Earl of Leicester's movement for landward extension of the Elizabethan ethos in his military expedition to the Netherlands in 1586 had failed; his nephew Philip Sidney lost his life in that expedition; and the whole enterprise was checked by the queen who withdrew Leicester from his command in disgrace. Leicester never got over this; he quietly died in 1588. Thus Leicester and the Sidney circle, Dee's supporters in the old days, were no longer there except for some survivors, such as Edward Dyer, Sidney's closest friend, who had been in touch with Dee and Kelley in their recent adventures.

Shunned and isolated, Dee was also confronted with a growing witch-hunt against him. The cry of 'conjuror' had always been sporadically raised but in the old days the queen and Leicester had protected his studies. Now the enemies were increasingly vocal. Dee felt obliged to defend himself in a letter to the Archbishop of Canterbury, printed in 1604 but written earlier. It is illustrated with a woodcut (Plate 12) which shows Dee kneeling on the cushion of hope, humility, and patience with his head raised in prayer to the cloudy heavens wherein can be seen the ear, eye, and avenging sword of God. Opposite to him is the many-headed monster of lying tongues and unkind rumour, its heads malevolently turned in his direction. He earnestly assures the archbishop that all his studies have been directed towards searching out the truth of God, that they are holy studies, not diabolical as his enemies falsely assert. From his youth up it has pleased the Almighty

> to insinuate into my hart, an insatiable zeale, and desire to knowe his truth: And in him, and by him, incessantly to seeke, and listen after the same; by the true philosophical method and harmony: proceeding and ascending . . . *gradatim*, from things visible, to consider of things inuisible; from thinges bodily, to conceiue of thinges spirituall: from thinges transitorie, and momentarie, to meditate of things permanent: by thinges mortall . . . to have some perceiuerance of immortality. And to conclude, most briefeley, by the most meruailous frame of the *whole world*, philosophically viewed, and circumspectly wayed, numbred, and measured . . . most faithfully to loue, honor, and glorifie alwaies, the Framer and Creator thereof.[23]

One hears in these words the voice of the pious author of the Mathematical Preface, rising with number through the three worlds. But the admired Dee of other days, mentor of Elizabethan poets, must now defend himself from being a black conjuror of devils.

The implications of the angel-conjuring side of Dee's doctrine had come out more prominently during his continental mission; probably rumours of this, and of Jesuit opposition to it, had reached England. Elizabeth and her advisers, always nervous of committing themselves to the rash projects of enthusiasts, would now be understandably nervous of Dee. Elizabeth had withdrawn her support from Leicester's continental enterprise; Leicester and Sidney were both dead. No wonder that Dee's position in England was very different from what it had been before his continental journey and that many people might now refuse to believe that the famous mathematician was a Christian Cabalist, and not a conjuror of devils.

Of Dee's three periods, the first one, the successful one, has been the most explored. We are all now familiar with the idea that John Dee, dismissed in the Victorian age as a ridiculous charlatan, was immensely influential in the Elizabethan age, an influence which is far from being, as yet, fully assessed or understood. Of the second period, the period of the continental mission, we are beginning to know a good deal more than formerly, enough to realise that it had some very large religious or reforming scope, and that its influence long persisted in ways difficult to decipher. The third period, the period of failure verging on persecution of this once so admired and important figure, has been the least studied of all. What I now say about it must be provisional, awaiting further much-needed research. For the third period is most essential for the understanding of Dee as a whole.

Dee was very poor after his return and in great anxiety as to how to provide a living for his wife and family. A former friend with whom he was, apparently, still in contact was Sir Walter Raleigh, with whom Dee dined at Durham House on 9 October 1595.[24] Raleigh, however, was himself out of favour, and would be unlikely to be able to help him to a position. At last, in 1596, he was made warden of a college in Manchester, whither he moved with his wife and family. It was an uncomfortable place and he had difficulty with the fellows of the college. In fact the Manchester appointment seems to have been something like a semi-banishment where he was, for reasons not quite clear, unhappy.

One of his activities when at Manchester was to act as adviser about cases of witchcraft and demonic possession. He had books on these subjects in his Manchester library which he lent to enquirers investigating such cases. One of the books which he

thus lent was the *De praestigiis daemonum* by Weyer,[25] the friend of
Agrippa, in which it is argued that witchcraft is a delusion,
witches being only poor, melancholy old women. Another book
which Dee lent was the *Malleus maleficarum*, a work which is very
positive as to the reality of witches.

It would seem strange that the conjuring suspicions against
Dee should have taken the form of turning him into an expert on
demonology to be consulted in trials, but such seems to have
been the case.

The reality of witches and witchcraft was being forcibly
maintained in these years by no less a person than the King of
Scotland, soon to succeed Queen Elizabeth as James I. In his
Daemonologie (1587),[26] James is profoundly shocked by the
'damnable error' of those who, like Weyer, deny the reality of
witchcraft. He refers the reader to Bodin's *Démonomanie* where he
will find many examples of witchcraft collected with great diligence. And for particulars about the black arts the reader should
consult 'the fourth book of Cornelius Agrippa'. This was the
spurious fourth book of the *De occulta philosophia* which James
accepted as genuine (Weyer had said that it was not by Agrippa).
James has much more to say about 'the Divel's school' which
thinks to climb to knowledge of things to come 'mounting from
degree to degree on the slippery scale of curiosity', believing
that circles and conjurations tied to the words of God will raise
spirits.[27] This is clearly 'practical Cabala' interpreted as a black
art, a fruit of that tree of forbidden knowledge of which Adam
was commanded not to eat.

James's work, if read in Manchester, would not have helped
Dee's reputation.

Dee appears to have been away from Manchester from 1598 to
1600; eventually he returned to his old house at Mortlake, living
there in great poverty, though still partially in touch with 'great
persons'.

The accession of James I in 1603 boded little good for the

reputed conjuror. Nevertheless Dee made desperate appeals to the new monarch. In a printed pamphlet, dated 5 June 1604, John Dee appeals to the king asking that those who call him a conjuror should be brought to trial: 'Some impudent and malicious forraine enemie or English traytor . . . hath affirmed your Maiesties Suppliant to be a Conjuror belonging to the most Honorable Priuie Counsell of your Maiesties most famous last predecessor. . . .'[28] Note that Dee suspects foreigners or traitors of fomenting the rumours against him, and that he hints that such rumours might implicate the late queen and her council.

All was in vain. Dee was not cleared. He died in great poverty at Mortlake in 1608.

The last act of Dee's extraordinary story is the most impressive of them all. The descendant of British kings, creator (or one of the creators) of the British imperial legend, the leader of the Elizabethan Renaissance, the mentor of Philip Sidney, the prophet of some far-reaching religious movement, dies, an old man, in bitter neglect and extreme poverty.

I am not interested here in the sensationalism which has gathered round Dee's story and which has tended to obscure his real significance. That significance, as I see it, is the presentation in the life and work of one man of the phenomenon of the disappearance of the Renaissance in the late sixteenth century in clouds of demonic rumour. What happened in Dee's lifetime to his 'Renaissance Neoplatonism' was happening all over Europe as the Renaissance went down in the darkness of the witchhunts. Giordano Bruno in England in the 1580s had helped to inspire the 'Sidney circle' and the Elizabethan poetic Renaissance. Giordano Bruno in 1600 was burned at the stake in Rome as a sorcerer. Dee's fate in England in his third period presents a similar extraordinary contrast with his brilliant first, or 'Renaissance', period.

The Hermetic–Cabalist movement failed as a movement of religious reform, and that failure involved the suppression of the Renaissance Neoplatonism which had nourished it. The Renaissance magus turned into Faust.

9

SPENSER'S NEOPLATONISM AND THE OCCULT PHILOSOPHY: JOHN DEE AND *THE FAERIE QUEENE*

Of the Elizabethan poets, the one who has been placed within a recognisable thought movement is Edmund Spenser, usually described as a Neoplatonist. This label, as formerly used, left out the Hermetic–Cabalist core which modern scholarship has revealed within Renaissance Neoplatonism, as formulated by Ficino and Pico. Notwithstanding the immense literature on Spenser, his Neoplatonism has not yet been tackled on modern lines, though much has recently been brought to light of which the older Spenser criticism never dreamed. Alastair Fowler has argued for intricate numerological patterns in The Faerie Queene, and for an astral or planetary pattern in its themes.[1] Angus Fletcher has drawn attention to the Hermetic–Egyptian setting of Britomart's vision in the Temple of Isis.[2] Thus there are movements stirring towards new solutions of Spenser's philosophy, if one can use that word of his outlook.

In this chapter, I make the attempt to place Spenser's thought within the history of the occult philosophy, as outlined in this book. I want to suggest that Spenser inherited much more than Neoplatonism as formulated by Ficino and Pico. He inherited the movement towards reform in later Christian Cabalists, like Reuchlin, Giorgi, Agrippa. He inherited the intensified Cabalist–Neoplatonism, or Cabalist–Neopythagorism, with its emphasis on number, of which John Dee was a leading representative. He inherited the thought of a 'more powerful philosophy', leading to a world-wide reforming movement, with Queen Elizabeth I in the leading role in which Dee saw her.

To a very serious Puritan like Edmund Spenser, the reforming side of the occult philosophy would have been likely to make a strong appeal. It will be argued in this chapter that a major influence on Spenser was the De harmonia mundi by the Christian Cabalist and Platonist, Francesco Giorgi.

In an earlier chapter in this book, the thought arose that Giorgi's philosophy might have been welcome to Tudor reformers because of the stand taken by the Friar of Venice on the subject of the divorce of Henry VIII. I cannot pursue that thought further here, beyond merely reminding of it, and reminding further that Giorgi's work was in the library of John Dee, and that we have had reason to think that it was a strong influence on the thought of Dee himself. Giorgi's work was particularly attractive to poets. His style has an intense lyrical and poetic quality. The French poets of the period had found Giorgi a most congenial philosopher; his influence would naturally extend to their contemporaries, the Elizabethan poets.

The first three books of The Faerie Queene were published in 1590 but the poem had been begun more than ten years earlier, as we know from letters exchanged between Spenser and Gabriel Harvey, printed in 1580.[3] At that time, Spenser was in contact with John Dee's pupils, Philip Sidney and Edward Dyer, both of whom are mentioned in the Spenser–Harvey letters. He was thus in touch with the leading poets of the Dee circle and could have become aware in this way of Giorgi's work. Seeking for a contemporary philosophy on which to base his panegyric of the queen and her imperial reform, Spenser might well have been drawn to the work on world harmony by the Friar of Venice. The French translation of 1578 can hardly have influenced the conception of Spenser's poem, by then probably well begun, moreover, Spenser and his friends were adverse to Anjou and to the French match with which the French translation may have been connected. Yet the French translation is likely to have increased contemporary awareness of Giorgi's work.

The Spenserian Hymnes[4] have always been taken as the clearest statement of the poet's Neoplatonism. The Hymnes were first published in 1596, that is six years after the first instalment of The Faerie Queene and in the same year as the second instalment. Spenser may have intended the Hymnes as an explanation of, or apology for, the philosophy behind The Faerie Queene. The Hymnes abound in references to Plato and to Platonic philosophy; their cult of heavenly love and beauty is Platonic in conception. Yet their basic structure is that of an Hermetic ascent and descent through the spheres of the universe.

In the Hymne of Heavenly Beauty, the poet rises through the three worlds; the elemental world; the celestial world, that round 'sown with glittering stars' wherewith God has encompassed this All; the intellectual world where the Platonic ideas merge with the angelic hierarchies. In the Hymne of Heavenly Love, he descends through the three worlds, beginning at the top where the Trinity reigns over a host of angels bright. The Hymnes culminate in outpourings of Christian devotion, in a rendering of the Gospel story in poetic language.

Just so does Giorgi's De harmonia mundi rise at the end – after his elaborate account of the three worlds – to an intense

Christianity,[5] suffused in lyrical and erotic devotionalism, influenced by Giorgi's familiarity with Cabalist mystical texts. To my mind, it is in Spenser's lyrical evangelicalism in the *Hymnes* that the influence of Giorgi is most apparent, the influence of a Franciscan Cabalist.

The recent developments in Spenserian scholarship which I have mentioned – the work of Alastair Fowler and of Angus Fletcher – have concentrated on eliciting numerological patterns in *The Faerie Queene* and on emphasising Spenser's use of the temple as a basic image. Both these preoccupations, the numerological and the templar, which are at bottom the same, are found in the highest degree of elaboration in the work of Giorgi. We have seen how the prefaces to the French translation by the La Boderie brothers stress the numerological and architectural imagery in Giorgi's work. His book, they say, presents the plan or model from which the Architect of the Universe worked. It is like the Temple of Solomon, the meaning of which is understood by those who know how to 'Pythagorise and Philosophise by Mathematics'.[6]

Spenser's description of the House of Alma (*Faerie Queene*, Book II, ix, 22) is an allegory of the human body and soul presented in architectural terms. The plan of the House of Alma is described as follows:

> The frame thereof seemed partly circulare,
> And part triangulare, O worke divine;
> Those two the first and last proportions are,
> The one imperfect, mortall, foeminine:
> Th'other immortall, perfect, masculine,
> And twixt them both a quadrate was the base
> Proportioned equally by seven and nine:
> All which compacted made a goodly diapase.

The actual figure which Spenser is here describing is difficult to determine, but the general meaning would appear to refer to the three worlds. The cube, or quadrate, is the elemental world of the four elements; the seven is the celestial world of the seven planets; the nine is the supercelestial world of the nine angelic hierarchies, which form into the triangle of the Trinity. All three worlds are present in man as well as in the universe. Hence the geometry and architecture of the House of Alma would be an expression in architectural terms of the little world of man. The geometry of the house as a whole formed a 'goodly diapase' or octave. The stanza is fundamental for Spenser on the universal harmony, and for his understanding of its allegorical expression in architecture. Fowler has wrestled with this stanza, using Giorgi in his attempts to interpret it.[7] Those who understand how to philosophise and Pythagorise by mathematics should be able to see the proportions of the Temple of Solomon rising behind it.

By a remarkable effort of the imagination, Spenser had absorbed the framework, the groundwork, of the type of thought which in the Italian Renaissance was productive of great creative works of art and architecture, the world in which Francesco Giorgi had lived. He expresses these ideas creatively through his poetry. It is his grasp of the basic ideas, his understanding of the numerology of universal harmony, of the perfect templar proportions of the great world of the universe and the little world of man, which gives that Renaissance quality of harmony to Spenser's poetry.

Let us now turn to the astral, or planetary, themes, which Fowler has tried to discover in The Faerie Queene. He thinks that the seven books of the poem refer in some way to the seven planets.[8] We have to remember that Spenser intended the poem to have twelve books[9] of which only six and part of a seventh were published. Caution must therefore be exercised in any attempt to interpret a work which was not fully executed as planned. Nevertheless I agree that Fowler is right in principle in seeking for planetary themes though I do not agree with his detailed interpretation. He tries to make the order of the planetary themes in the poem correspond to the order of the planetary week – Sun-day, Moon-day, Mars-day, and so on. The planetary-week order works for some of the books of the poem but not for all of them. Many years ago I drew up – for my own private edification, though I sometimes discussed it with students – a plan of what appeared to me to be the order of the planetary themes in The Faerie Queene. This, of course may also be wrong, but before bringing out my own ideas on the subject a general question must be raised.

The books of the poem are said by Spenser to be about certain, rather curiously chosen, virtues. Spenser's poem is profoundly ethical, as well as profoundly religious, and, in a way, profoundly Christian. Through what philosophy could the seven planets, with their associations with astrology, so opposite in its fatalistic determinism to the moral free-will which the poem teaches, have been so important for Spenser that he used them as basic themes in the moral and religious scheme of his ethnical poem? The answer is to be found in the planetary-angelic-Sephirotic schemes of Francesco Giorgi, though these were not original to him.[10] We have been through this system before, but it needs to be repeated again here in relation to Spenser.

In the highest supercelestial or intellectual world, Giorgi puts the Sephiroth, or emanations of Cabala, the Platonic ideas, the Christian angelic hierarchies. All are as it were fused in that highest world, and they pour down their influences through the middle world of the stars – and by the stars Giorgi means the seven planets and the twelve signs of the zodiac. These stars give different characteristics to the influences but they are none of them in themselves bad. Saturn and Mars are not bad or unfortunate, as in astrology. All the influences of the stars are good as they pour down from the divine creator, though they have different virtues. It is only the bad reception of the

1 Gentile, Jew, Moslem and Christian under the Trees of the Lullian Art.
Illustration to Ramon Lull, *Liber de gentili et tribus sapientibus* (written 1274
in Arabic), in Lull, *Opera omnia*, Mainz, 1721–42

debunt omnes terrarum populi,quòd nomē Tetragrammaton vocatū erit super te. Qui qui-
dem aceruus orationis ex istis tribus videli-
cet,Nomen Tetragrammaton Vocatum, simul
collectus,omnino iuxta Cabalam Hebræorum
per שׁ Schin frequenti vsu intelligitur, vt si
vltima respondeat primis,nihil aliud hæc pro-
phetia cōtineat,quàm si audieris vocē יהוה,
hoc est quando Tetragrammaton fiet audibile,
id est, effabile, tunc nomen Tetragrammaton
vocatum per שׁ Schin,erit super te,haud secus
atq; si diceret, Si nomen ineffabile Tetragram
maton oporteat fieri effabile, necessario vocabi
tur per consonātem quæ appellatur שׁ Schin,
vt fiat יהשׁוה, qui erit supra te,caput tuū
& dominus tuus. Benedictus sit Deus & pa-
ter domini nostri יהשׁוה Ihsuh Christi,
qui desuper instillat nobis cognitionem veri
nominis vnigeniti filij sui & saluatoris nostri,
vel secundū Græcos sanatoris nostri.Hoc enim
nomen à medendo & sanando deriuant Græ-
corum autores. Hebræorum verò grammatici
à saluando, vt idem esse יהשׁוה Ihsuh pu-
tent quod saluator. Atqui saluator commune
nomen est, יהשׁוה Ihsuh autem maximè
propriū, ita quod nulli alteri nisi filio Dei in-
carnato conueniat.Facit hoc varietas literarū
ex quibus dictio constat, quali à seculo non est
audita.

2 The Tetragrammaton and the Name of Jesus. Page from Johannes
Reuchlin, *De verbo mirifico* (1494), edition of Lyons, 1552

reconciliati, aut recapitulari omnia. Sed cum producta quælibet contineantur in Christo homine, etiã rationes producentes, & operantes, quæ sunt
in Archetypo continent in Christo Deo: De quibus omnibus exarare longum nimis eset, & ulterius progrederemur, q̃ præsens exigat opus. Quomodo aūt principalia nomina Dei, & quæ frequentius in scriptura sacra
aperte repetunt /in hoc nomine יהוה. Iesu cōtineant, adumbrabimus. Hoc
nomen quadriliterum est celeberrimum/& frequẽratissimũ, quod sic scribitur יהוה. nec exprimi potest: sed quando legitur, pronuntiatur Adonai.
Huius itaq̃ nominis duæ literæ pcipuę, ya atq̃ ı cõtinent in nomine יהו
Duo uero ה maximo mysterio mutātur in ש: Dicūt.n. secretiores theologi, q̃ summus opifex Deus spiritualia omnia produxit per quandam uim
significatã in priori ש: Corporalia uero per uirtutẽ signatam in posteriori
ה. Et cum omnia per uerbum humanatum, quod nominatur Iesus effecta
sint/uirtutes, aut proprietates ipsæ signatæ per illa duo ה includunt in eo.
Sed quia Iesus datus, & missus est nobis tanq̃ redẽptor, & ductor ad uerã
quiete̅, quæ est uita æterna, imo factus est ipsa quies nˉra, ideo in loco illoꝝ
duoꝝ ה significantiũ rationes principii in nomine יהו. Iesu ponitur ש, q̃
est principium ושב sabat, & ipsum significat, quod interpretatur requies.
Ecce quot & quanta mysteria importantur in tribus literis huius nois יהו.
I E S V: Nam ı diuinitatem significat, ut est notissimũ apud ipsos theologos ı arborem uitę, & ש requiem: denotat utraq̃, q̃ Iesus noster est Deus oˉs
uiuificans utraq̃ uita, & tandẽ beatificãs in requie illa æterna. Extat quoq̃
illud nomen quadrilitеꝝ alio mysterio in nomine Iesu, per uiam y̅ numerorum adiũcto nomine matris, a qua substãtiam corporis traxit: Nam
quatuor literę illius nominis reddunt in numero.26. & nomẽ matris, quod
est מרים miriã dãt.290: Qui numerus iunctus cũ illis.26. cõstituit.316, quẽ
etiam numerũ dant literæ nominis יהו. In quo denotat nominatũ ipsum
a patre Deo, matreq̃ humana processisse. Per hanc eandem uiam numerorum concludimus conclusum in Iesu illud terrificum nomen שדי sadai:
cuius literæ in numero dant.314: Cui numero si addatur binarius, qui corporaturam significat, cõstituit.316. qui est numerus literarum nominis יהו.
ut nuper diximus, Data ẽ quo huic uirtus illius nominis שדי sadai, quod
semper terrificũ fuit in hostes humani generis: Vnde in Psalmo.90.qui factus est ad terrendos illos hostes, dicit Propheta: In uerba Sadai morabit:
Pro quo nos habemus: In protectione Dei cœli commorabitur. Cum igit̃
Christus cognosceret ipsius nominis uirtutẽ in suo fuisse conclusam Apostolis mysterium reseruauit dicens: In nomine meo dęmonia eiicient, & cętera quę sequˉuntur. Est quoq̃ in nomine Iesu hoc nomen אל quod Deum
significat: & אלה quod idem est cũ suo plurali אלהים. quis aliquãdo hoc

Dauid

CHRI
STVS

mondes est pourueu de sa racine, quarré & Cube, tout ainsi que l'Vniuers, comme il apparoist par les nombres qui sont hors les rondeaux, par là peux-tu entendre l'Armonie & conuenance de tout, & comme peut estre vray le dire d'Anaxagore, qui mettoit omnia in omnibus & singula in singulis.

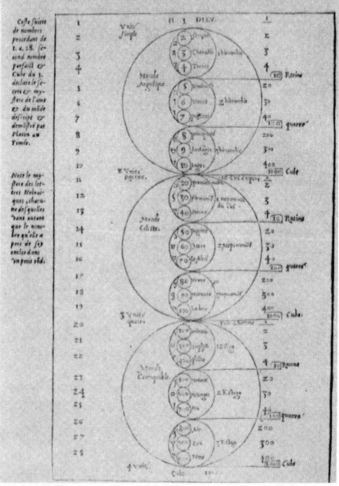

4 Numerological relationships between the Three Worlds. Diagram illustrating discourse by Nicolas Le Fèvre de la Boderie in Francesco Giorgi *L'Harmonie du monde* (French translation by Guy Le Fèvre de la Boderie of *De harmonia mundi*), Paris, 1578

5 Albrecht Dürer, *Melencolia I*, engraving, 1514

6 Albrecht Dürer, *St Jerome*, engraving, 1514

7 Lucas Cranach, *The Melancholy Witch*, painting, 1528

FRANCISCI GEORGII

VENETI

MINORITANAE FAMILIAE

DE HARMONIA

MVNDI TOTIVS

CANTICA

T R I A

Talia probariot, fpiritus quibus fpirat.

8 Francesco Giorgi, *De harmonia mundi*, Venice, 1525. Title-page, with note by the censor that the work abounds in arguments of Platonists and Cabalists and is therefore to be read with caution

decantat ipsum arbitrum undis:Sic etiam planetar; ordo exquirit:ut post
Lunam terream sit Mercurius aqueus:Venus aerea:Sol igneus.Et iterũ/
Mars igneus:Iupiter aereus:Saturnus aqueus:Signifer; cœlũ terreũ:Pri/
mum mobile igneum.Quo ordine etiã Angelicos montes succedunt:Hav
bent n̄ Angeli naturam terream cum Luna:Archãgeli aqueam cũ Mer/
curio:Principatus aeream cũ Venere:Potestates igneam cũ Sole:Virtutes
iterum igneam cum Marte:Dominatões aeream cum Ioue:Throni aqueã
cum Saturno:Cherubini terream cum firmamento:Seraphim igneã cum
primo mobili:& cum Archetypo in ignea ut Spiritui sancto conueniunt:

Moses
Throni uero cũ filio,qui est aqua supramundana, de qua omniũ philoso-
phou,& theologou facile Princeps Moses pertractat:quando aquas sub
globo,aut cortina cœlos; segregat ab iis,quæ desup erant:Quæ sunt aquę
Angelicæ Deo/teste Dauide/laudantes:Sunt & summa affluẽtia bonita-
tis diuinę,quæ ne plus q̃ inferiou; gradus,& opera met; nitur effundat/in
expolita est cõtinens illa cœlestis:in qua tãq̃ in tribunal/quodã diiudica-
tur/q̃cum ex ipsa aqua cuiq; tribui debeat. Sed huiusmodi arcana Moses
sub esta reclusit: pribus/populisq; illis / quibus in figura omnia continge/
bant:Ex qbus multigen̄s,& occulti hmis sacramétis antiqui philosophi,
& uates aliquos cortices extrahentes sibi/multa uendicarunt:adeo/ut cre
datur Rythagoræ, Socratis,Platonis,Aristotelis/& alios; sapiẽtiã/quæ a
summo fonte Deo per Mosen ad mortales emanauit,ut ipse Moses,& nõ

Cicero
Socrates (sicut scribit Cicero) sapientiã uocauit:ut de cœlo/& primus lit
tris publicis comendauerit:Sed clarius hæc explicata habent a Christo/&
eius asseclis/ quibus cade credidit. Et forsitã hæc aqua sapiẽtiæ salutaris
diffusius adhuc propinabit mortalibus/ quãdo superiores Dei ministri in
aqueũ cœli atriũ conuenient omnes/quibus a supremo fonte datur facul/
tas aperiendi excelsos illos canales/nũc ob infœlicia tempora conclusos:
immo obsurata merita illou;/qui his deterioribus offuscati infœlicesq; te/
nebræ offecit;illã supremam lucé,& aquam apprehendere nequeunt:nec
merent:Quos canales iubeat Deus sua clemẽtia aperiri: quia terrena fa/
ciesã in summa ariditate reperit,& propinos;/sicut propinauit Messiq;
merito sumptus ex aquis dicit:Profundaq; ipsam Dei filius aqua supre
ma per ministros in culiculum aquã colligendos/sicut olim tanta copia
propinauit discipulis,ut flamina de uentre eou; scaturiret: aquæ iuuenu;
ũde fieret fons saliens in uitã æternam. Sed ad nostrũ Mercuriũ redeun/
do,naturã lapic aqueã:Nam sicut hæc laudã do auterã obtegente macula:
ut appareat nuda rei formatific ille Hermes uerus interpres ãmouet testã
extranei idiomatis/obscuritatem ænigmatũ/& parabolas;,aut cuiuscunq;
detrusi sermonis difficultaté:Et apiés ea,quæ in penetralibus arcanis Dei:
& naturæ recondita sunt,nudam offert ueritatem contuendam.Et ut cum

K

10 John Dee, *Monas hieroglyphica*, 1564, title-page

11 John Dee, *General and rare memorials*, 1577, title-page

12 Dee and his Enemies. Title-page of Dee's *Letter* addressed to the Archbishop of Canterbury, 1604 (written earlier)

13 Faustus conjuring a Devil. Title-page of Christopher Marlowe, *Doctor Faustus*, edition of 1620

14 Matthias Gerung, *Melancolia*, painting, 1558

15 William Shakespeare, memorial bust, Stratford-on-Avon

16 Rembrandt, *The Inspired Scholar*, etching, c. 1651–3

influence by the evil will of the recipient which turns their intrinsically good influences into vices.

This system does not do away with free-will. It is against the determinism of judicial astrology, as was Pico della Mirandola. When well-received by the will of the recipient, the planetary influence is a virtue; when badly received it is a vice. Thus the opposites of the seven planetary virtues are the seven deadly sins. This system is traceable in Dante's *Divine Comedy*, where the spheres of Hell are the spheres of Heaven in reverse. Spenser's poem is also a divine comedy, a universal presentation of conflict between good and evil in a cosmic setting. The Spenserian knights, representing virtues, have to fight the bad opposite sides of their temperaments, the seven deadly sins.

As we have seen, Giorgi sets out a list of the planets in their association with angels and other entities,[11] and in what follows I shall compare Giorgi's list with the astral themes of the books of *The Faerie Queene*. I shall quote these in what I think is Spenser's order, suggesting that Giorgi's list is illuminating for the interpretation of Spenser's meaning.

The first book of *The Faerie Queene* is about the Red Cross Knight who represents Holiness and is accompanied by the lady, Una. It is a solar book (as Fowler agrees), full of solar imagery.

For Giorgi, the Sun represents the Christian religion, also the theological virtue of Charity.[12] It will be remembered that the episode of the House of Charity occurs in Spenser's first book which would thus be presenting, in its solar astral theme, a religion of love and charity. Red Cross and his companion Una, or the *Monas*, would thus be Christianity struggling to illuminate a dark world, dominated by its evil opposite. The angelic hierarchy to which Sol corresponds in Giorgi's scheme is that of the Powers.

Spenser's Book II is on Sir Guyon, or Temperance. It seems obviously a Mars book. Mars is frequently named; fire imagery is constant; and a kind of wrath or sternness prevails.

In Giorgi's list, Mars corresponds to the angelic hierarchy of the Virtues; the Friar expounds connections between the cleansing power of fire and that of virtue.[13] Spenser's placing of Mars–Virtues after Sol–Powers is thus consistent with a visionary scheme in which a righteous wrath must find a place, and knights must fight in defence of the Solar religion.

Book III is on the female knight, Britomart, representing Chastity. Spenser himself states that its subject is the same as that of Raleigh's poems to Cynthia, that is to Diana, the Moon. It is a Luna book on Chastity. In Giorgi, Luna corresponds to the hierarchy of Angels, and to Malkuth, or the Kingdom, among the Sephiroth of Cabala.[14]

Book IV, on Cambel and Triamond, or Friendship, describes fighting opposites, and is dominated by the image of fighting opposites reconciled, the Caduceus. It must surely be the Mercury book. Giorgi puts Mercury with the hierarchy of the Archangels; he says that Mercury and the Archangels propose divine numbers to us for contemplation.[15]

The fifth book, dedicated to Saturn and Justice, to Astraea and the Golden Age, is quite obviously the Saturn book. Saturn, as defined by Giorgi,[16] is the 'revalued' Saturn of the Renaissance, promoted from his unhappy medieval position to being the star of profound scholars and highest intellectual insight. Whilst emphasising the deep studies of the Saturnian, Giorgi stresses still more the importance of Saturnian leadership in religion. The Saturnian religion, says Giorgi, is the form of religion from which all others derive. The people who have received the fullest inspiration from Saturn are the Hebrews. Giorgi equates the Law revealed to Moses, when he ascended to Binah, one of the highest of the Sephiroth, with the Justice of Saturn. The angelic hierarchy to which Saturn corresponds is the Thrones.

Book VI, with its courtly hero, Sir Calidore, or Courtesy, and its vision of Venus and the Graces, is the Venus book. In this book, Spenser gives to the complex religious and ethical themes of his poem the colour of courtly Neoplatonism, as does Giorgi when discussing Venus. Giorgi on Venus[17] combines three trains of thought. He sees first of all the planet Venus, star of love, whose gifts of grace and beauty, when rightly received and not turned by evil will to lust, are so attractive. Then comes the Neoplatonic Venus, representing the beauty of Him through whom all things are beautiful, with many references to Plato, particularly *Phaedrus* and *Symposium*. And finally there is the angelic Venus, for Venus is at her best when the angelic hierarchy of the Principalities favours her. Then indeed Venus shines forth, full of grace and charm, courteous and gentle. Such Venereans are agreeable to both God and man.

Spenser's unfinished seventh book would presumably have been the missing Jupiter book. The full twelve which were planned must surely have had reference to the twelve signs of the zodiac which shine in the sphere of fixed stars, to which corresponds, in Giorgi's list, the angelic hierarchy of the Cherubim.[18]

But how are we to reconcile this astral interpretation with the fact that Spenser himself states in the letter to Raleigh printed with the first instalment of *The Faerie Queene* that he intended the twelve books to portray the twelve private and moral virtues, as defined by Aristotle, and that if these books were well received he might go on to write twelve more on Aristotelian political virtues? These Aristotelian virtues have always given trouble to the critics; Holiness and Courtesy are not Aristotelian virtues; it is not easy to see how this Aristotelian scheme was to be fitted in to the scheme of the poem.

The operative word is 'twelve'. Spenser is thinking numerologically. As Giorgi recounts, following numerological tradition, twelve can include with the signs of the zodiac many other dozens, such as the Twelve Tribes of Israel,[19] and the Twelve Apostles.[20] Why not twelve Aristotelian virtues?[21]

Moreover, the appearance of Aristotelian virtues within Spenser's Neoplatonic and numerological schemes is consistent with Giorgi's exposition, in the *De harmonia mundi* of his manner of reconciling the philosophy of Aristotle with that of Plato.

In a chapter on how the Peripatetics accord with other philosophies on essential things, and on those two Princes of Philosophy, Plato and Aristotle,[22] Giorgi explains that both Plato and Aristotle teach a way to God, but that Aristotle starts at the bottom of the ladder with the elements, whereas both Plato and the Pythagoreans begin with number which gives them an advantage. This is a greatly over-simplified statement of the argument which, however, brings out the point that Giorgi thinks of Aristotle's philosophy as a kind of Hermetic ascent, rising from the sphere of earth through the spheres of the other three elements, thence up through the spheres of the planets to the highest divine realms. This Hermetic interpretation of Aristotle is greatly assisted by the fact that Giorgi believes that the Pseudo-Aristotelian *Problemata*, a work which he knows and cites, is actually by Aristotle.[23] As we have seen, the Pseudo-Aristotle of the *Problemata* was the source for Agrippa's theory of inspired melancholy, as set forth in his *De occulta philosophia*.

It certainly helps the conflation of Aristotle with the Giorgi type of astral Neoplatonism if one believes that Aristotle taught that Saturnian melancholics are inspired by Platonic *furor*. And in speaking of heroic virtue, Giorgi notes that Aristotle has said that through the exercise of virtue man can rise to union with the intelligences.[24] This may also be a reference to the Pseudo-Aristotle, and it indicates how Spenser's 'Aristotelian virtues' could allude to much that is hardly to be found in the genuine Aristotle.[25]

Yet there was a sense in which genuine Aristotelian teaching on virtue could be worked into the universal harmony. Aristotle in his *Ethics* defines justice in terms of proportion, an idea which suggests proportion as an ethical quality. As John Dee noted in his Preface to Euclid of 1570: 'Aristotle in his *Ethikes* . . . was fayne to fly to the perfection and power of numbers for proportions arithmeticall and geometricall.'[26] Thus the Aristotelian virtues could be worked into numerological schemes. To the student of Giorgi, accustomed to find Aristotle always included with the Neoplatonists as fundamentally in accord with them, Spenser's inclusion of Aristotelian virtues in an astrally based scheme of universal harmony, comes almost as a final proof that Spenser's source was the *De harmonia mundi*.

The question of the influence of Giorgi on Spenser is complicated by the fact that Spenser is adapting the thinking and outlook of the Friar of Venice to his panegyric of Queen Elizabeth I and her imperial reform, the main concern of *The Faerie Queene*.[27] Spenser tells Raleigh that the whole poem was planned in honour of the queen. The dedications of the individual books refer to the queen as the supreme example of the virtue which they celebrate. And the astral themes, the astral plan of the poem, are dedicated to the same object.

The suggestion that I would make is that the planetary themes of the poem should be seen as arranged, not in the fixed order of the planetary week (as Fowler has argued) but in an order deliberately selected to express the idea and purpose of the poem, the presentation of an ideal portrait of a religious and moral leader, of Queen Elizabeth I and her imperial reform. That portrait has a variegated planetary and angelic colouring. Lighted by a Sun of Christian religion and Christian Charity (Book I), it includes red glints of Martial firmness (Book II). The white Chastity of the Moon (Book III) expresses the purity of the Virgin Queen's reform. Mercury (Book IV) includes all colours and can reconcile opposites with spiritual alchemy. The Justice of Saturn (Book V) represents the wise rule of Astraea. And with Venus (Book VI) this complex movement, or religion, or personality, takes on the colouring of a courtly cult, a court ruled over by the messianic figure whom the poem as a whole celebrates.

The work of Francesco Giorgi will not alone account for the

inspiration of *The Faerie Queene;* I have been making enormous omissions. Though Giorgi has chapters on the Just Empire of the Prince, and on the rule of champions (or knights),[28] he naturally has nothing about the sacred British-Imperial descent of the Tudors and its associations with Arthurian chivalry, so important an element in Spenser's poem. The Giorgi influence must somehow have merged with an Arthurian-British element to form a kind of 'British Israel' mystique. Such a linkage would be quite possible in the highly charged atmosphere of sacred destiny, of religious mission, with which Elizabethan Englishmen maintained their morale in their dangerously isolated position. And it seems obvious that the circle whence such ideas could have emanated can only have been the circle of John Dee.

Dee was a Christian Cabalist and a British imperialist. Though in the Preface to Euclid he cites Agrippa rather than Giorgi on the three worlds, yet Giorgi's schemes are the same in principle as those of Agrippa, though less overtly magical. The emphasis on number, the architectural imagery, and Vitruvianism, all this could have come to Spenser from the Dee circle, together with British-Arthurian legend and Cabala. Giorgi's *De harmonia mundi,* though in itself an important guide to Spenser, is perhaps most important because it leads back to Dee, or to the Dee circle, as the great formative influence on Spenser.

Eleven years before the publication of *The Faerie Queene,* Spenser had published his *Shepherd's Calendar* (1579), a poem which already contains elements of the epic – the cult of the queen, the Puritan outlook. And it is based on a twelve, the twelve months, illustrated with twelve cuts of the signs of the zodiac. The commentator on the poem, the mysterious 'E.K.', discusses the question of in what month the world was created and refers to the opinion of 'the best Rabbins'. The poem is in fact truly a calendar with a learned background. It is surely significant that, at about the same time that Spenser was writing his *Shepherd's Calendar,* John Dee was exercising his mathematical, astronomical, and astrological knowledge on the project of the reform of the calendar.[29] It seems probable that Spenser was in contact with Dee or members of his circle when composing his *Shepherd's Calendar*, absorbing the fund of scientific knowledge which he was to use in *The Faerie Queene*, and evolving its astral and numerological allegories.

Seen as a whole, the argument which I am putting forward is that Spenser's philosophy was based on the Neoplatonic Christian Cabala of Giorgi and Agrippa, but that this had been modified by passage through the influences of the Tudor Reformation. Basically, it was a reflex of the philosophy of John Dee who had expanded these influences in new scientific and politico-religious directions. Dee was the true philosopher of the Elizabethan age, and Spenser, as its epic poet, reflected that philosophy.

It has been said of Spenser's epic that it expresses a 'prophetic moment', after the Armada victory, when the queen appeared almost as the symbol of a new religion, transcending both Catholic and Protestant in some far-reaching revelation, and transmitting a universal Messianic message. It would seem from the present investigations, fragmentary and incomplete though they are, that an influence of Christian Cabala underlies the profound seriousness of the courtly Puritanism which was Spenser's religion, and which he infused into his vision of the religious role of Elizabethan England. The identification of this influence on Spenser will help to link Elizabethan thought with later movements, such as the 'Rosicrucian' philosophy of Robert Fludd, or the Cabalist influence on Milton and the Puritans.

A word must be said of that other Hermetic–Cabalist missionary, Giordano Bruno, in relation to Spenser. In an extraordinary way, the missions of Dee and of Bruno overlap, or run parallel to one another. Dee leaves for the continent just before Bruno arrives in England in 1583. Whilst in England (when Dee was abroad) Bruno preaches a Hermetic–Cabalist philosophy which has some reference to a Messianic role for Elizabeth.[30] Dee and Bruno both visited Prague,[31] whence Bruno went to Rome to his death, and Dee eventually returned to disgrace in England.

Bruno, like Dee, is very strongly influenced by Agrippa (much less so, if at all, by Giorgi). He preaches an 'Egyptian' Hermetic reform in which Cabalist magic, almost entirely derived from Agrippa's *De occulta philosophia*[32] has a place. The comparison of Dee and Bruno and their respective influences has not yet been seriously undertaken, though there would certainly be much to learn from such a comparison which would also be important for assessing the possibility of an influence of Bruno on Spenser. I mention only one point which may be relevant.

In his *Spaccio delle bestia trionfante*, Bruno outlines a vast moral reform in which the good sides of stellar influences predominate over the bad sides.[33] Virtues associated with the constellations mount to heaven and rule, whilst the bad opposite vices descend and are extinguished. Thus a universal celestial reform is effected, associated politically with England and France and opposed to Spain. One wonders whether this scheme may have influenced Spenser's presentation of reform in terms of victory of good planetary influences over bad in his epic of reformed chivalry. There are, however, notable differences between the Brunian and the Spenserian outlook, though there would have been much in Bruno's 'Egyptianism' to interest Spenser.

Dee, Bruno, and Spenser, in their widely differing ways, all represent those European stirrings of protest against the reactionary suppression of the Renaissance.

As I said in the previous chapter, it is most important when thinking of Dee to keep constantly in mind his three periods. Particularly is this true when thinking of Spenser in relation to Dee.

The Faerie Queene was conceived and partly written during Dee's first period, when he was such an important centre of influence, favoured by the queen and Leicester, imparting scientific and mathematical knowledge to Elizabethan navigators and scientists, pursuing his historical studies and connecting these with hopes for 'British Empire' linked to Arthurian legend, presiding over his wonderful library frequented by all the cognoscenti of the day. Those were the days when Spenser began to think about *The Faerie Queene* and began to write the poem.

Spenser was continuing to write it during Dee's absence on his continental mission. How much did Dee's friends in England know about his activities abroad between 1583 and 1589, the date of his return? So far as I know, this question has never been asked. There was one person who would have known all about it, namely Sidney's friend Edward Dyer who took some undefined but important part in Dee's activities abroad during those years. Rumours of Dee's missionary activities abroad, if they reached influential circles at home, might well have aroused those fears of foreign complications which shadowed the Elizabethan aspirations and caused the queen and her advisers to draw back from commitments which might involve them in dangerous confrontations with powerful enemies. The recall of Leicester in 1586 was just such a nervous drawing back from involvement. And when Dee arrived home in 1589 from his foreign exploits, coldness and withdrawal awaited him.

It is very important to remember that *The Faerie Queene*, conceived and written during Dee's successful and expansive periods, was actually published, the first part of it, in 1590, one year after Dee's return to England, when his third period of semi-banishment and fall from favour had begun. The members of the 'Sidney circle', much diminished by the deaths of Leicester and of Sidney himself, were no longer there to hail the arrival of Spenser's epic. The poem entered a harder world and one cautiously and doubtfully disposed towards the enthusiasms of former years. The encouragement of Spenser had been taken up by Walter Raleigh, with whom the poet was in contact in Ireland

and who is mentioned as a close friend and adviser in the prefatory matter to The Faerie Queene. And it was Raleigh who introduced Spenser at court in 1592. But no rewards or favours were forthcoming for the author of the great epic of the Elizabethan age. Spenser went back to his semi-banishment in Ireland, returning to London in 1599, but only to die in poverty and neglect.

Moreover, misfortune also overtook the friend at court who had encouraged Spenser and his poem. Walter Raleigh lost the royal favour and was banished from court in 1592, ostensibly on account of his marriage.

I believe that much in the chilly reception of The Faerie Queene can be explained if it is realised that the poem expressed Dee's vision for Elizabethan England, an expansionist vision which had become too dangerously provocative by the time it was published. After Dee's activities abroad, he received no reward on his return home, and was never adequately rewarded for his outstanding contribution to the greatness of Elizabethan England. Semi-banishment, ill-success and poverty were to be his fate in his third period. No wonder that a similar fate befell the author of The Faerie Queene.

I try in this book as far as possible to avoid detailed linking to historical situations, concentrating on the thought evolving in those situations. The above brief and inadequate sketch seemed necessary to place Spenser and his poem within the Elizabethan situation, but I now return to the wider, and necessarily vaguer, effort to place them within the history of European thought, and of the partial breakdown of the Renaissance under the pressures of the later sixteenth century.

The hopes of some vast all-embracing reform through Hermetic–Cabalist influence and particularly through the influence of Christian Cabala, belonged to the earlier sixteenth century, though they were never forgotten nor completely discarded amid the disappointments of the later sixteenth century.

We have seen that one of the dangers was the reaction against Renaissance magic, the obsessive fear of dangerous spiritual forces, which swept over Europe, one of the manifestations of which was the witch craze. We saw that the cry of 'conjuror' was strongly raised against Dee, and operated strongly against him, in spite of his protestations as to the purity and whiteness of his magic.

The Faerie Queene is a great magical Renaissance poem, infused with the whitest of white magic, Christian Cabalist and Neoplatonic, haunted by a good magician and scientist, Merlin (a name sometimes used of Dee), and profoundly opposed to bad magicians and necromancers and bad religion. The Spenserian magic should be read not only as poetic metaphor (though it is that) but also in relation to contemporary states of mind in which such attitudes could become polarised in terms of the religious differences. In fact, they are so polarised in Spenser. The white magic of the pure imperial reform is opposed to the bad necromancy of its enemies. Thus, even for Spenser, the cries of 'conjuror' raised against Dee would not have been without danger. As a great magical Renaissance poem *The Faerie Queene* came rather late in time and ran into the period of the witch crazes.

The label, in terms of European trends, which seems to me most applicable to *The Faerie Queene* is 'Rosicrucian', the movement representing the late form of Renaissance Magia and Cabala, of which Dee had been an exponent and which he had been preaching on the continent whilst Spenser was writing his poem. It is not for nothing that the poem opens with Red Cross and Una (the *monas*). German Rosicrucian writers of the early seventeenth century were aware of deep-rooted connections with Dee's *monas*,[34] and some echoes of Spenser's chivalric formulation can be detected in that literature.[35]

In studying Spenser's poem, and the reactions to it, we are thus dealing with major European currents of religious thought and aspiration.

10

ELIZABETHAN ENGLAND AND THE JEWS

We have been thinking about a Christianised Jewish influence, about Christian Cabala which was so important an element in the Renaissance tradition descended from Ficino and Pico. We have argued that there was a strong influence of Renaissance Christian Cabala in Elizabethan England, adapted to the outlook of Elizabethan religious imperialism.

Now a question arises, which I endeavour to face in the present chapter, though in a superficial way and without the equipment in Hebrew scholarship necessary for adequate exploration of a problem of such importance. The question is: were there any Jews in Elizabethan England, and if there were any, what would their attitude have been to the Christian imitation of Jewish mysticism in Christian Cabala?

To attempt an answer, however inadequate, necessitates some survey of the whole vast subject of the dispersion of the Jews after the Expulsion of 1492 from Spain, and the influence of this upon the Jews themselves. We have already mentioned that a new type of Cabala developed among the exiles, one slightly different from the pre-expulsion Spanish Cabala which influenced Pico, and more centred on expectation of a coming Messiah who would end the misery of the exile and persecution and re-establish God's people in the holy land. This intense movement of Lurianic Cabala had a very strong hold on the Jews of the post-Expulsion era, penetrating rabbinic scholarship[1] and gradually becoming a popular movement of great strength which culminated eventually in the appearance of the so-called false Messiah, Sabbatai Sevi, in 1665.[2] This movement was working up in sixteenth-century Jewry, gaining in strength in the seventeenth century, in the way which has been traced and described in the researches of Scholem, shedding a new and searching light on the whole period.

Another new factor in the history of Judaism in the period was the fact that the persecutions and dispersions gave rise to new kinds of contact between Jews and Christians. Total separation became less possible to maintain in a world of such perpetual flux and migration and in which conversion was an issue of life and death for the Jew.

The fierce persecution of the Jews in Spain and Portugal gave rise to the phenomenon of the 'marrano', a term of contempt used in those countries of the crypto-Jew, who, under an exterior of pretended conformity to the ruling religion, secretly preserved his Judaism.[3] The only form of life which made it possible for Sephardic, or Spanish, Jews to survive in what had hitherto been their homeland was to live under a mask of pretended Christianity. Very many refused to adopt this course, preferring to be burned alive in the *autos-da-fé*, and to endure other terrible tortures, rather than give up their convictions. The extraordinary heroism of the Sephardic Jews in the face of the persecutions of the Inquisition which went on in Spain and Portugal, even into the late seventeenth century, is one of the most remarkable records in the history of human endurance.

Yet many also were the New Christians, or marranos, who, though accepting forced conversion to Christianity, managed to keep alive in secret and to pass on to their children for generations their ancestral religion. In Portugal, whither many Spanish Jews had fled after 1492, the mass forced conversions drove hordes to baptism at the fonts under circumstances of appalling cruelty. On such a vast scale were these Portuguese conversions that the term 'Portuguese' became almost the equivalent of 'crypto-Jew' or 'marrano'. The marranos distinguished themselves greatly in the professions, particularly as doctors of medicine, and in their remarkable flair for finance. They were useful citizens for any country to acquire, and in the exodus from the Iberian peninsula they were scattered far and wide.

By far the greater number of the Jewish exiles went to the east and found a refuge in the Ottoman empire. The Crescent was infinitely more tolerant of Jews than the Cross; within the Turkish domains, they were allowed to profess their religion openly. 'No one was persecuted for his religion in Solyman's time, when the Inquisition was carrying on its deadly work in Spain and the Netherlands.'[4] The centre of gravity of Judaism shifted from the west to the east, from Spain to Turkey. The relative freedom of the Jewish immigrants in Turkey allowed them to rise, through their ability, to positions of high influence. Joseph Nasi, Duke of Naxos, a marrano refugee, was at one time considered virtually the ruler of the Turkish empire. Alvaro Mendes, also a Sephardic Jew, was very powerful at the Turkish court; he was one of the prime movers in the epoch-making alliance between England and Turkey against Spain, was in close contact with Burleigh, and was knighted by Queen Elizabeth.[5] In his career and political attitudes one can recognise a tendency of the Jewish exiles who were naturally inclined to favour with their skills and wide financial connections those opposed to their cruel enemies and persecutors, the Spaniards.

Many of the exiles went to Italy. One of the most notable

products of Italian Neoplatonism, the *Dialoghi d'amore* of Leone Ebreo, was written by a distinguished Sephardic exile. Some of the Italian states were more favourable to the Jews than others. They were welcomed at the court of the Este at Ferrara, also at Mantua, and, to some extent, in Naples. The very important Jewish community in Venice was a centre of Hebrew learning and publishing.

In France[6] the Jewish refugees were not molested but they could not publicly profess their religion, though there were marrano communities, particularly in the neighbourhood of Bordeaux. The mother of Michel de Montaigne, essayist and mayor of Bordeaux, was a marrano refugee, Antoinette Lopez.

In England,[7] there were officially no Jews throughout the Elizabethan period. They had been expelled from England in 1290. There is no doubt, however, that, as in other European countries, there were always some Jews present in England and the number may have increased in Elizabethan times through the general increase in trade and commerce in which they acted as agents. It is certain that some Jewish refugees found their way to England after the expulsions from Spain and Portugal. They would have had, however, to conceal their religion and to live as crypto-Jews or marranos. What was the effect on marranos in England of the Venetian Christian-Cabalist influence in connection with the divorce of Henry VIII is a problem which has not yet been examined. In Elizabethan England the situation was that an influence of Christian Cabala was present at court and in learned circles in a country in which Jews were, officially, not allowed to exist. Yet we hear, unofficially, that two Jewish uncles of Michel de Montaigne, Martin and Francesco Lopez, were at one time present in the marrano colony in London.[8]

The question arises as to whether the adoption of Christian Cabala might have been a possible compromise for the marrano in England. A good many Christian Cabalists on the continent were converted Jews.[9] Giorgi's *De harmonia mundi*, with its

'Judaising' tendency,[10] might have provided a bridge to conversion for the English marrano.

The most notorious Elizabethan Jew was the Portuguese doctor, Roderigo Lopez, employed as their physician by the Earl of Leicester and by the queen herself. This Portuguese New Christian had qualified in medicine in his native country. In London, he became a member of the College of Physicians, before which he delivered the annual anatomical lecture in 1579, and was the first house physician appointed at St Bartholomew's hospital.[11] Suddenly accused of plotting to poison the queen, Doctor Lopez was hanged at Tyburn in 1594 amid the howls of a violently antisemitic mob.[12] I have no intention of trying to enter here the dark labyrinth of the Lopez case, though I would suggest that perhaps the case has been studied too much as a local Elizabethan issue, and with too little reference to the general picture of the marrano diaspora.

In contrast to the tragic story of Doctor Lopez, a more pleasing picture of the reception of marrano refugees in Elizabethan England is extant.[13] Unfortunately the story derives from late sources and must be discounted as partly legendary, though Cecil Roth thought that the legend contained an element of truth.

The story relates that in the year 1593[14] a brother and sister, Manuel Lopez Pereira and Maria Nuñez, whose parents had been victims of the Inquisition, left Portugal with their uncle, Miguel Lopez, and a large party of marranos, to seek a refuge in northern lands. Their ship was captured by an English ship and brought to an English port. An English nobleman fell in love with the beautiful Maria Nuñez and sought to marry her. Queen Elizabeth, on hearing the story, expressed a wish to see the lady, and was captivated by her beauty. She invited her into the royal coach, drove about in London with her, and ordered her ship and all its passengers to be set free. In spite of this flattering welcome, Maria would not accept the tempting offer she had received. 'Leaving all the pomp of England for the sake of

Judaism, as the old record puts it, she pursued her way with her companions to Amsterdam.'[15] Here in 1598 they were joined by her mother and other members of her family and the famous Amsterdam Jewish community grew in part from this foundation.

This legend is worth pondering over. Queen Elizabeth was not in the habit of putting other ladies forward to her public as beauties, of promenading with them through London as (almost) equal in beauty to herself. The legend does not quite make sense as personal reminiscence, but it would make sense as allegory of philosemitic tendencies in the English queen, of a Jewish spiritual beauty associated with that of the reformed Imperial Virgin.

The most liberal of the northern Protestant countries in its reception of the Jewish refugees was Holland. Amsterdam rose to a position of prominence in wealth and commerce, and this city offered prospects, unknown elsewhere, not even in Turkey, to the marranos. In Amsterdam it was possible to live openly as a Jew, to frequent the synagogues openly, to establish schools and training colleges of Jewish learning for the re-education in Hebrew scholarship of a people who had been forbidden access to their own traditions for generations. The amazing story of the Jewish community in Amsterdam has been told by Cecil Roth.[16] To it came in large numbers marranos from the Iberian peninsula. Remarkably advanced schools were established, academies were founded. This culture, based on the revival of Hebrew studies, included poets, and dramatists, in an astonishing Hebraic Renaissance.

Why were the Jews not received in Elizabethan England, as they were in the other main power which resisted their persecutors, Holland? Why, after the defeat of the Armada, was that victory not followed up by the reception of the Jews, resulting in strengthening of trade and economic power in that curious mingling of practical affairs with religious enthusiasm which was characteristic, both of the Puritan millennial, and the Jewish messianic outlook? The project of the return of the Jews to England had to wait until Cromwellian times when it was urged with enthusiasm by Menasseh ben Israel, rabbi of the famous Amsterdam community founded during the reign of Elizabeth I.

It is not impossible that the reception of the Jews may have been mooted in Elizabethan times by secretly philosemitic influences, but rejected owing to the growth of unfavourable attitudes. May that be the meaning of the strange imaginary Elizabeth-portrait of the Fairy Queen parading through London in her coach with a dark Jewish beauty beside her? The legend which associated an abortive visit to England with the founding of the Amsterdam community may not be without significance.

Let us now return to the question with which this chapter began.

Were there any Jews in Elizabethan England? The answer is that there certainly were, though probably not very many. If they maintained the practices of their religion, this could only have been done in the utmost secrecy. They would have to have been crypto-Jews, marranos, publicly professing the public form of Christianity in England.

What would their attitude have been to the Elizabethan form of Christian Cabala? This is, of course, impossible to answer with any degree of precision now, nor would an open answer have been possible at the time. Yet it can be pointed out that Elizabethan England was a power which resisted the persecutors, and that the Elizabethan imperial reform included Christian Cabala as an ingredient of the Elizabeth cult, perhaps making possible for a patriotic English Jew an easy transition to the religion of his adopted country.

11

THE REACTION: CHRISTOPHER MARLOWE ON CONJURORS, IMPERIALISTS AND JEWS

Christopher Marlowe holds a most important place in English literature through his brilliant poetic gift and also as Shakespeare's exact contemporary (born in 1564) and his forerunner in the creation of poetic drama. He died a violent death, stabbed under curious circumstances, in 1593, a time when Shakespeare was beginning to emerge in his full stature. No study of Shakespeare can begin without some reference to Marlowe, the predecessor, and his mighty line. Hence the literature on Marlowe is enormous.

In this chapter I plunge into the daunting and dangerous sea of Marlowe studies, hoping to avoid shipwreck by clinging firmly to the themes of this book. Three of Marlowe's most famous plays are on these themes. One is about an occult philosopher, fiercely attacked in a violent reaction against occultism. Another is about a world-imperial figure, presented as barbarous and cruel. A third is about a Jew; it is one of the most tremendous antisemitic fantasies in literature.

Marlowe's famous play, Doctor Faustus, is closely based on the English translation of the German Faust-Buch (1587). The first known edition of this translation was published in 1592, which leads scholars to assume that Marlowe probably wrote the play in the last year of his life, that is to say in 1593. The earliest known performance of the play was in 1594, though there may have been earlier ones. Between 1594 and 1597 over twenty performances are recorded in Henslowe's diary. The play was evidently an immense success. The first printed edition was in 1604; a later edition of 1616 shows variants from the 1604 text. The various editions of Faustus have presented many problems to textual scholars.

The diabolical apparatus used in the productions caused great excitement and terror.[1] Shag-haired devils with squibs in their mouths ran roaring over the stage; drummers made thunder in the tiring-house; technicians made artificial lightning in the heavens. It was reported in the seventeenth century that there had been a visible apparition of the Devil on the stage in Queen Elizabeth's days during a performance of Faustus. We can see for ourselves on the title-page of the 1616 edition (Plate 13) Faustus standing within a circle marked by the symbols of the seven planets and the twelve signs of the zodiac, conjuring up a devil.

The play has been much studied in modern times as a literary phenomenon but such an approach must surely lose something of its original impact. Though there are no actual witches in the play, it belongs, with its vivid infernal imaginings, to the atmosphere of the witch craze then raging on the continent. In an earlier chapter we saw that Jean Bodin in his Démonomanie associated his attack on witches with his violent disapproval of Pico della Mirandola and Cornelius Agrippa for having made what he considered a bad use of Cabala.[2] Marlowe definitely presents his

Faustus as a student of Agrippa. His play belongs into the reaction against Renaissance magic, particularly as formulated by Agrippa.

The original Faustus was a historical personage, contemporary of Trithemius, Reuchlin, and Agrippa, who pretended to humanistic status (giving himself the classical pseudonym of Faustus) but who was really a magician of a popular type, much disapproved of by Trithemius.[3] His legend as a diabolist soon started and it became part of the attack on Agrippa to class him with Faustus, as is done, for example, by the Jesuit Martin del Rio in his attack on Renaissance magic, published in 1599.[4] The association was really unfair to Agrippa who was genuinely a learned Renaissance magus, disciple of Trithemius. The association of Faustus with Agrippa is central to Marlowe's play and is part of its general denigration of Renaissance magic.

When Marlowe's Faustus is discovered in his study, he is learning logic from Aristotle in order to dispute well. Having achieved this, he tries a greater subject, medicine, and works at Galen. He has great success as a physician but this is not enough; he turns to the law and to Justinian. After all, divinity is best; he takes up Jerome's Bible. Now he lights on yet other books. These metaphysics of magicians and necromantic books are heavenly. Lines, circles, letters, characters, these are the books that Faustus most desires. Power, honour and omnipotence are promised to the 'studious artisan'. All things will be at his command. 'A sound Magitian is a Demi-god.'[5]

This survey of all human learning, and the dismissal of it as vain, sounds like an echo of Agrippa's *De vanitate*. The moral which Marlowe draws from the 'all is vanity' text is, however, very different from that of Agrippa. For Agrippa, the only learning which was not vain was to know Jesus. Marlowe fills the void left by the vanity of learning with bad magic, with the magic taught in Agrippa's other work, the *De occulta philosophia* interpreted, not as Christian Cabala, but as wholly bad, a summoning of diabolical powers.

A good angel urges Faust to 'lay that damned book aside', clearly the book of Agrippa which he is studying.

> Philosophy is odious and obscure,
> Both Law and Physicke are for petty wits:
> Divinitie is basest on the three,
> Unpleasant, harsh, contemptible and vilde:
> 'Tis magick, magick, that has ravisht me

Faust resolves that he

> Will be as cunning as Agrippa was
> Whose shadows made all Europe honour him.[6]

Faust stands between two angels, one good who urges him to lay the damned book aside, one bad who encourages him to go forward in 'that famous Art, wherein all Nature's treasury is contained'.[7] Faust has been doing angel-conjuring in order to learn natural philosophy from the angels. Being impure in heart he has attracted a bad angel. His magic cannot be a white magic. It transpires that he intends to make a political use of the spirits he raises from whom he will learn the secrets of all foreign kings, and levy soldiers with the wealth the spirits bring, who will 'chase the Prince of Parma from our land'. His German friends encourage him, promising that the spirits will bring wealth greater than the gold from America that 'stuffes old Philips treasury'.[8] That is to say, the conjuring will bring wealth to be used to raise armies against the Catholic King of Spain.

Faustus resolves to conjure, and is advised to go to some solitary place with the books of Bacon and Albertus, the Hebrew Bible and New Testament. People wonder where Faustus is and enquire of his disciple, Wagner, who sets his countenance 'like a

Precisian', and replies in a style which mocks the Puritan mode of speech. 'Truely my deer brethren, my Maister is within at dinner.'[9] In his 'canting' Puritan style, Wagner is lying to conceal the fact that his master is doing black magic.

Faustus enters to conjure, with a circle inscribed with anagrams of Jehovah's name, figures of the heavens, characters of signs and planets. He is doing practical Cabala which has the effect of raising Mephistopheles. Faust finds him too ugly and urges him to

> Go and returne an old Franciscan Frier,
> That holy shape becomes a devill best.[10]

Mephistopheles obeys and appears as a devil in the habit of a Franciscan friar. Have we now moved from parody of Agrippa to parody of Francesco Giorgi, the Franciscan Friar of Venice?

After the appearance of the diabolical Franciscan Friar, Faustus abjures Christ and the Trinity, as demanded by Mephistopheles. This, of course, completely overturns 'Christian Cabala', and the claims of Pico, Reuchlin, and Giorgi that the most powerful name in Cabala is now the Name of Christ. Faustus's magic is not Christian Cabala but entirely black. Mephistopheles himself warns Faustus against it, by describing his own torments in Hell.

When Faustus is next discovered in his study he is continuing his unlawful researches. Mephistopheles returns; Faustus signs the contract giving up his soul in exchange for knowledge and power. He feels qualms after the signature, but Mephistopheles distracts his mind with a theatrical show; devils enter in rich apparel and dance.

Good and bad angel try again, but Faustus's heart is hardened and he cannot repent though his misery is great. He might ere now have killed himself had it not been the beautiful music which he has conjured, making blind Homer sing for him and hearing the sound of Amphion's harp. He turns to ask

Mephistopheles about divine astrology, about the elements, and the spheres of the planets. He still has scholarly instincts, and can hear echoes of the universal harmony, although damned.

Awaiting damnation he calls on Christ, and there comes the famous line

See see where Christs bloud streames in the firmament.[11]

But that Name cannot help Faustus now; he is taken to Hell by devils.

It seems unlikely that the audience, by this time convulsed in superstitious terrors, could possibly have missed the moral of this play, but, just to make sure, the moral is stated at the end. It is a warning to avoid unlawful things

Whose deepnesse doth intice such forward wits,
To practise more then heavenly power permits.

To arrive at Marlowe's *Doctor Faustus* within the sequence of the argument of this book is to gain rather a different impression of the play from the one usually current. It begins to look less like the thought of an heroic individual soul, struggling with problems of science or magic versus religion, and more like a piece of propaganda constructed in view of a current situation. This play was not written to be read by literary critics looking for mighty lines in the quiet of their studies. It was written to be produced in the popular theatre, with horrific diabolical effects, to audiences working up into hysteria. In fact, as already remarked, it belongs to the atmosphere of the contemporary witch crazes in which the building up of Cornelius Agrippa into a black magician played a significant part.

We are in fact witnessing in this play the reaction against the Renaissance. Cornelius Agrippa's occult philosophy was, as we know, compounded of Renaissance Magia and Cabala, out of

Marsilio Ficino and Pico della Mirandola. The dismissal of Agrippa as a black magician is a dismissal of the traditions of Renaissance magic and science.

It is interesting to examine in this play the mechanics (so to speak) of the reaction. The medieval formula of fear of sorcery is applied to a situation which is not medieval. Faustus is not a medieval sorcerer; he is a Renaissance scholar who has taken all learning for his province with a particular bent towards the natural sciences. The medieval anti-sorcery formula, ignorantly applied to the Renaissance scholar, produces Faustus, the genius with an artificially-induced neurosis.

This is the pattern which was being followed in the European reaction against the Renaissance, of which Marlowe's *Doctor Faustus* is a striking example. Yet, though the theme was general, the individual situations in which it was applied varied. What was the individual situation which Marlowe's play reflects? Or, to put it differently, who was the victim aimed at in his ferocious play?

Earlier chapters in this book may suggest an answer to this question. John Dee, returned from his continental mission in 1589, was faced with growing outcries against him as a conjuror, and felt surrounded by enemies who refused to believe that his Christian Cabala was 'white'. Marlowe and his *Doctor Faustus* must surely have been an important factor in the opposition to Dee, fomented from the public performances of this sensational play. Audiences would inevitably have recognised Faustus as an unfavourable reference to Dee. Had not Dee publicly proclaimed in his mathematical Preface to Euclid that he was following Cornelius Agrippa?[12] The turning of the Dee of his first period, mathematician and scientific expert, leader of the Elizabethan Renaissance, into the Dee of the third period, the banished conjuror whom the queen and the court are afraid to encourage, was a process in which Marlowe's propaganda in the theatre may have played a considerable part.

Marlowe associates the bad occultism of Faustus with the

Puritans; he makes references to gold-making to be used against the King of Spain which sound uncannily like phrases in the later Rosicrucian manifestos which were inspired by Dee's mission on the continent.[13] Could Marlowe, in his capacity of political agent, have known something about Dee's second period abroad? At any rate, he certainly knows something about Christian Cabala as propagated by Henry Cornelius Agrippa and by 'Franciscan Friars' and he is violently against it as diabolical.

Puritan Christian Cabalists might therefore have felt threatened by *Doctor Faustus*. We must tread cautiously among these hidden aspects of the Elizabethan situation, though they probably contain the real truth about what was going on. There was a philosophy and an outlook which we associate with the Elizabethan age, the philosophy of Spenser, which looked to Queen Elizabeth I as the Protestant saviour of Europe. And there were opposite currents, entirely opposed to that philosophy and that outlook. Marlowe's *Doctor Faustus*, with its obvious allusion to Dee as conjuror, tended to undermine the Elizabethan Renaissance, and can hardly have been welcome to the survivors of the Sidney circle, or to Edmund Spenser, or to Walter Raleigh, his patron, or indeed to the queen and her government.

Judging from the standpoint of the history of the occult philosophy in the Elizabethan age it would seem that the world of John Dee, of the Sidney circle, of Spenser, Raleigh and *The Faerie Queene* is a world diametrically opposed to that of Marlowe's *Doctor Faustus*. Or rather, *Faustus* looks something like an attempt to overwhelm Elizabethan Christian Cabala in a witch craze. The purity of the white magical reform, the fairy world in which Spenser places the royal image of the imperial reform, is infinitely remote in its mythical Arthurian outlines from the hard doctrinaire patterns of the European witch craze.

Marlowe's *Tamburlaine* was first published in 1593 and 1597. According to Henslowe's diary, it was performed many times in the 1590s. The date of composition has been suggested as 1587–9.[14]

The theme of *Tamburlaine* is an imperial theme on a tremendous scale. The shepherd boy, born under Venus, star of love, and Saturn, star of empire,[15] dreams that he will become Monarch of the East and he does so become, conquering country after country. He wears an 'emperiall crowne'; spectacular triumphant entries accompany his progress. The mighty line about riding in triumph through Persepolis[16] spreads the aura of a Renaissance triumphal entry around the progress of Tamburlaine towards world rule. Chivalric pageants in his honour, with cosmic themes, are suggested by the monarch's sun-bright armour and by the extraordinary image of the meteors tilting in heaven in honour of his victories.

Tamburlaine is a Saturnian; his colours are black.[17] His vast aspiration towards universal knowledge and universal rule are those of an inspired melancholic, cultivating the 'revalued' Saturn of the Renaissance, star of profound students and of the golden age of empire:

> Our soules, whose faculties can comprehend
> The wondrous Architecture of the world:
> And measure every wandring plannets course:
> Still climing after knowledge infinite,
> And alwaies mooving as the restles Spheares,
> Will us to weare our selves and never rest,
> Until we reach the ripest fruit of all,
> That perfect blisse and sole felicities,
> The sweet fruition of an earthly crowne.[18]

This is the humour of Renaissance melancholy, aspiring to profound knowledge and imperial rule. Yet there is a sense in which Marlowe's presentation of the theme is satirical.

The imperial theme according to Marlowe needs to be

compared with other Renaissance imperial themes in order to bring out its peculiarities. The Empire of Charles V aroused visions of world empire for the House of Hapsburg.[19] The propaganda of Guillaume Postel in France aroused visions of the Monarchy of the East for the French king.[20] The imperial theme and its imagery was adapted for the propaganda of Queen Elizabeth I and was very familiar to the Elizabethan public. In Marlowe's use of it there is a striking absence of the main accessory of the imperial theme, namely that it represented the establishment of a just rule and the maintenance of peace and all the virtues.

Tamburlaine's rule, though it is adorned with all the glorious trappings of imperial pageantry, is not just. He is a cruel tyrant and there is no word about virtue in all the play. The horrors of his cruelty are displayed on the stage. He spreads war and not peace.

Marlowe would appear to be undermining imperial themes through his presentation of the tyrant Tamburlaine. This play, published at about the time of John Dee's return to England, clearly does not belong at all to the world of Dee's build-up of 'British Empire'. On the contrary, the effect of *Tamburlaine* would be to devalue the imperial idea, and to dismiss any suggestion of connection of imperial triumphing with the establishment of justice and virtue. Raleigh's and Spenser's poetic cult of Elizabeth as representative of the religious and reforming aspect of empire is in sharp contrast to Marlowe's frenzied emphasis on imperial cruelty and tyranny.[21] Since there is so much in the pageantry of the play which an Elizabethan audience would recognise as reflecting pageantry in honour of the queen, this contrast may even have been intended to be dangerously subversive.

The first recorded performance of Marlowe's play *The Jew of Malta* was in 1592. It has been conjectured that it may have been written in 1589 or 1590. There has been much discussion as to whether some of the later passages in the play are by other hands than Marlowe's. There were very many performances of this popular play during the 1590s. The first printed edition was in 1633.[22]

Barabbas, the Jew, is first seen in his counting house with heaps of gold before him. His survey of the brilliant gems in his possession includes the famous line 'Infinite riches in a little roome'[23] which, in its context, means an easily portable investment. He tells of his widespread commercial activities, of the trading fleets and argosies which are adding to his enormous wealth. But the Jew is not allowed to keep his money; the Governor of Malta confiscates it in order to pay tribute levied by the Turk. Enraged, Barabbas seeks a way of concealing the rest of his fortune. His house has been taken from him and turned into a nunnery; in it, some of his wealth is hidden. He persuades his beautiful daughter, Abigail, to pretend to become a nun in order to find the money and throw it out to him. In the shadow of the silent night, the Jew waits under the balcony for the money bags which Abigail throws down. Thereafter the plot thickens to show the Jew committing every possible kind of crime. He compasses the death of his daughter's lover, who is a Gentile; he poisons all the nuns in the nunnery; he poisons wells, spreads diseases, treacherously betrays and murders both friends and enemies, inspired not only by love of money but by hatred of Christians.

Clearly, this play is antisemitic propaganda, using all the old legends about poisoning wells, and so on, in the framework of a cleverly constructed play, written with a poetic gift for language, like all Marlowe's propaganda pieces. As in the case of *Doctor Faustus*, a quiet literary approach hardly covers the impact of *The Jew of Malta*. We should imagine this play being performed in the public theatre and watch the rising passions as the audience turns into an antisemitic mob.

An important point about Marlowe's Jew needs emphasising. He is not a medieval Jew, though the traditional medieval slanders are brought out against him. He is a modern, post-Expulsion, Jew using his widespread trading connections to build up a fortune. He can see, as results of the Christian faith, only malice and excessive pride, which do not fit with the profession of Christians. He would rather be a Jew than a Christian:

> They say we are a scatter'd Nation:
> I cannot tell, but we have scambled up
> More wealth by farre then those that brag of faith.
> There's *Kirriah Jairim*, the great Jew of *Greece*,
> *Obed* in *Bairseth*, *Nones* in *Portugall*,
> My self in *Malta*, some in *Italy*,
> Many in *France*, and wealthy every one:
> I, wealthier farre then any Christian.[24]

Though maliciously intended to excite envy and hatred, there is truth in this account of the extraordinary developments in wealth from trade fostered by the Jews, and from which the countries which received them benefited, as Holland was experiencing, or about to experience, at this very time.

If English audiences, excited by Marlowe's propaganda, had rushed out into the streets searching for Jews to bait, they would not have found any. At whom, then, was the propaganda aimed?

There was certainly one well-known Jew in England, the Portuguese marrano Doctor Roderigo Lopez, formerly physician to the Earl of Leicester and high in the queen's favour. It was in 1593 that Lopez fell into difficulties and was accused of attempting to poison the queen. Elizabeth was a long time making up her mind to sign his death warrant but she did so at last. Bakeless repeats the story that Lopez, executed in June 1594, a year after Marlowe's death, asserted in his dying words that he loved the queen as he loved Jesus Christ; but the crowd screamed, 'He is a Jew.'[25]

It would be difficult to prove that Marlowe had Lopez in mind when he wrote *The Jew of Malta*, yet it is a fact that the sensational execution of Lopez revived interest in the play which became again exceedingly popular, with many performances to large houses from 1594 onwards.[26]

The antisemitism of the play must surely have been somewhat uncomfortable for the queen who had employed and encouraged Lopez, the Jew (as she had earlier encouraged Dee, the conjuror). And one remembers now again the curious story about Maria Nuñez, the Portuguese Jewess supposedly received with open favour by the Queen (in 1593, according to the late source) but who decided to pass on to Amsterdam with her companions, becoming one of the legendary founders of the Amsterdam community.

One wonders whether the whole Lopez affair may have been, as it were, the tip of an iceberg beneath which larger matters were concealed. Was the real crisis caused by a suspicion that some philosemitic persons in very high positions were considering the possibility of the admission of the Jews to England?

Only three plays of Marlowe's have been considered in this chapter, much has been left out, and the chapter should be read as only a first attempt at a new and somewhat revolutionary approach to Marlowe. Yet enough has been said to indicate that Marlowe's propaganda belongs with the contemporary revolution from Renaissance magic, and from the magical religious reform encouraged by Hermeticists and Cabalists. Marlowe is modern; he belongs to the contemporary mood of rigidity and reaction which was sweeping Europe.[27]

Elizabethan England was in a curious position in which her late Renaissance was overtaken, almost immediately, by reaction. Spenser's *Faerie Queene* is a magical, fully Renaissance poem, coming so late in time that it is overtaken almost immediately, or simultaneously, by the reaction. For surely Marlowe's chief target was the Fairy Queen, and all that that conception implied of white magic, imperial reform, and Christian Cabala.

12

SHAKESPEARE AND CHRISTIAN CABALA: FRANCESCO GIORGI AND *THE MERCHANT OF VENICE*

We have now arrived at one of the most famous plays of the world's most famous dramatist. There is certainly no need to begin this chapter with an abridged account of the plot of *The Merchant of Venice*; everyone knows that story about Shylock, the Jew, and his pound of flesh. Yet the story is not always accurately remembered. The merchant of Venice designated by the title as the play's main character is not Shylock, the Jew, as so often supposed, but Antonio, the Christian. No one ever forgets the pound of flesh, but not everyone remembers why it was so important, because it was a legal point, the Law being the real theme of the play. Relationships between Jews and Christians in Venice are vitally connected with the main theme. And the play's marvellous poetry reaches a supreme climax at the end, when Jessica, the Jewess, now a Christian, and wedded to the Christian,

Lorenzo, gazes in Venice at the night sky, brilliant with stars, and hears her lover's exposition of the universal harmony.

The Merchant of Venice[1] was first printed in 1600. The date at which Shakespeare wrote it is uncertain, though it must have been earlier than 1598 when the play is mentioned by Francis Meres; it is probably not later than 1596 because of its mention of a wreck which took place in that year. At any rate, it can be safely said that it belongs to the 1590s and to a time when the Lopez case was still topical, for it is generally agreed that Shakespeare had in mind Marlowe's Jew of Malta. There are reminiscences of Marlowe's play in both the plot and the language of The Merchant of Venice.[2]

There are basic differences between Marlowe's and Shakespeare's presentation of the Jew. Barabbas is simply an object of hatred and disgust, loaded with all the traditional Jew-baiting accusations, a figure designed to foment antisemitism of the crudest kind. Shylock is a dignified human being; Shakespeare makes clear the central importance to him of his religion and does not heap the usual slanders on him. Nor does he minimise his faults, the chief of which is hatred, hatred of Christians. There is an intention of murder in his demand for the pound of flesh. But this savage state of mind is accounted for by the insulting way in which he has been treated, which is vividly described. Ordinary antisemitism did not describe what it was like to be a Jew scorned by Christians. Shylock has been warped by persecution.

Nevertheless, the fierce obstinacy with which he demands his legal right against his debtor, refusing any other payment but the pound of flesh agreed upon, puts him in a highly unfavourable light as a merciless stickler for the Letter of the Law.

In his usual way, Shakespeare was using for his story existing materials.[3] The tale about the Jewish usurer who demanded his pound of flesh was well known; the actual form of it which

Shakespeare used he derived from an Italian version of it, printed in 1558, which he followed closely. With this second-hand material, Shakespeare combined an equally well-worn story of three caskets, one of which contained something of great value. From these hackneyed anecdotes, Shakespeare produced his work of astonishing genius, containing some of the most exquisite poetry he ever wrote.

The plot of the play is not credible in a realistic sense. Though it tells a fascinating tale, it is, as has been said, a fairy tale, not a story of real life. Or it is an allegory, a story with a hidden meaning, an allegory or a fairy tale about the Law, the Torah.

The central scene is the trial scene in which Shylock demands his pound of flesh, but is confuted by the beautiful Portia, disguised as a lawyer. In her unforgettable sermon, Portia pleads that Justice be tempered with Mercy:

> The quality of mercy is not strain'd,
> It droppeth as the gentle rain from heaven
> Upon the place beneath . . .
> It is an attribute to God himself;
> And earthly power doth then show likest God's
> When mercy seasons justice: therefore Jew,
> Though justice be thy plea, consider this,
> That in the course of justice, none of us
> Should see salvation: we do pray for mercy.[4]

These words have been interpreted as an allegory of the Law, of the rigorous Jewish Law of the Old Testament superseded by the New Testament Law of Love. The last act of the play is seen as the solution of the confrontation between Shylock and Portia in the trial scene. Jessica and Lorenzo, the Old Law and the New, are united in love and they talk of music, 'Shakespeare's recurrent symbol of harmony'.[5] This is very interesting but it leaves out

Francesco Giorgi, the Cabalist Friar of Venice who must surely have been in the minds of the Jews and Christians in Shakespeare's play.

A recent commentary on the play by Daniel Banes, published in 1975–6,[6] is written with full knowledge of Giorgi's *De harmonia mundi* and other Cabalist writings. Banes is convinced that *The Merchant of Venice* is very strongly influenced by Giorgi's work, which he suggests that Shakespeare could have known in the French translation.[7] Banes's argument contains many valuable insights but unfortunately he weakens his strong case (or so it seems to me) by seeking to equate the characters in the play with the Sephiroth of Cabala. He gives throughout his commentary diagrams illustrating the interactions between the characters and ends by finding these remarkably summarised and completed by the diagram of the Sephirothic Tree in which the Sephiroth are diagrammatically interrelated. Banes completes the Sephirothic Tree by adding the names of characters in *The Merchant of Venice* to the names of the Sephiroth. This is a somewhat high-handed procedure but it does lead Banes into some interesting suggestions.

He sees the trial scene as a diagram with Shylock on one side, Antonio on the other, and Portia in an intermediate position. Shylock represents the Sephira *Gevura* or *Din*, JUDGMENT SEVERITY; Antonio corresponds to *Hesed*, LOVING KINDNESS; Portia is equated with *Tiphereth* BEAUTY or MERCY who mediates between the two opposites of Severity and Kindness and attempts to reconcile them with Beauty-Mercy. Banes points out with many quotations that Mercy is not a monopoly of Christians but is enjoined in Jewish law and in Cabalist mysticism.[8]

Portia's attempt to convert Shylock to Mercy would thus be argued on Jewish–Cabalist lines, not necessarily on Christian lines. It might be added (though Banes does not say this) that Shylock's experiences as a Jew would not have impressed him favourably with Christian ideas of mercy; Portia might have been showing her usual tact in slanting her arguments in a Jewish direction. As we know, she did not succeed in converting him by these arguments; other arguments had to be used, and in the end Shylock became a forced convert, a marrano.

The theme of conversion, so vital an issue of the times, arises constantly in his play about Jews and Christians in Venice. The 'Judaising' philosophy of Francesco Giorgi endeavoured to meet that issue.

The other most significant and best-remembered scene of the play is the scene where Lorenzo sits with Shylock's daughter, Jessica,[9] gazing at the night sky. The Christian lover tells the Jewess about the universal harmony:

> Sit Jessica, – look how the floor of heaven
> Is thick inlaid with patens of bright gold,
> There's not the smallest orb which thou behold'st
> But in his motion like an angel sings,
> Still quiring to the young-eye'd cherubins:
> Such harmony is in immortal souls,
> But whilst this muddy vesture of decay
> Doth grossly close it in, we cannot hear it.

Then 'Enter Musicians' to the accompaniment of the famous lines on the power of music.[10]

The music of the spheres was, of course, a commonplace handed down from Plato through the Middle Ages; the actual context in which Shakespeare makes his supreme formulation of the theme is the Venice of Francesco Giorgi, visited in Shakespeare's Venetian play. Thus, it may be suggested that the immediate inspiration for this outburst was the universal harmony of the Friar of Venice, the book which we have already found to be so influential in the Elizabethan age. Think of

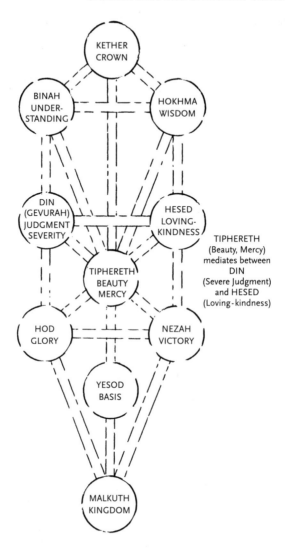

Figure 1 THE SEPHIROTHIC TREE
(The Hebrew names of the Sephiroth are transliterated, with approximate English translations.)

Giorgi's poetic expositions of the theme through canticles and tones in his vast volume. Think of his analyses of how the hierarchies of angels go with the spheres of the planets, how the hierarchy of the cherubim belongs with the highest of the celestial spheres, the sphere of fixed stars. Universal harmony heard in Venice, reconciling Christians and Jews – surely the influence of the Friar of Venice lies behind this scene, the influence of the famous Christian Cabalist, author of the *De harmonia mundi*.

Whilst the influences of Christian Cabala, and particularly the influence of Giorgi, begin to seem fundamental for the main Jewish–Christian themes of the play and its imagery, we have not yet integrated the theme of the caskets into these themes. What is the significance of the three caskets among which Portia's suitors had to choose? It was not the golden casket nor the silver one which was the winning choice which gained Portia's hand, but the casket of lead, chosen by Bassanio.

When Bassanio chooses the casket of lead[11] and becomes the chosen lover of this great, rich, powerful, and wonderfully wise lady, Portia, the themes of universal harmony break out, to be taken up again so exquisitely at the end of the play, when the Shakespearean magic is turned on at full strength, and the effects of music and musical language spread beneficent influences, harmonising all discords.

It has been suggested that the three caskets represent the three great religions, as in Boccacio's story of the three rings. Of Portia's three suitors, one, the Prince of Aragon, appears to be a Spanish Christian; another, the Prince of Morocco, is a Moor, and therefore a Moslem in religion. The third, Bassanio, should represent Judaism, and it is therefore to be expected that he should choose the casket of lead. For lead is the metal of Saturn, who represents, according to Giorgi, the religion of the Jews.

The observation of Banes,[12] who quoted Proverbs 8: 10–11, in relation to the choice of the caskets is significant:

> Choose my discipline, and not silver;
> Choose understanding, and not fine gold;
> For wisdom is better than rubies.

Bassanio in choosing lead chooses the divine discipline, the Judaic Law, the Torah, and with that choice he gains Portia, the Christian Princess.

In this play, Shakespeare would seem to be moving among the mysteries of Wisdom–Torah, and the personifications of it in that wealth of imagery and of religious songs of love in which the persecuted Sephardic Jews expressed their religion, banned in their homeland. The wonderful series of nights of love, 'on such a night as this', with which Lorenzo woos Jessica may reflect such an atmosphere.[13]

It is now clear that *The Merchant of Venice* is in no sense an anti-semitic play in imitation of Marlowe's *Jew of Malta*. On the contrary, it is something like a reply to Marlowe. Shylock and Barabbas are at opposite poles as presentations of the Jew. The audiences at *The Merchant of Venice* heard the universal harmony pealing forth from work of the Cabalist Friar of Venice. The audiences at *The Jew of Malta* were inclined to become antisemitic mobs. The two plays are as unlike as they can possibly be, except for the fact that they both have a Jew and his daughter as central characters, a fact accounted for if Shakespeare is deliberately replying to Marlowe.

Shakespeare's play, with its evocation of Venice, of Jews and Christians in Venice, of a Jewish-Christian marriage, distils a very different atmosphere from Marlowe's appeal to the antisemitic mob. It reminds one of the musical philosophy of the Cabalist Friar of Venice. It could live with the Spenserian magic, as Marlowe's play could not. And the Spenserian magic was being renewed in the years in which Shakespeare's play was written. In 1596, Spenser published the *Foure Hymnes* with their emphasis on Neoplatonic mysticism, with Cabalist undertones, centred on Elizabeth as the Venus of heavenly beauty.

It would seem from *The Merchant of Venice* that Shakespeare, like Spenser, found the Christian Cabalist philosophy of the Friar of Venice congenial.

13

AGRIPPA AND ELIZABETHAN MELANCHOLY: GEORGE CHAPMAN'S *SHADOW OF NIGHT*

One of the most mysterious poems of the Elizabethan age is George Chapman's *The Shadow of Night*. It opens by describing a 'humour of the night', a sad and weeping humour, but devoted to abstruse studies. The profound contemplations of the Night are then contrasted with the foolish and pointless activities of the Day. These experiences lead finally to a vision of the Moon, rising in magical splendour out of the darkness of the Night. The poem is in two parts, *Hymnus in Noctem* and *Hymnus in Cynthiam*. Many have been the attempts to unravel the hidden meanings of this most strange work. What is that darkness and that weeping humour through which the poet arrives at his moonlit visions?

Bent on concealing, rather than revealing, his meaning Chapman nowhere uses the key word which would have set enquirers on the right track, the word 'melancholy'. The humour is a dark humour, a weeping humour, a humour of the night; these are surely all indirect ways of saying that it is a melancholy humour. Chapman is describing the inspired melancholy and its stages, as set out in Agrippa's *De occulta philosophia*. Moreover, I hope to be able to show through the illustrations to this chapter, that Chapman was influenced by Dürer's visual imagery in his formulation in poetic imagery of the theme of the inspired melancholy.

Published in 1594, Chapman's poem will be seen here as a defence of the occult philosophy and its profound studies, a reply to the attack on such studies by Marlowe whose death had occurred in 1593, but whose *Doctor Faustus* was still delivering a message dangerous to those who had formerly supported scientific movements associated with Agrippa–Dee.

This brief introduction must suffice, for the moment, to place Chapman's poem before the reader in the context of the other studies in this book, and to introduce the surprising and novel character of the elucidation of the poem here attempted.

In his letter before the poem,[1] Chapman speaks of certain noblemen, and others, who have devoted themselves to deep studies thereby drawing science out of the neglect which was killing it. These men and their friends are devoted with exceeding rapture of delight to the deep search for knowledge. Shod with the winged sandals of Mercury and 'girt with Saturn's adamantine sword', they are intent on cutting off the head of ignorance and on 'subduing their monstrous affections to most beautiful judgment'. That Saturn, the Saturn of the Renaissance, star of highest and deepest learning and of profoundly ascetic life, is the guiding star of this group gives the clue to their place in the history of thought. These Elizabethan noblemen and their learned friends are Saturnians, following the 'revalued' Saturn of the Renaissance in their devotion to deep scientific studies and lofty moral and religious aims.

Once the Saturnian character of the deep search for

knowledge is realised we again have the clue to the meaning of Chapman's poem as concerned with melancholy, the Saturnian humour. The following analysis will endeavour to show that the inspired melancholy herself appears in it, with her black face and surrounded by her instruments of skill, painted by Chapman in word pictures which recall Dürer's engraving of *Melencolia I* (Plate 5).

Would it have been possible for Chapman to have seen that engraving? Certainly. Unlike paintings, engravings could easily travel. Robert Burton had seen Dürer's *Melencolia I*, which he mentions by name and describes in his *Anatomy of Melancholy*.[2] Burton's book was not published until 1621, yet his mention of the engraving shows that it could travel to England and might have done so earlier. Elizabethan noblemen might have owned copies of it. John Dee himself, student and admirer of Dürer,[3] might have acquired copies on his continental travels.

Chapman's sad Humour of the Night is the source of inspiration; she presides over the court of skill; through her, all secrets are reached:

> now let humour give
> Seas to mine eyes, That I may quicklie weepe
> The shipwracke of the world: or let soft sleepe
> (Binding my senses) lose my working soule,
> That in her highest pitch, she may controle
> The court of skill, compact of misterie,
> Wanting but franchisement and memorie
> To reach all secrets. . . .[4]

Chapman is invoking a melancholy humour to lead the 'working soul' through inspired *furor* (the senses being asleep) to reach her highest pitch when she controls the court of skill. The entranced figure of Dürer's Melancholy, freed from the sleeping senses (the sleeping dog), reaching her highest pitch in the court of skill, presents in visual images the theme which Chapman translates into poetic images.

The extraordinarily intense atmosphere of Dürer's engraving finds a parallel in the intensity of Chapman's words. He appeals to all serious poets to steep themselves in the Humour of the Night, the humour of inspiration:

All you possess with indepressed spirits,
Indu'd with nimble and aspiring wits,
Come consecrate with me, to sacred Night
Your whole endeuors, and detest the light . . .
No pen can any thing eternal write,
That is not steept in humour of the night.[5]

The pen wielded by the poet in the Night of Inspiration, as described by Chapman, may be compared to the engraver's tool wielded by the artist in the Night of Inspired Melancholy, as depicted by Dürer. Chapman's words, 'the court of skill', used to describe the surroundings of his Melancholy-Night figure, would describe admirably the setting of Dürer's *Melencolia I*, surrounded by instruments and figures referring to her learned activities and meditations. The man of genius, whether the artist or the poet, is the inspired melancholic. This is the theory of the Pseudo-Aristotelian *Problemata*, retailed by Agrippa in the *De occulta philosophia*.[6] Dürer's engraving depicts the melancholic inspiration of the artist-scientist. Chapman's poem describes, in terms of very similar imagery, the melancholic inspiration of the poet.

Night and melancholy have in common the fact that both are dark. Chapman's Night is personified as a female figure with a *facies nigra*:

Mens faces glitter, and their hearts are blacke,
But thou (great Mistresse of heauens gloomie racke)

Art blacke in face, and glitterst in thy heart.
There is thy glorie, riches, force, and Art.[7]

This dark figure with the black face, secretly indued with power
and wealth and all the force of Art, has a Düreresque intensity.
We think of Dürer's Melencolia I, with her swarthy face, her
money-bags, and the symbols of her mental power.

There is another curiously close parallel to Chapman's 'melancholy' imagery in a picture which the authors of Saturn and
Melancholy reproduce as among the compositions which have
obviously been influenced by Dürer's engraving. This is the picture attributed to Matthias Gerung (Plate 14 in this book) and
dated 1558. It shows in the centre a winged female figure in the
melancholy pose, head on hand. Her dark robes mingle with the
patch of darkness within which she is seated. Immediately in
line with her, near the lower edge of the picture, is a philosopher
measuring with compasses the globe of the world and surrounded by darkness. Indubitably, these two figures together
reflect Dürer's 'Melencolia' and her characteristic interest in
abstruse studies. The influence of Dürer's engraving is also
apparent in the rainbow in the background.

In other respects, Gerung's composition would seem to have
no relation at all to Dürer's engraving or to the theme of
melancholy. It is filled with quantities of figures engaged in
many kinds of activities. There are soldiers exercising near
their tents; people at banquets; dancing; having baths; engaged
in many kinds of sports and pastimes. These active figures
seem to be unrelated to the two meditative, melancholy figures.
As the authors of Saturn and Melancholy observe, describing this
picture:

> in a richly variegated and undulating landscape we see every
> possible activity of urban, rural, and military life; but though
> realistically conceived, these representations appear to have no

connection of any kind with each other or with the notion of melancholy.[8]

George Chapman can throw light on this problem, for in his *Hymnus in Noctem* he paints a word picture of an antithesis between Day and Night, in which the busy occupations of the Day are contrasted with the meditative Night of Melancholy, the former being empty and foolish, the latter profound and holy. He describes the coming of Night, which is the Day of deep students, and conversely the coming of Day and its idle occupations, contrasting with the studies of Night:

> And as when hosts of starres attend thy flight,
> (Day of deepe students, most contentfull night)
> The morning (mounted on the Muses stead)
> Ushers the sonne from Vulcan's golden bed,
> And then from forth their sundries roofes of rest,
> All sorts of men, to sorted taskes addrest,
> Spread this inferiour element: and yeeld
> Labour his due: the souldier to the field,
> States-men to counsell, Iudges to their pleas,
> Merchants to commerce, mariners to seas:
> All beasts and birds, the groues and forrests range,
> To fill all corners of this round exchange,
> Till thou (deare Night, o goddesse of most worth)
> Lets thy sweet seas of golden humor forth
> And Eagle-like doth with thy starrie wings,
> Beate in the foules and beasts to Somnus lodgings,
> And haughtie Day to the infernall deepe,
> Proclaiming silence, studie, ease and sleepe.[9]

These lines are surely a poetic counterpart to the Gerung picture. They explain the 'sorted men to sorted tasks addressed' of the picture as the occupations of Day, or of the active life, which are contrasted with the Night of contemplation and study. Like the Gerung picture, Chapman's lines describe Night as the inspired melancholy, contrasted with the empty and uninspired occupations of the Day. The basic theme is, of course, related to the conventional debate between the active and the contemplative lives.

For Chapman, the followers of Night with its studious peace, as opposed to the noisy bustle of the Day, its pure contemplative visions as opposed to vulgar activities, are the followers of virtue, who reject the 'whoredoms' of the 'painted light'.[10] So, in the Gerung picture, the gentle melancholy Night, and her attendant the deep student who is measuring the globe, are marked off by Night and darkness from the 'fooleries' of Day, and pursue their meditations undisturbed.

In the Gerung picture, a conflict is going on in the sky between several not very clearly defined mythological figures. One of these appears to be shooting at the Sun, thereby hastening the advent of the darkness of Night which is spreading in gloomy clouds. In Chapman's poem, Hercules is urged to shoot at the Sun, to stop his lustful activities, and to 'cleanse the beastly stable of the world' by descending from heaven:

> Fall Hercules from heauen in tempestes hurld,
> And cleanse this beastly stable of the world:
> Or bend thy brasen bow against the Sunne . . .
> Now make him leaue the world to Night and dreames.
> Neuer were vertues labours so enuy'd
> As in this light: shoote, shoote, and stoope his pride
> Suffer no more his lustful rayes to get
> The Earth with issue: let him still be set
> In Somnus thickets: bound about the browes,
> With pitchie vapours, and with Ebone bowes.[11]

How strangely close this seems to the Gerung picture, where

someone (Hercules, if Chapman's interpretation is accepted)[12] is shooting at the Sun, where dark tempests are preparing to hurl the shooter from the sky, where the vanquishing of the Sun and Day bring in the Melancholy Night of study, contemplation, and virtue.

It is difficult to resist the impression that Chapman had seen something like the Gerung picture. What he might have seen is an engraving by Dürer, now lost, of which the Gerung picture was a copy. Was there a lost Dürer engraving of *Melencolia II*, the second stage of inspired melancholy, and was the Gerung picture a copy of it? Did Chapman see the *Melencolia I*, which we know, hanging beside a *Melencolia II*, lost except for the copy of it by Gerung? And was it those two images which he combined in the imagery of his poem?

Though these researches into the archaeology of esoteric imagery may have seemed over-elaborate, or a digression from the main theme of this book, we are not losing sight of the goal. On the contrary, these researches are leading directly into something which belongs very much to our main theme. For if Chapman is defending inspired melancholy he is defending Cornelius Agrippa and the occult philosophy, defending Cabala and magic as profound studies leading towards scientific, moral, and religious truth, presenting a view of Agrippa-studies, or of Agrippa–Dee studies, which is an answer to Marlowe's witch-hunt against Agrippa–Dee, a refusal to accept the prohibition of *Doctor Faustus* against deep studies as leading inevitably to Hell and damnation.

As the authors of *Saturn and Melancholy* have convincingly argued,[13] Dürer was influenced in his conception of inspired melancholy by Agrippa's account of it in the *De occulta philosophia*. And Agrippa was following the classification of inspired melancholy into three stages in the Pseudo-Aristotelian *Problemata*.

The first stage was in the imagination of the artist or poet, inspired by the demons of creative *furor* to produce works of genius. This is the *Melencolia* I of the Dürer engraving, reflected in Chapman's poem by the dark-faced figure in the court of skill.

The second stage in the Agrippan classification was concerned with moral insight, the political melancholy of the utopian dreamer, profoundly dissatisfied with the world as it is. The Gerung picture might well be an echo of a *Melencolia* II expressive of this kind of moral melancholy. It shows the Saturnian melancholic in his scholarly retirement contrasted with the senseless occupations of active men, their meaningless wars, their stupid sports, their vulgar amusements. The Gerung picture, understood as *Melencolia* II in this sense, would correspond in the world of Elizabethan melancholy to the 'malcontent' humour,[14] the humour of Hamlet, 'the nighted humour'[15] with which the Prince of Denmark surveys the lustful activities of the Day.

Chapman's *Hymnus in Noctem* begins in the first stage of inspired melancholy and appears to move into the second stage at about the middle of the poem, though images from both stages overlap throughout. There is much other material which tends to obscure the outline of the argument, which can, however, be identified as concerned with the Agrippan stages of melancholy, profoundly influenced by Düreresque imagery.

The *Hymnus in Noctem* is immediately followed by the *Hymnus in Cynthiam*. In this hymn to Cynthia, or the Moon, we can study how Chapman assimilates his imagery to the Elizabeth cult. Cynthia, the Moon, is 'our empresse', that is Queen Elizabeth I, appearing in all the purity of her imperial reform. The Moon is already rising at the end of *Hymnus in Noctem*. She ascends as a glorious bride; associated with her, 'enchantress-like', is 'the dreadful presence of our Empress'.[16] A note by Chapman states that this alludes to Elizabeth's 'magicke authority'. In the *Hymnus in Cynthiam* the magic moon has fully risen in her 'all-ill-purging purity'. She does not banish Saturn. On the contrary, Cynthia's chastity performs the same 'adamantine' function as Saturn's sickle. Through a parallel between the castration of Saturn and the chastity of Cynthia, the Moon,[17] the latter becomes identified with the Saturnian theme of the poems.

The greater part of the *Hymnus in Cynthiam* is taken up by the description of a shadowy hunt. The nymph Euthemia (Joy) takes the forms of wild beasts which draw after them a pack of hunting dogs. The names of the dogs are taken from the account of the Actaeon fable by Natalis Comes in which the dogs of Actaeon are moralised as the senses.[18] In the shadow-hunting, the dogs of the senses hunt after false joys. The hunt lasts during the Day, but ends when Night returns. Thus the dogs, or senses, are the evil forces of the Day which sleep in the Night of inspired melancholy.

The moon-lit visions of the *Hymnus in Cynthiam* belong to the political aspect of Melancholy, its aspirations after Saturnian golden ages, its messianic expectations. This prophetic grade of the inspired melancholy (the third in the Agrippan formulation) is brought into line with the cult of Queen Elizabeth I as the Virgin of the Imperial Reform. All are enjoined to worship this Moon, in her moral aspect as an example of Chastity, in her political aspect as set against the Sun which now represents the European political and religious powers antagonistic to Elizabeth–Cynthia, who is adjured to

> Set thy Christal, and Imperiall throne . . .
> (Girt in thy chaste, and never-loosing zone)
> Gainst Europe's Sunne directly opposite
> And give him darkness that doth threat thy light.[19]

The enemy of Cynthia is here revealed as an evil Sun of papacy and Spanish aggression.

A still more definite link with the symbolism used of the queen is disclosed in the lines which allude to the imperial device of the Emperor Charles V which was constantly used of Elizabeth and her imperial reform:

> Forme then, twixt two superior pillars framed
> This tender building, *Pax imperii named.*[20]

Here is the familiar image of the two columns of the famous imperial device used as the framework for the vision of the chaste Moon of Empire to which Chapman's series of visions of the inspired melancholy has been leading.

And this Night of the Elizabethan Moon is full of white magic. The vision of the 'dreadful person of our Empresse' is bathed in white magical moonlight; she appears 'enchantress-like'; she is adjured to exercise her magic powers:

> Then in thy clear and Isie Pentacle
> Now execute a Magicke miracle.[21]

Chapman's poems have led eventually to Elizabeth as the central figure in a political vision of Reformed Empire, seen in the Night of inspired melancholy and its very white magic. The intense emphasis on chastity in the Elizabeth cult is here seen as the necessary guarantee that the magic of her cult is a white magic, religious and Cabalist.

Chapman would appear to be moving in a Spenserian thought world, forming pictures of, or invocations to, the royal messiah. As with Spenser, the picture is composite. It is a predominantly Lunar picture, but influences of Saturn are combined with those of Luna. It would appear to be a picture predominantly severe and ascetic. Can one say that it is a Puritan portrait, in black and white? Certainly there is probably a Puritan influence on Chapman and on his Lunar-Saturnian poem, yet, as we saw in the case of Spenser, such an outlook could include softer influences, influences of the heavenly beauty of Venus, as well as of the severity of Saturn. The same is true of Chapman.

A year after the publication of *The Shadow of Night*, with its glorification of the Saturnian melancholy, Chapman published a richly erotic poem, *The Banquet of Sense*. The critics have found it difficult to reconcile this poem with the strenuously ascetic *Shadow of Night*. There is, I think, no problem if the two poems are approached through the occult psychology in which the various planetary characteristics are combined or tempered with one another to form the complete personality. The Venus influences of *The Banquet of Sense* are not an invitation to lust. The descriptions of the beauty of the body are expressed in language which is intended to recall that of the Canticle. The address at the end to a 'dear soverign' includes a vision of her perfections raised to heaven,

> Deckt in bright verse, where Angels shall appeare
> The praise of vertue, loue, and beauty singing.[22]

The Venereal theme is raised to a celestial and angelic level, as in Spenser's *Hymnes* (published in the following year). This poem is, so to speak, a Venus picture to hang beside the Saturn and Luna pictures, not so much as a contrast to them, but as a mitigation of their severity. As in *The Faerie Queene* the portrait as a whole includes a Venus version, as well as Saturnian or Lunar versions, so in Chapman's mind the pictures modulate into one another. The severity of the Saturnian Law is mitigated by the influences of Beauty–Venus.

Or one can think of the contrast between *The Shadow of Night* and *The Banquet of Sense* in terms of the familiar themes of contemplative and the active lives. The comparison is not between a holy asceticism and an evil and lustful life of the senses. In the night of melancholy, the senses sleep to allow full reception of intuitive vision. In the active life of day, perception is through the senses and sense-impressions. In one of its aspects, the *Banquet* is a study of sense-impressions. To view this poem as an immoral 'descent' from the asceticism of the *Shadow* is to misunderstand both poems which are comparing the approach to knowledge through intuitive revelation, when the senses are in abeyance with the approach through sense-impressions. Perhaps the most helpful of the commentators on Chapman's poems is Milton, who in Il *Penseroso* and L'*Allegro* is presenting the same contrast between the Night of inspired melancholy and the active life of Day. [23]

The main direction of this chapter has been towards suggesting that Chapman's poems are a restatement, in obscure form, of Spenserian themes. Marlowe's attack is replied to; an effort is made to re-express the occult philosophy in its relation to the Elizabethan imperial theme.[24] And Chapman's formulation of the imagery of the inspired melancholy is a vindication of the Dee tradition. The noble Saturnian melancholics are carrying on the Dee science and magic in the obscurity of their melancholy night.

So we arrive at the hypothesis which has been so much mooted, that there was a group of noblemen-scientists and their friends, pursuing deep philosophical and mathematical studies, and that Chapman was a member of this group and alludes to it in his poem. The group has been known as 'the School of Night' because of a suggestion that Shakespeare may hint at it under that title.[25] If there was such a group, it has been argued that it may have consisted largely of thinkers associated with Raleigh and his enterprises, namely the famous Thomas Hariot, the Earl of Northumberland (mentioned by Chapman in his preface) and other advanced Elizabethan thinkers.

The contribution which the present study makes to the problem is that it should now be possible to take it out of the sphere of personal allusion within a small coterie into the world of general history of thought. This is because of the identification of the subject of Chapman's poem as the inspired melancholy, as defined by Agrippa and illustrated by Dürer. We can now realise that Chapman and his friends were Saturnians, following the revalued Saturn of the Renaissance in their devotion to deep studies, their utopian moral aims, and their prophetic vision in which Queen Elizabeth I appears as the messianic figure expected in this remarkable Elizabethan transformation of the occult philosophy.

The Shadow of Night may have been close to Raleigh's long poem, now mostly lost, glorifying the queen as Cynthia in imagery which was probably related to Spenser's imagery in the 'Luna' episode of The Faerie Queene. The Saturnian deep devotion to scientific studies in a night of inspired melancholy, combined with a courtier's devotion to a lady beautiful as Cynthia–Venus, might well result in Raleigh's type of personality, the personality of an Elizabethan knight – passionate inspired melancholic and master of esoteric love poetry.[26]

We know from references in his History of the World that Raleigh was conversant with Hermetic literature.[27] The list of books (undated) which he once owned includes works such as the commentary on Pico's Cabalist Conclusions by Archangelo de Burgo Novo, and a copy of that significant work by Reuchlin, the De verbo mirifico.[28] Raleigh is likely to have been influenced by the wide and deep religious outlook stimulated by Cabalist influences. The Jesuits called Raleigh and his school a 'school of atheism' which indicates that Raleigh's religious outlook was not welcome to the missionaries of extreme Counter-Reformation.

We are witnessing here a phenomenon of profound European importance, the retreat into deeper occultism of the traditions of Renaissance magic and occultism, threatened and attacked by reactions, such as that led by Christopher Marlowe. A parallel, though not perhaps a very close one, to this Elizabethan situation might be the situation around the Emperor Rudolf II who was retreating at about this time into profound melancholy under the guidance of his Cabalist confessor, Pistorius.[29] Rudolf was retreating in ever greater alarm from the rigidly Counter-Reforming activities of his relatives, the Spanish Hapsburgs, and their Jesuits.

The elusive spiritual kinship between Rudolf and Elizabeth was related to the similarity in their situations, as outposts of a liberal Renaissance outlook amidst a rising tide of reaction. The Düreresque imagery in which Chapman's melancholy is expressed may even reflect a similar cult of Agrippan melancholy at the imperial court, passing into Elizabethan England through the familiarity of Dee, and of the Sidney circle, with the Rudolfine atmosphere.

The Elizabethan melancholy is related to the wider European phenomenon of the convulsive experiences through which Renaissance traditions were passing under the pressures of the reaction.

14

SHAKESPEAREAN FAIRIES, WITCHES, MELANCHOLY: KING LEAR AND THE DEMONS

Shakespeare was writing his plays in, roughly, the twenty years covered by the last decade of the sixteenth century and the first of the seventeenth. These were the years during which, in Europe, Renaissance Neoplatonism and its associated occultisms were being heavily attacked by the forces of reaction. At the turn of the century, in 1600, occurred the symbolic burning of the Hermetic philosopher, Giordano Bruno.

In England these stresses and strains were strongly present. On the one hand a late and particularly powerful form of Renaissance Neoplatonism was developed in the Dee movement, was reflected in the late Renaissance magical poem *The Faerie Queene*, and was used in the propaganda for Elizabeth I. On the other hand, the reaction was also present. The Jesuit missions had spread the Counter-Reformation attitudes. Though England was spared the worst of the continental witch-hunts, the atmosphere of the reaction is felt in Marlowe's *Doctor Faustus*.

These problems had come sharply to the fore in Elizabethan England on the return of Dee from his continental mission in 1589. Dee is discouraged; Raleigh falls from favour in 1592. The thought-movements characteristic of earlier years suffer a rebuff.

Plaintive protests were made by poets at the failure to continue the movements of former times, when Leicester and Sidney were the leaders of the Elizabethan Renaissance. That remarkable collection of poetry *The Phoenix Nest*,[1] published in 1593, begins with a lament for Leicester, continues with elegies on Sidney, and includes poems by Dyer, Raleigh, and other members of their circle, poems infused with melancholy and with allusions to Cynthia, to chastity, and to the Spenserian Elizabeth-cult. These poems seem to plead for something, perhaps for return to the Spenserian–Elizabethan outlook and philosophy and politico-religious traditions.

To this period belongs Chapman's secret rehabilitation of those traditions, studied in the last chapter. And Spenser himself, disregarding the court discouragement of Raleigh and Dee, continued in 1596 with the publication of *The Faerie Queene*, and reaffirmed, with the publication in the same year of his *Foure Hymnes*, his 'Elizabethan Neoplatonism'.[2]

If it can be accepted as a fact, as I believe that it can, that the thought of *The Merchant of Venice* is influenced by the Christian Cabala of Francesco Giorgi, then it would follow that Shakespeare would be sympathetic to the Spenserian outlook. Can one interpret other Shakespearean plays, themes, or images as related to this outlook?

This book is not about Shakespeare, any more than it is about Spenser, Marlowe, or Chapman. Like the mentions of those poets, it is only an attempt to situate Shakespeare within the general themes described in this book. The present chapter selects a few plays and themes for discussion, and that in a most summary manner. It is in no sense a final solution or presentation but only a first attempt to look at some familiar Shakespearean phenomena from the point of view of traditions and attitudes which this book has tried to investigate.

Shakespearean fairies are related to the Fairy Queen through their loyalty and through their fervent defence of chastity. The curious fairy scenes in The Merry Wives of Windsor refer to the queen, to the Order of the Garter, and to the Garter Chapel at Windsor. This play was first printed in 1602; the date of composition is unknown; there is a reference in it to the visit of the Duke of Württemberg in 1592. The fairies are employed to point a moral of chastity. They punish Falstaff for his lust; they write the motto of the Order of the Garter in flowers and decorate the Garter Chapel. They are defenders of chastity, of a chaste queen and her pure knighthood. They are enjoined to perform a white magic to safeguard her and her order of knighthood from evil influences.

These Elizabethan fairies are not, I believe, manifestations of folk or popular tradition. Their origins are literary and religious, in Arthurian legend and in the white magic of Christian Cabala. The use of fairy imagery in the queen cult was begun in the Accession Day Tilts, and relates to the chivalric imagery of the Tilts.[3] As taken up by Spenser in The Faerie Queene, the fairy imagery was Arthurian and chivalric, and also an expression of pure white magic, a Christian Cabalist magic.

The Shakespearean fairies emanate from a similar atmosphere; they glorify a pure knighthood serving the queen and her imperial reform. To read Shakespeare's fairy scenes without reference to the contemporary build-up of the Virgin Queen as the representative of pure religion is to miss their purpose as an affirmation of adherence to the Spenserian point of view, a very serious purpose disguised in fantasy.

*

The supreme expression of the Shakespearean fairyland is *A Midsummer Night's Dream*. This play was first printed in 1600; it was probably written for a private performance at a wedding, perhaps in 1595 or thereabouts.

This magical play about enchanted lovers is set in a world of night and moonlight, where fairies serve a fairy king and queen. Into the magic texture is woven a significant portrait of Queen Elizabeth I. Oberon, the fairy king, describes how he once saw Cupid, all armed, flying between the cold moon and the earth:

> A certain aim he took
> At a fair vestal, throned by the West
> And loos'd his love shaft smartly from his bow,
> As it should pierce a hundred thousand hearts.
> But I might see young Cupid's fiery shaft
> Quench'd in the chaste beams of the wat'ry moon,
> And the imperial votaress passed on,
> In maiden meditation, fancy free.[4]

Shakespeare's picture of Elizabeth as a Vestal Virgin, a chaste Moon who defeats the assaults of Cupid, an 'imperial votaress', is a brilliant summing up of the cult of Elizabeth as the representative of imperial reform.[5] A well-known portrait of Elizabeth presents the imagery in visual form. Elizabeth holds a sieve, emblem of the chastity of a Vestal Virgin; behind her rises the column of empire; the globe beside her shows the British Isles surrounded by shipping, alluding to her enthronement 'in the West'. It is a portrait of the Virgin of imperial reform, of which Shakespeare gives a verbal picture in the lines just quoted, using the same imagery.

As I have pointed out in *Astraea*,[6] both the 'Sieve' portrait and Shakespeare's word-picture in the *Dream* are Triumphs of Chastity on the model of Petrarch's *Trionfi*, and the triumph refers both to purity in public life and in private life, to Elizabeth both in her public role as the representative of pure imperial reform, and in her private role as a chaste lady. It is exactly in such a role that Spenser presents Elizabeth, so he tells Raleigh in the letter to him published with *The Faerie Queene*. As Gloriana she is a most royal queen or empress, as Belphoebe she is a most chaste and beautiful lady. Shakespeare's word-picture presents Gloriana–Belphoebe, the Virgin of pure Empire, enthroned by the West, the chaste lady who triumphs over Cupid.

The appearance in the sky of the *Dream* of this Spenserian vision strikes the key-note of the magical-musical moonlight of the play. The moon is Cynthia, the Virgin Queen, and the words 'the chaste beams of the watery moon' might also allude to Walter Raleigh's cult of her as Cynthia. Puns on 'Walter', pronounced 'Water', were usual in referring to Raleigh. Spenser was following Raleigh, so he says, in the 'Luna' book of *The Faerie Queene*. Hence the allusions of the Shakespearean lines would be both to Elizabeth as Spenser's Gloriana–Belphoebe, and also to Raleigh's cult of her as Cynthia, adopted by Spenser.

Thus the complex phenomenon which floats in the night sky of the *Dream* relates the play to the Spenserian dream-world, the Spenserian magical cult of the Imperial Virgin, with its undercurrent of Christian Cabala.

What of Shakespeare and the other poet whom we have studied in this series, George Chapman? There has been much speculation concerning possible echoes of Chapman and his poem about night in Shakespeare's *Love's Labour's Lost*. This play was first printed in 1598. The date of its composition is uncertain, perhaps about 1594–5.

The play is a complex tissue of topical allusions. The phrase 'the school of night' has attracted attention as possibly containing some hidden meaning. One of the lovers loves a dark woman, with a black complexion, which he extravagantly praises. This evokes the criticism

> O paradox! Black is the badge of hell,
> The hue of dungeons and the school of night.[7]

It has been thought that this might be an allusion to Chapman's poem or rather to a school of mathematicians and philosophers, possibly including Walter Raleigh, whose ideas Chapman's poem might reflect.[8] Shakespeare has been thought to have been satirising this group in his words about a 'school of night'.

I have no intention of pursuing again here in terms of personalities the various hares which the words 'school of night' have started. However, a new light is surely thrown on this problem by the identification, made in the previous chapter, of the subject of Chapman's poem *The Shadow of Night*. We now know that the poem is about the inspired melancholy, as defined by Agrippa, the dark Saturnian humour, characterised by a dark complexion, the 'black face' of the melancholy temperament. Chapman, we suggested, is reflecting in his imagery about blackness the Dürer engraving of melancholy with her *facies nigra* in her court of skill. Shakespeare's allusion to a dark woman, associated with a 'school of night', might therefore be allusion to the inspired melancholy, perhaps having some personal connotations as well, but which might be explained, or studied, on a non-personal level as concerned with the topic of burning contemporary interest, the inspired melancholy.

That there is allusion to the inspired melancholy in the play has been recognised. Armado's pretensions to greatness because of his melancholy have been seen as a parody of the theory. But, though parodied in the sub-plot, the inspired melancholy is a basic feature of the main plot.

Berowne falls madly in love with the dark Rosaline. This love, black as pitch, has taught him to be melancholy with the furor of inspired melancholy. On hearing Berowne's extravagant language in honour of his dark and heavenly Rosaline, the King exclaims, 'What zeal, what fury hath inspired thee now?' He recognises the inspired melancholy and the reason why Berowne's love is black – 'Thy love is black as ebony'. There follow the quick exchanges on blackness: 'No face is fair that is now full as black', cries Berowne, to which the King rejoins:

> O paradox? Black is the badge of hell,
> The hue of dungeons and the school of night.

Berowne agrees that 'Devil's soonest tempt, resembling spirits of light', yet continues his praise of blackness.[9]

The 'school of night' need not be a reference to any particular group of people. Profound Saturnian or Cabalist studies always carried with them the danger of becoming involved with bad spirits, or devils, instead of good spirits, or angels, of reaching hell rather than heaven. The words may be no more than the usual warning to Cabalists of the dangers inherent in their attempts to reach the highest heights. Marlowe in his anti-Agrippan *Doctor Faustus* had heavily underlined the dangers of the occult philosophy, and there may be echoes of his attack in the King's words.

Berowne, however, was clearly a good Saturnian, not a wicked conjuror, for through his love, though black, he hears the universal harmony

> as sweet and musical
> As bright Apollo's lute, strung with his hair;
> And when love speaks, the voice of all the gods
> Make heaven drowsy with the harmony.[10]

He assures his friends that in forswearing their oaths in order to follow their loves they are being truly religious:

> For charity itself fulfils the law:
> And who can sever love from charity.[11]

Portia might have used this as the text of her sermon on the Law.

This play is an astonishing example of the incredible virtuosity with which Shakespeare uses esoteric imagery. The plot is ridiculous; the fantastic comic characters move in a world as impossible as that of the lovers. The true plot and meaning are in the other-worldly logic of the imagery.

Many fascinating vistas for further pursuit of esoteric argument in Shakespeare are opening up, but there is no room nor time here for more than a few more glances at a few more plays. Much must be omitted with reluctance, for example the part played by a Renaissance Friar in *Romeo and Juliet*. I intend to concentrate now on the more obvious of the allusions to the Saturnian theme of the inspired melancholy.

As has been outlined in earlier chapters, Agrippa's account of the inspired melancholy involved three stages, a stage of imaginative insight into all arts and sciences, illustrated in Dürer's *Melencolia I*; a stage of moral insight, of which we have argued that Gerung's picture of Melancholy sheltering amongst the shades of Night against the foolish occupations of the Day might be a Düreresque reflection. We thought to see both stages reflected in Chapman's poem, both *Melencolia I* in her court of skill, and also that phase of inspired melancholy which saw into moral corruption and loathed 'the beastly stable of the world'.

The Melancholy Jacques in *As You Like It* (first printed in 1623, date of composition uncertain – about 1599 has been conjectured) recalls classical and Agrippan theory of melancholy through his very name, suggestive of Ajax, the example of melancholy madness.[12] He represents the inspired melancholy of the moralising kind. From his retirement 'under the shade of melancholy boughs'[13] in the Forest of Arden he watches scenes from the life of man from the cradle to the grave, described in his famous speech. Jacques's insight, his moralising on the time, is akin to folly; he has learned it from Touchstone, the Fool, and he claims the license of a fool to speak his mind. He is the melancholic who is inspired to speak the truth:

> give me leave
> To speak my mind, and I will through and through
> Cleanse the foul body of the infected world.[14]

One is reminded of Chapman's words

> Fall Hercules from heaven in tempests hurled
> And cleanse the beastly stable of the world.

Now that we know that these words of Chapman's refer to the inspired melancholy in the second of the phases described by Agrippa, their resemblance to the words of the Melancholy Jacques become still more striking and we begin to see Jacques and his Melancholy as in tune with that mourning, weeping, Saturnian, malcontent humour which Chapman describes.

The Melancholy Jacques is but a preparation for the appearance of the most famous melancholic of all time, Hamlet, Prince of Denmark.

The tragedy of *Hamlet* (first printed in 1603, probably written in 1600) opens in the deepest darkness of the night and with the appearance of an awful apparition. The ghost was a thing seen in the night; the problem was to decide whether it was an invention of the devil or a prophetic inspiration giving dreadful insight into the true state of society.

In the world of *Hamlet* the occult atmosphere is intensely strong. In the darkness of his night, Hamlet wrestles with his melancholy problems. Is his melancholy the inspired melancholy, giving prophetic insight into an evil situation and telling him how he is to act rightly and prophetically in that situation? Or is it a symptom of weakness like the melancholy of witches, making him prone to diabolic possession and the deception of evil spirits? These are the questions asked in *Hamlet* and they were the questions which were raging at the time.

There can be no doubt that Hamlet belongs to Melancholy Night, but is it a good melancholy of inspired vision or a bad melancholy of witchcraft and evil? Hamlet himself is not at first sure, and he questions the Ghost:

> Be thou a spirit of health or goblin damn'd
> Bring with thee airs from heaven or blasts from hell.[15]

When the Ghost reveals to him the story of the murder and of his uncle's guilt he cries, 'O my prophetic soul',[16] but yet he continues to doubt himself and the validity of his vision.

> The spirit that I have seen
> May be the devil. . . . And perhaps
> Out of my weakness and my melancholy,
> As he is very potent with such spirits,
> Abuses me to damn me.[17]

This is the theory of the diabolic possession of witches.

Hamlet tests the ghost's story with the play, and the effect of the play on his mother and uncle proves to him that the ghost had in fact given him a truly inspired insight into an appalling moral situation.

Like the Melancholy Jacques who must 'cleanse the body of the infected world', or like Chapman's Hercules who must 'cleanse the beastly stable of the world', Hamlet regards the situation with which he has to deal as a 'nasty sty'.

Hamlet's black humour is proved to be, not the blackness of Hell or of a witches' school of night, but the melancholy of a prophet in a world so badly disobedient to the Law that the universal harmony is inaudible, or broken, like sweet bells jangled out of tune and harsh.

*

With the accession in 1603 of the King of Scotland to the throne of England the witchcraft problem became more acute than ever, for this monarch believed intensely in witches and believed that plots had been hatched to harm him by witchcraft. He also did not believe that Christian Cabala of the type defined by Cornelius Agrippa was harmless. In his book about demonology he had classed Agrippa with bad conjurors and devils and sorcerers.[18] We know, too, that James was against Agrippa's disciple, John Dee, who appealed to him in vain to be cleared of bad conjuring.[19] He would surely have been against the Spenserian fairy world of white Cabala; he did in fact condemn fairies as bad spirits[20] and he disliked Spenser's poem which he believed contained criticism of his mother.[21]

In short, on the problem of Melancholy, on whether it is the inspired melancholy or the bad melancholy of witches, King James would have been likely to side with Marlowe in seeing it all as damnable, seeing Agrippa as the diabolical conjuror, Dee as his deluded follower, The Faerie Queene as no white-magical prophecy of a messianic role for England but as belonging to the outmoded flattery of his predecessor on the English throne, which involved the denigration of his mother, Mary, Queen of Scots.

A dark night of melancholy witchcraft broods over Scotland in *Macbeth* (first printed in the folio of 1623, probably written between 1603 and 1606, after the accession of James). The world of Macbeth and his wife is a school of night indeed, where witches incite to murder. The deep damnation of this deed is trumpeted against by angels, by 'heaven's Cherubins',[22] whose universal harmony is heard only in the form of judgment. The magic is bad, an evil necromancy. A few escape from this black night of Hell, amongst them the ancestor of King James, but there are no good fairies and we are very far from the Spenserian world.

In *King Lear*, on the other hand, written at about the same time or a little later (printed in 1608, 1619, 1623, probably written 1604–5), Shakespeare has gone to Spenser for his subject. There were earlier plays about King Lear which he knew, and of course he knew the main historical source, Holinshed. Nevertheless it remains a fact that the story of King Lear and his ungrateful daughters, and of the faithful Cordelia, is told at some length in *The Faerie Queene*[23] where it forms part of the 'British Chronicle' which is the preparation in history for the appearance of Gloriana and her messianic role. Spenser was of course repeating Geoffrey of Monmouth. The British Chronicle, and the legend of the descent from Brut of British kings, was being adapted to James by contemporary propagandists,[24] as Shakespeare certainly knew. He was following this process himself in choosing a 'Brutan' theme,[25] a theme of sacred British descent, for his play, but what is a little strange is that he chose an ancient British monarch whose story was such a dire tragedy, and a story of ingratitude.

In Shakespeare's telling of the story, the theme of ingratitude is heightened to cosmic proportions. The British monarch has given away his empire to wicked and ungrateful people. They owe everything to him, yet they turn him out into a frightful storm, utterly destitute and friendless save for a Fool and for a person who seems to be an escaped lunatic, possessed by devils.

The wild figure of Tom o' Bedlam gesticulating beside Lear on the blasted heath was an addition by Shakespeare to the story and one which introduced the theme of demonology to the melancholy scene. The extraordinary thing about these demons in the night of *Lear* is that they are faked. Tom o' Bedlam is really Edgar in disguise; he is deliberately simulating demoniac possession.[26]

The problem of why Shakespeare chose to give as companion to Lear in his destitute state a man who was *pretending* to be possessed by devils has never been satisfactorily solved. For the

names of the devils supposed to be in possession of Tom o'
Bedlam, Shakespeare was using a compilation by Samuel Harsnett, *Declaration of Egregious Popish Impostures*, published in 1603. This
is a polemical work in which a Jesuit is accused of having
induced a sense of demonic possession in some persons, pretending afterwards to exorcise them. It is certain that Shakespeare was using this account, for words and phrases from Harsnett occur in relation to Tom o' Bedlam, and the names of the
devils which are supposed to infest him are taken directly from
Harsnett.[27] The devil-names from Harsnett would probably have
been recognised by Shakespeare's first audience as referring to a
case of faked demonic possession and faked exorcism. That is to
say, Shakespeare through the device of Edgar's impersonation of
Tom o' Bedlam, brings in an allusion to demonology and witch-
scares, not in order to arouse terror in the audience after the
manner of Marlowe, but to raise the question in their minds as
to whether such scares could be falsely raised, or manipulated
against a victim for political or politico-religious reasons. Or, as
Harsnett badly puts it in his title, as 'Egregious Popish
Impostures'.

At this point an amazing thought presents itself. To whom was
Shakespeare referring in this figure of an ancient British monarch, treated with base ingratitude, haunted by false accusation
of demonic possession? There was a living survivor of the great
days of the Spenserian dream whom this description would
pretty exactly fit – John Dee.

The architect of the idea of British Empire had been John Dee,
in his first period, when he had been at the centre of the Elizabethan age, and one of the inspirations of Spenser's poem. Dee
claimed to be himself descended from British kings, belonging
himself to the tradition which Spenser had traced, and of which
the story of Lear was one of the episodes.

Dee in his third period, during which Shakespeare wrote *Lear*,
was banished from court and society, suffered total neglect and

bitter poverty, and might well have felt himself to be the victim of base ingratitude. He who had given so much received no reward. He was moreover pursued by scares against him as a black magician and sorcerer, though he himself never admitted this charge, proclaiming himself a Christian, as no doubt he was, a Christian Cabalist.

The tragedy of *Lear* may be, in its deepest historical and spiritual aspect, the tragedy of the imperial theme of the Elizabethan age, sung by Spenser as its epic poet, nourished by the work of Dee, but now broken and dispelled in this dark hour of disillusion and despair.

15

PROSPERO: THE SHAKESPEAREAN MAGUS

In his last period, the period of the so-called romantic plays, Shakespeare appears to emerge from his tragic mood into a happier atmosphere. I have argued in my book on Shakespeare's last plays[1] that the more hopeful feeling was encouraged by the energetic line of thought and leadership being displayed by the young Prince Henry, ardently anti-Spanish and intent on reviving the Elizabethan outlook to which his father was unfavourable. Prince Henry patronised and encouraged members of the old Elizabethan school. George Chapman was his protégé. Raleigh was still in the prison to which he had been consigned at the beginning of the reign, pursuing his Saturnian studies with the Earl of Northumberland and Thomas Hariot, but he was a favourite with the young prince.

The fairy imagery revived in the prince's circle. Thomas Dekker's play *The Whore of Babylon*, presented by Prince Henry's company of players in 1607,[2] attempts to recreate Shakespearean fairy imagery. The personage of Titania is said to figure 'our late

Queen Elizabeth', her evil opposite being Babylon or Rome. Prince Henry's actors are living in the Spenserian world, and remembering its continuation in *A Midsummer Night's Dream*.

In the masques in honour of Prince Henry ('Barriers' and 'Oberon') the prince appears in an Arthurian setting as descendant of ancient British kings, reviver of chivalry, aided by the magic of Merlin who rises from his tomb to assist the Fairy Prince and his subjects, 'the nation of the fays'.[3] The Spenserian fairyland becomes the ideal world of the Fairy Prince who is continuing the traditions of the Elizabethan Fairy Queen. The sudden death of the prince in 1612 was a fearful blow to his supporters.

Prince Henry's sister, Princess Elizabeth, was associated in the public mind with the late queen of the same name as another pure Protestant heroine.[4] *The Tempest* was produced before the Princess Elizabeth as one of the shows in the festivities celebrating her marriage to the Elector Palatine, the Protestant wedding, much misliked by pro-Spanish interests.

Thus it was within 'the Elizabethan revival within the Jacobean age' that *The Tempest* (performed in 1611 and 1612, first printed in 1623) presented in Prospero, magus and conjuror, Shakespeare's last word on the occult philosophy.

That Prospero's magic reflects the influence of Agrippa's *De occulta philosophia* was indicated by Frank Kermode in 1954 in his introduction to the Arden edition of *The Tempest*. Other studies have argued that this presentation of a Dee-like Agrippan magus was part of the Elizabethan revival.[5] The magical play presents, in new and fascinating guise, old and familiar arguments. That the magic of Prospero is a white magic is underlined in the emphasis on chastity in Prospero's advice to his daughter's lover, and elsewhere in the play. The white and pure magic of Prospero is contrasted with the black magic of the evil witch, Sycorax, and her son. Prospero is using the *De occulta philosophia* to call on good spirits (the name, Ariel, is mentioned in Agrippa's book),[6] and he overcomes and controls the bad magic of the witch.

Surely contemporary audiences must have picked up the underlying trend of this play as a return to the magical world of the late Virgin Queen, her chastity and pure religion, now continuing and revived by the younger generation. Her philosopher, the white magician Doctor Dee, is defended in Prospero, the good and learned conjuror, who had managed to transport his valuable library to the island. The presence of the Dee-like magus in the play falls naturally into place as part of the Elizabethan revival. That was the world to which Shakespeare had belonged, the world of the Spenserian fairyland, the world of John Dee. He gladly falls in with the revival of the thought and imagery of that world and writes under its influence his most magical play.

Prospero, the beneficent magus, uses his good magical science for utopian ends. He is the climax of the long spiritual struggle in which Shakespeare and his contemporaries had been engaged. He vindicates the Dee science and the Dee conjuring. He allays the anxieties of the witch craze and establishes white Cabala as legitimate.

How profound is the change in atmosphere from Lear, the British Spenserian king, abandoned in a storm and mocked by faked demons, to Prospero, firmly in control of his magical island through his white conjuring.

It is strange that, save for one Italian writer,[7] students of Shakespeare's *Tempest* have failed to draw attention to the fact that another play about the occult sciences appeared at about the same time. This was Ben Jonson's *The Alchemist*, first performed (so far as we know) by the King's Men, Shakespeare's company, in 1610, first printed in 1612. Shakespeare's conjuror, Prospero, is noble and beneficent; Jonson's Subtle, the alchemist, is a charlatan and a cheat. Yet both are drawn from Doctor Dee.

There is an undoubted satirical allusion to Dee's *Monas*

hieroglyphica in Jonson's play, and Dee's mathematical preface to Euclid is parodied throughout.[8] Jonson pokes very clever fun at alchemists, magicians, mathematicians, scientists – all to him equally ludicrous – and in the end Subtle and his gang are cleared out of the house they have made the centre of their nefarious practices by the returning owner. But not before the clever fun has pretty obviously pointed to 'the Elizabethan revival within the Jacobean age' as the object of the satire.

An influential female member of Subtle's gang is a whore. One of his dupes is a weak-minded poet who is fooled by the gang. They fake a vision for him in which Subtle is disguised as a priest of Fairy, and the Fairy Queen is impersonated by the whore. It is an exact reversal of Dekker's *Whore of Babylon*, an attack on the Spenserian revival. Jonson is writing from the point of view of the reaction, of the enemies of Elizabethanism, of Elizabethan occult science, of Spenser and his fairyland.

Yet – and this is a most strange phenomenon – Jonson had himself written the masques in honour of Prince Henry, building up the Elizabethan and Arthurian fairy legend around him. As a possible solution to this problem it may be suggested that King James, who greatly feared Spain and the Jesuits and was most nervous of his son's active Protestantism, might have been not displeased by Jonson's indirect way of sabotaging the cause which he had publicly supported in the masques. And James sincerely disliked Dee and feared anything savouring of magic. It is significant that Jonson became a favourite at court and wrote many masques flattering James and insinuating contempt for occultists, alchemists, mathematicians, and Rosicrucians.[9]

A play which should be carefully compared with Jonson's *Alchemist* is Marlowe's *Doctor Faustus*. Marlowe and Jonson are writing from similar attitudes, attitudes of reaction against the occult philosophy and with particular reference to Dee. Marlowe's reaction is the obvious one of raising a witch-hunt against conjurors. Jonson may seem less crude in attacking alchemists with ridicule rather than with threatened persecution, but his satire is really extremely harsh and threatening. Jonson's switch to alchemy as the main subject of ridicule or reproach reflects the enormous contemporary development of the alchemical side of occult philosophy (already present in Agrippa's work) through the influence of Rosicrucianism.

Shakespeare's language in *The Tempest* is infused through and through with spiritual alchemy and its theme of transformation:

> Full fathom five thy father lies
> Of his bones are coral made.

Though Shakespeare never wielded a wand, nor thought of himself as a magus, he is a magician, master of the spell-binding use of words, of poetry as magic. This was the art in which he was supreme and which Prospero symbolises.

Ben Jonson thought differently of the poet's art. For him it must be polished by careful criticism. As we know, Jonson criticised Shakespeare for wanting art, for being uncritically verbose. 'He never blotted a line', said his admiring fellow-actors. 'Would he had blotted a thousand', replied Jonson, the critic.[10] The preface to *The Alchemist* contains warnings against contemporary poets who 'presume on their own naturals', 'deride diligence', and 'utter all they can, however unfitly'. This sounds very much like Jonson's normal style of criticism of Shakespeare on, apparently, purely literary grounds.

The presence of this type of criticism in the preface to *The Alchemist*, the play which is really an attack on Dee and the occult tradition, may cause one to think again about Jonson's literary criticism. Perhaps it went deeper than the literary surface. Perhaps it was an attack on magical poetry, on poetry inspired by the occult philosophy.

The monument to Shakespeare in the parish church of Stratford-on-Avon (Plate 15) has been much criticised as unworthy of its subject, but it is undoubtedly a memorial bust erected to the poet soon after his death by people who knew him. What have these friends sought to emphasise? Surely they have tried to show through the fixed gaze, the trance-like expression, the half-open mouth, the poet who uttered from inspiration, who never blotted a line.

To attempt to sum up the second part of this book is difficult. I shall try only to mention some main points in these brief last paragraphs.

The occult philosophy in the Elizabethan age was no minor concern of a few adepts. It was the main philosophy of the age, stemming from John Dee and his movement. Dee's Christian Cabala lies behind the Cabalist Neoplatonism of Spenser's epic, whence the imagery flows through the age. The fierce reactions against Renaissance occult philosophy are also most strongly felt in England. The continental controversies are present in the attitudes of the poets, in Marlowe's Faust figure, unleashing a form of the witch craze in the heart of the Elizabethan world. Chapman darkly replies in his defence of inspired melancholy, and these profound problems are constantly present to Shakespeare.

In my book *Shakespeare's Last Plays* I suggested that the Elizabethan age is mysterious, that we do not know where it came from or whither it went. 'What was the philosophy of the Elizabethan age? Who were its characteristic thinkers? How far were they influenced by Renaissance philosophy or Renaissance magic?' This book tries to suggest at least a preliminary answer to these questions. The philosophy of the Elizabethan age was the occult philosophy of the Renaissance which received a new and powerful formulation in that age, all the more powerful and impressive because it came at a time when the reaction against it was raging.

Shakespeare's great creations – Hamlet, Lear, Prospero are seen as belonging to the late stages of Renaissance occult philosophy, struggling in the throes of the reaction. This is what I take to be the 'Shakespearean moment', the hour when the Renaissance begins to pass through the crucible of the reaction. Hamlet's melancholy is haunted by these dangers. Lear is overcome by them. Only Prospero reaches a partial solution, and Prospero is a late formulation in creative art of the occult philosophy of the Renaissance.

Part III

The Occult Philosophy and
Rosicrucianism and Puritanism

The Return of the Jews to England

Part II

INTRODUCTION

We have tried to answer the question of whence came the Elizabethan occult philosophy. We have now to ask ourselves whither
did it go, through what movements or tendencies did it pass into
the future. In the following brief and inadequate essays, the
attempt will be made to trace it into Rosicrucianism, into
Puritanism, and into the growth of philosemitism which made
possible the return of the Jews to England.

The philosophy of Christian Cabala as expressed by Giorgi and
Agrippa is very close to the so-called Rosicrucian philosophy, as
expressed in the Rosicrucian manifestos and by Robert Fludd,
and as studied in my book *The Rosicrucian Enlightenment*. We can now
better understand the history of Rosicrucianism by linking it
with the history of Christian Cabala as carried into the Elizabethan age. The first chapter of this third part is devoted to
linking the studies of the present book with those of *The
Rosicrucian Enlightenment*.

Puritanism as it developed in the seventeenth century will
be linked, in the second chapter, with the Elizabethan type of

Puritanism and messianism. An effort will be made to present Milton as emerging from Elizabethan occult forms of Puritanism, and as switching the underlying Cabalist themes of Spenser's *Faerie Queene* into the overtly Hebraic themes of *Paradise Lost*. Milton as the preacher of a messianic role for England is seen as descending from Elizabethan messianism.

In the third and last part, the difficult task is attempted of seeing all these movements as fundamentally Hebraic in character, preparing the way for the return of the Jews to England.

16

CHRISTIAN CABALA AND ROSICRUCIANISM

At the end of the chapter on Francesco Giorgi in the first part of this book, the suggestion was raised that Giorgi's philosophy may be closely related to the philosophy of Rosicrucianism. It is certain that Robert Fludd's vast volumes on the universal harmony, the *Utriusque cosmi historia* published at Oppenheim in 1617–19, are heavily influenced by Giorgi and represent, in essence, the Giorgi philosophy in a later form.[1] Fludd, as we know, was associated with the Rosicrucian movement.[2] Was, therefore, the influence of Giorgi which we have traced in the Elizabethan age and called an influence of Christian Cabala really the same as an influence of Rosicrucianism, a movement possibly connected with secret societies and particularly with Freemasonry?[3]

I remind of this possibility, but I am not discussing in this book the secret society aspect. What I am trying to do is to maintain this whole subject on a level of history of ideas which can be investigated in a historical way as deriving from certain texts and formulations which can be historically ascertained.

Though the influence of Giorgi's philosophy may eventually have become associated with secret groups, it does not seem to have been so associated from the beginning. As we have seen, Giorgi as the well-known Franciscan Friar of Venice was an openly acknowledged influence in the early sixteenth century. He represented a Renaissance philosophy operating at the heart of major Renaissance movements. It was a European Renaissance philosophy, not at the beginning particularly associated with England, and not a secret society, but spreading openly as the teaching of a pious Franciscan friar who had absorbed Renaissance influences.[4]

It was certainly not called a 'Rosicrucian' philosophy in Giorgi's time. How then did it acquire that name and the associations which go with it?

Many suggestions as to the origin of the name have been made,[5] but in moving along the historical line which we are following the suggestion which seems most likely is that the Giorgi type of Christian Cabala acquired this name when it became associated with Elizabethanism, with the Tudor Rose, with Dee's scientific British imperialism, with a messianic movement for uniting Europeans against the Catholic-Hapsburg powers.

With the Giorgi type of Christian Cabala was associated in the Dee movement the Agrippa type, more deeply magical, alchemical as well as Cabalist. The Agrippa movement may have been a secret society type of movement from the start. The Dee movement as a whole took on an English and Protestant flavour, Protestant in the sense of a movement of protest of the Renaissance occult traditions against the Catholic reaction.

The epic poem which celebrated this movement was Spenser's *Faerie Queene*. A central character in that poem is the Red Cross Knight. Spenser's poem, I would suggest, is already a Rosicrucian poem, with Red Cross as the moving spirit of occult

Protestantism. In fact we know that later German Rosicrucian writers associated Spenser's poem with their movement.

Thus Rosicrucianism was present in England in the form of Spenserianism, before the name 'Christian Rosenkreutz' appeared in Germany as the central character of the German Rosicrucian manifestos, published in 1614–15.

How did the English knight, Red Cross, turn into the German 'Christian Rosenkreutz'? The transition is fairly clear and has been indicated in my book.[6] The German Rosicrucian manifestos reflect the philosophy of John Dee which he had spread abroad in the missionary venture of his second, or continental, period. One of the Rosicrucian manifestos contains a tract which is closely based on Dee's *Monas hieroglyphica*. Thus the Dee philosophy, which lies behind Spenser's poem, when carried abroad by Dee would quite naturally translate Red Cross into Christian Rosenkreutz.

We discovered in an earlier chapter that a valuable guide to the meaning of Dee's *monas* is Giorgi's *De harmonia mundi* with its abstruse combintations of numerology, astrology, and Cabala. Suggestions concerning *ros* (dew) and *crux* which have been made to explain the name 'Rosicrucian' can be found in Giorgi's work. Hence the intuition which sees in Giorgi's philosophy the root of Rosicrucianism is vindicated.[7] Giorgi is a source of Dee who is the source of the Rosicrucian manifestos. The Dee movement, the Spenserian movement, the Rosicrucian movement, are closely related.

In what I have called 'the Elizabethan revival in the Jacobean age',[8] the Dee tradition revives, and of this revival Prospero is the symbol, symbol of the magical Renaissance philosophy reviving in a milieu which attempted revival of the Elizabethan outlook. Its bold affirmation of that philosophy makes of *The Tempest* almost a Rosicrucian manifesto, made, it is true, several years before the printed German manifestos,[9] but expressive of the occult philosophy in its Elizabethan manifestation.

Much of this I have said, or hinted, in *Shakespeare's Last Plays*. It needs to be emphasised here because the history of the occult philosophy in the Elizabethan age is really the history of Rosicrucianism, though not called by that name. It acquires that name when it is exported, when, as a result of Dee's mission, it spreads on the continent, when it becomes associated with the unfortunate Winter King and Queen of Bohemia. It is strangely significant that *The Tempest* was acted before that couple on the eve of their departure. Shakespeare gave them the blessing of his Rosicrucian manifesto; Prospero represents the Elizabethan occult philosophy, revived, and about to be exported as Rosicrucianism.

I have described in *The Rosicrucian Enlightenment* the atmosphere and culture of the court of Frederick and Elizabeth of the Palatinate at Heidelberg, and have endeavoured to convey its culture as 'Rosicrucian', an export of the Elizabethan occult philosophy to Germany. Utterly crushed by the armies of the reaction and by the beginning of the Thirty Years' War, the exported Rosicrucian culture was also subjected to terrible witch-hunting. The secret society aspect would have become important under the pressures of persecution, but this story has not yet been unravelled. In fact, the whole later history of the occult philosophy, both in England and abroad, is profoundly obscured by the convulsions of the religious conflicts and propaganda.

One can better understand the hatred and horror which this movement aroused in its enemies when one remembers that Christian Cabala, as understood by its earlier adherents, was a form of evangelical Christianity supported by a philosophy 'more powerful' than scholasticism, the occult philosophy. It represented a powerful spiritual force, associated with Christianity, but opposed to the forces of reaction, whether Catholic or Protestant. As such it was violently detested and hounded as diabolical, to be exterminated like the witches it encouraged, blackened as abominable and satanic.

Yet it was, in its origins, the occult philosophy of the Renaissance which had inspired some of the most exquisite productions of Renaissance culture.

In 1623, Marin Mersenne published in Paris his *Quaestiones in Genesim*, one of the key works marking the transition out of Renaissance modes of magical thinking into those of the scientific revolution. In this Genesis commentary, Mersenne fiercely attacks Renaissance Neoplatonism and its allied occultist tendencies, mentioning by name and with strong disapproval the famous Renaissance philosophers associated with this outlook – Ficino, Pico, and many others, and particularly Francesco Giorgi who comes under attack both for his *De harmonia mundi* and for his *Problemata*. Mersenne devoted a whole work, published in 1623, to refuting Giorgi's *Problemata*; and he severely attacks the *De harmonia mundi* at many points in the *Quaestiones in Genesim*.[10]

Mersenne's attitude reminds one of that of Bodin, who objected so strongly to the association by Pico (and still more by Agrippa) of astral and Hermetic magic with Cabala. By placing his attack within the context of a commentary on Genesis, Mersenne may possibly be intimating disapproval of the traditions of Christian Cabala as a degradation from true religious Cabala.

Much happened between 1580, when Bodin published his *Démonomanie*, and 1623, when Mersenne published his attack on Renaissance philosophies. In that interval the whole development of the Elizabethan age had taken place, the whole extension of the Dee philosophy and its stimulating power on that age – all this had happened and was over by the time Mersenne wrote. Not only that, but the extension of that movement as a Rosicrucian mission on the continent had taken place and was over by 1623, the German Rosicrucian movement crushed, the Palatine and his wife fled, and the Counter-Reformation, led by the Jesuits, was spreading over the whole area.

The year 1623 marks the hour when it might well appear that the Counter-Reformation had triumphed throughout Europe, when rumours of a union of Protestant princes against it were heard no more, when, with these disasters, the philosophies of the Renaissance were also overwhelmed, wiped out in the tides of witch-hunting which followed the victors.

That Mersenne was well aware of the contemporary relevance of his attack on Renaissance philosophies is shown by the fact that he devoted particular attention to the attack on Giorgi's philosophy, and also that a large part of his polemic is aimed against Fludd and the Rosicrucians.

The early seventeenth century advances amidst clouds of witch-hunting which still make it difficult for the historian to trace what is really going on. The Mersenne controversies come at the moment when those clouds are thickest, which is also the moment when the 'scientific revolution' is getting under way.

In an article[11] published several years ago I compared Francesco Giorgi's *De harmonia mundi* with Mersenne's *Harmonie universelle*:

> Giorgi's *Harmony of the World* is full of Hermetic and Cabalist influences. . . . Mersenne is a seventeenth century monk, friend of Descartes. . . . Mersenne attacks and discards the old Renaissance world; his *Universal Harmony* will have nothing to do with Francesco Giorgi of whom he strongly disapproves. Mathematics replaces numerology in Mersenne's harmonic world; magic is banished; the seventeenth century has arrived.

And I suggested that 'the emergence of Mersenne out of a banished Giorgi' is one of those transitions from Renaissance to seventeenth century which are fundamental turning points in the history of thought. I added that 'to understand Mersenne and Mersenne's rejection of Giorgi, one must know where Giorgi came from. He came out of the Pythagoro–Platonic tradition plus Hermes Trismegistus and the Cabala.'

The studies in the present book may add a little more to our understanding of the historical circumstances surrounding Mersenne's controversy with Fludd and the Rosicrucians. Rosicrucianism was a movement which vindicated Renaissance occultism against the attacks of the Counter-Reformation and so became involved in the witch scares. Mersenne writes from an atmosphere of horror and dread of 'the Rosicrucians' whom Jesuit propaganda had depicted as frequenters of witches' sabbaths[12] – a similar kind of atmosphere to that raised by Christopher Marlowe in his devil-infested *Doctor Faustus*. Mersenne's attack on Giorgi, Fludd, and the Rosicrucians is an attack on Christian Cabala with its heretical associations, and which appeared in a very different light to Mersenne to that with which it had been invested by Spenser and the Elizabethan poets. Compare the universal harmony echoed by Shakespeare in *The Merchant of Venice*, and inspired by Giorgi, with Mersenne's banishment of Giorgi from his version of harmony.

By eliminating Giorgi and all that he stood for in Renaissance tradition, Mersenne banished the astral linkings of universal harmony, cutting off at the roots the connections of the psyche with the cosmos. This appeased the witch-hunters and made the world safe for Descartes, which was what Mersenne was nervously trying to do.

I have argued in *The Rosicrucian Enlightenment* that Francis Bacon's movement for the advancement of learning was closely connected with the German Rosicrucian movement, having a similar mystical and millennial outlook, and continuing in England the movement which, exported to Germany, was to be so disastrously checked in 1620.[13] I emphasised that Bacon's *New Atlantis*, published in 1627, a year after his death, is full of echoes of the Rosicrucian manifestos, that Bacon is, in fact, defending the

Rosicrucian movement and seeing his own movement for the advancement of learning as in continuity with it.

On re-reading the *New Atlantis* after the studies in this book, one is more than ever struck by the Rosicrucian echoes in the work. And, moreover, the whole situation in Bensalem, the ideal city described in *New Atlantis*, now stands out much more clearly.

The ideal state or city which Bacon describes was a Christian Cabalist community. They had the sign of the Cross (a red cross) and the Name of Jesus, but their philosophy was not normal Christian orthodox philosophy, of any persuasion. It was the occult philosophy, half suspected of being magical, really good-angelical, and more powerful than normal philosophies. Yes, certainly more powerful because it is the Baconian science. The programme of learning and research set out in half-mythical, half-mystical, form in the *New Atlantis* is really the Baconian programme for the advancement of learning which finds a congenial setting in what one can now recognise as a Christian Cabalist utopia.

The *New Atlantis* is thus a basically important text for the study of the Christian Cabalist movement in relation to the growth of science. And it is very important in another way which I will try to hint at briefly.

The visitor to Bensalem, the city in *New Atlantis*, became acquainted with a merchant of the city, who was a Jew and circumcised, for the inhabitants have some Jews among them whom they leave to their own religion:

> Which they may the better do, because they are of a far differing disposition from the Jews in other parts. For whereas they hate the name of Christ, and have a secret inbred rancour against the people amongst whom they live; these [i.e. the Jews of Bensalem] give unto our Saviour many high attributes and love the nation of Bensalem extremely.
>
> And for the country of Bensalem, this man [the Jew] would

make no end of commending it, being desirous by tradition among the Jews there to have it believed that the people thereof were of the generations of Abraham, by another son . . . and that Moses by a secret cabala ordained the laws of Bensalem which they now use, and that when the Messiah should come, and sit on his throne at Jerusalem, the King of Bensalem should sit at his feet. . . . But yet setting aside these Jewish dreams, the man was a wise man and learned, and of great policy, and excellently seen in the laws and customs of that nation.[14]

The long discussion about the Jew of Bensalem, and of how, though remaining unconverted, he assimilated completely to the country, is of great importance in the sequence of studies in this book. I suggest that the reason why he was able to assimilate with such enthusiasm was because Bensalem was a Christian Cabalist country.

The *New Atlantis* thus throws light on the importance of Christian Cabala in effecting new and better relations between Christians and Jews. This new and better feeling may even be the continuation of attempts in Elizabethan times to soften with Christian Cabala the rigidities of the Shylock situation.

There is a marked contrast between the atmosphere surrounding the growth of Baconian science in England and that surrounding the contemporary development in France of the Cartesian mechanism encouraged by Mersenne. Baconian science grows in a warm and friendly Rosicrucian atmosphere. Mersenne is afraid of the heretical associations of Rosicrucianism which he earnestly tries to avoid.

I draw attention to this contrast without attempting to analyse it further, merely emphasising the importance of the history of Christian Cabala for the understanding, both of Mersenne's reactions, and of the constructive Hebraism of the Baconian movement.

17

THE OCCULT PHILOSOPHY AND PURITANISM: JOHN MILTON

The Elizabethan movement which we have studied, and of which Spenser's *Faerie Queene* was the epic expression, contained strong Puritan elements. We have seen that throughout its history from Pico onwards, Christian Cabala tended to carry with it reforming enthusiasms. Reuchlin connects it with the beginning of the German reformation; Egidius of Viterbo hoped much from Catholic reform. In England, the Tudor reform took up Cabalist elements, and the English representative of the Christian Cabalist philosophy, John Dee, associated it with Elizabethan imperial reform.

There was a definite Puritan reforming element in the movement, with its emphasis on moral purity, though the courtly Elizabethan Puritan may not correspond to the generally current picture of a Puritan. That magnificent courtier, the Earl of Leicester, was a leader of the Puritan party, so was his nephew, Philip

Sidney, the chivalric hero, so was the main poet of the Sidney–Leicester circle, Spenser. The Spenserian movement was Renaissance in its culture. It expressed a Renaissance philosophy turned towards Puritan reform, and infused with what has been called 'Puritan occultism', that is to say a Puritan version of the occult philosophy.

This outlook, particularly as revived in the renaissance of Elizabethanism in the circle of Prince Henry and his sister,[1] could pass easily into Puritanism proper, into the Puritanism of the Revolution and of its great epic poet, Milton. Milton's vision for England was that of a nation of chosen people,[2] chosen in the Hebraic sense, chosen to lead Protestant Europe against the power of the Papal Antichrist. Spenser had envisaged Elizabethan England and its queen as chosen for just such a religious role. The great difference was, of course, that Milton was not a monarchist, like Spenser, but a republican. Nevertheless there is a profound basic similarity between the religious outlook of Spenser and that of Milton. Now that the messianic elements in Spenser's *Faerie Queene* have been recognised, the processes through which the Elizabethan chivalrous epic could be transformed, in Milton's hands, into the Biblical epic of *Paradise Lost* become more understandable.

Milton frequently expressed great admiration for Spenser as a religious and moral teacher, and we know that his early plans for the poem which he intended one day to write were that it should be on a chivalrous theme, a tale of King Arthur and his knights.[3] Thirty years later, when he at last wrote the immortal poem, its hero was not Arthur but Adam. He had transposed his early enthusiasm for the chivalrous epic of Elizabethan Puritanism into the tremendous Biblical epic reflecting his enthusiasm for the Puritan Revolution. The Rosicrucian revolution had not materialised; the Puritan revolution, its successor in ideology, succeeded, at least for a time. Milton devoutly believed in it and in the 'chosen' role of Englishmen, just as Spenser had devoutly believed in the movement of his time.

If, as has been argued in earlier chapters, Giorgi–Agrippa are the Christian Cabalist influences behind Dee and Spenser, the chief mediator of Christian Cabalist influence to Milton may well have been Robert Fludd, the Christian Cabalist philosopher of the early seventeenth century who was in direct descent from the Giorgi–Dee tradition and who was identified with the Rosicrucian movement. Recent scholarship has been pointing to Fludd as probably a main influence on Milton's world of angels and demons.[4] This seems all the more probable when we reflect on Milton's scheme of education based on the arts and sciences (set out in *Areopagitica*), a scheme basically related to music, to architecture, to the mathematical arts, as in the 'universal harmony' tradition of Giorgi, Dee, and the Christian Cabalists, and having no relation to scholastic Aristotelianism. Gassendi, when supporting Mersenne against Fludd and the Rosicrucians, bitterly complained of people who put angels and demons everywhere and despise Aristotle.[5] Milton could well be fitted under that heading and seen as on the angelic-demonic side in the great continental attack on Rosicrucianism, even though the continental thinkers may have been unaware of him and his poem.

That there was an influence of Cabala on Milton is now generally recognised. The suggestion of such an influence was a startling novelty when first put forward by Denis Saurat.[6] Saurat believed that 'Neoplatonism' was too easy an answer to the problem of Milton's sources, arguing that there is also a Cabalist influence on the poet. Saurat was looking for traces of genuine Jewish Cabala in Milton's poetry and believed that he had found echoes of characteristic doctrines of Lurianic Cabala in *Paradise Lost*.

Saurat's findings were much debated and questioned, and a more satisfactory solution of the problem was put forward in 1955 by the eminent Hebrew scholar Zwi Werblowsky.

Werblowsky states that an influence of Jewish, or Lurianic, Cabala on Milton cannot be proved, but that there was decidedly an influence of Christian Cabala upon him: 'Milton is influenced not by the Lurianic *tsimtsum*, still less by the *Zohar*, but by Christian post-Renaissance Cabala in its pre-lurianic phase.'[7] The example of such a Christian Cabala which Werblowsky gives is the works of Robert Fludd, and it is Fludd's Christian Cabala which he believes to have been the major influence on Milton.

The studies made in this book can supply, I believe, a missing link in the arguments of Milton scholars. The influence of Christian Cabala, via Agrippa–Giorgi–Dee, on Spenser's epic poem have not been known or recognised. The discovery of that influence complements the discovery of Christian Cabalist influence, via Fludd, on Milton's poem, for Fludd was the inheritor of the Elizabethan Cabalism which influenced Spenser.

Much now begins to fall into place and to become visible in clearer perspective. Milton inherited the Neoplatonic Christian Cabala of the Elizabethan age as expressed by its early seventeenth-century successor, Robert Fludd, the Rosicrucian. This sequence of ideas fits exactly with the poetic sequence, with Milton as the admirer of Spenser (whom he held to be a better teacher than Aquinas) writing an epic poem in which the Spenserian influence is expressed through the Hebraic–Cabalist–Biblical tradition which underlay Spenser's Arthurianisms and chivalry.

Moreover, Milton would now come out as the inheritor of Spensers' Hebraic type of patriotism. The writer of that excellent book, *Jerusalem and Albion*, believed that Milton 'by foisting on his contemporaries a particular messianic task unwarranted by the tradition of his people'[8] was guilty of a profound misjudgement. This statement is evidence of how lack of knowledge of Elizabethan messianism has caused a serious gap in the history of ideas. The idea of the messianic task was implicit in Elizabethan Spenserianism and its queen-cult. Milton was the inheritor of the thought of a special messianic role for England; he inherited it from Spenser and the Elizabethan poets, particularly perhaps from Raleigh. He could have found it also implicit in Bacon's Bensalem.

The evidences of continuity between the Miltonic and the Spenserian, or Elizabethan, messianism are many and various, and are particularly visible in Milton's earlier works, for example in *Comus* with its chastity theme. The Lady of *Comus* is a pure heroine of Puritan reform, like Queen Elizabeth I, or the Princess Elizabeth. However, it is impossible to do justice to this subject in a brief sketch, which I will conclude by recalling what I have said earlier concerning *Il Penseroso* as the Miltonic treatment of the inspired melancholy.

Milton describes the dark face of Melancholy, whose black hue hides the brightness of her saintly visage.[9] Saturn's daughter, pensive and ascetic, brings with her 'the cherub Contemplation'. In this divinely inspired Saturnian mood the poet enters into a Hermetic trance in which he has visions of

> What worlds, or what vast regions hold
> The immortal mind, that hath forsook
> Her mansion in this fleshly nook.

It is the trance of the inspired melancholy, as described by Agrippa and as depicted by Dürer.

And the Agrippan demons come into the Miltonic vision, for the trance leads on immediately to

> those Demons that are found
> In fire, air, flood, or underground,
> Whose power hath a true consent
> With planet or with element.

These words connect the poem with the demons in Agrippa's

analysis of melancholy,[10] the connection with which is further confirmed by the fact that Milton, like Agrippa, passes on to a third or prophetic stage of inspired melancholy. Having passed through ecstatic musical experiences, Milton foresees these as leading to a highest, or prophetic, initiation. He foresees himself reaching this in old age:

> Till old experience do attain
> To something like prophetic strain.

There can be little doubt that Milton knew of Agrippa's treatment of the inspired melancholy. (If he knew Fludd, he would certainly have known Agrippa, one of Fludd's main sources.) And he is applying it to the stages of his own inspiration, looking forward to prophetic experience in old age when he would write the great poems.

Did the knowledge of Agrippa's treatment of inspired melancholy come to Milton direct from the *De occulta philosophia* (or from the Pseudo-Aristotelian *Problemata*)? Or was it mediated to him through Chapman's treatment of the theme? The latter seems the more probable, in which case Milton was tapping the Elizabethan occult philosophy, as formulated by an Elizabethan poet, for his own formulation of the melancholy theme, so characteristic of the age of Elizabeth.

Milton would appear to be a Saturnian, but one who knew how to moderate the Saturnian melancholy with other influences. For in *L'Allegro* he depicts the positive attitude to the senses, moderating Saturn with Venus or Jupiter, like Chapman in *The Banquet of Sense*.

Milton's Puritanism is infused, like that of Spenser, with Renaissance influences. The remarkable combination in Milton of bold, indeed revolutionary, freedom with Renaissance traditions makes of him not a Puritan in the narrow sense, but a Renaissance Puritan, like Spenser, preserving within his

Puritanism the Renaissance traditions. It is this combination which would have made Milton so attractive to members of Italian academies whom he met on his visit to Italy. He was an Englishman who boldly resisted the tyranny of Antichrist, yet was vitally linked to the Renaissance culture, cultivated in the Academies, though frowned on by the seventeenth-century rulers of Italy. Milton's demons might have brought him into trouble in some circles yet they belong naturally to the outlook of the writer of a great Renaissance poem, concerned with the angelic and demonic forces of the cosmos. Such a poem could be written in Puritan England, but not in seventeenth-century Italy.

The Rosicrucian movement had failed on the continent. Refugees from that failure poured into Puritan England as the refuge from Antichrist. And the Puritan revolution took over some of the aspects of the projected Rosicrucian revolution. This is why there was a 'Puritan occultism', why an English translation of the Rosicrucian manifestos was published in Cromwellian England,[11] and why the philosophy of John Dee was cultivated by earnest Parliamentarians.[12]

18

THE RETURN OF THE JEWS TO ENGLAND

Since 1290 when Edward I expelled the Jews from England, there had been, officially, no Jews in the country.[1] The reigns of Henry VII, Henry VIII, Elizabeth, James I, and Charles I passed by without any acknowledged settlement of Jews being made. There certainly was some Jewish presence in the country during this long period, but a clandestine one and Jews were probably few in number. Only as a converted Jew, was it possible for a Jew to live openly in England, and even then possibly at some risk. In spite of the fact that Christian Cabala, actually representing an influence of Jewish mysticism on Christianity, was a strong influence in the Renaissance period, no Jew would have been officially allowed to practise his faith. Puritanism, with its Biblical inspiration and concentration on the Old Testament, encouraged the growth of philosemitism, but in spite of this, the settlement of Jews in Puritan England under the Protectorate was still not officially recognised, though Oliver Cromwell earnestly tried to have it authorised, and the Amsterdam rabbi Menasseh ben Israel came to England to urge it. It was not until after the Restoration that Charles II unobtrusively allowed Jews to live in England, the first recognition of their presence since the expulsion of 1290.

The extraordinary fact is that the whole movement of Christian Cabala in England – ultimately an influence of Jewish mysticism as adapted to Christianity in the Renaissance – passed without the presence of Jews being acknowledged, though there were, as we saw in an earlier chapter, undoubtedly refugees from the Expulsion of 1492 from Spain in the country, New Christians or marranos, small in number but influential. Even more surprising, the whole Puritan movement, and the Puritan Revolution, with its strongly Hebraic religion and culture, took place without the presence of Jews being acknowledged in England. The return of the Jews to England, and the preparation for their return by Menasseh ben Israel during the rule of Oliver Cromwell, was thus virtually a culmination of the gradual movement of a new attitude towards the Jews and their religion.

Menasseh ben Israel[2] was born in 1604, four years before Milton, and was brought to the Amsterdam community as a young child by parents escaping from the tortures of the Portuguese inquisition. In Amsterdam they were allowed openly to practise their religion, and to join in that cultural and religious awakening which the Dutch tolerance opened up for the Spanish and Portuguese refugees.

The Amsterdam community has been touched on in an earlier chapter when discussing the legend that it was founded by refugees who had been graciously received by Queen Elizabeth I in England in 1593 but had passed on to the greater religious freedom of Amsterdam. This legendary connection with England is interesting, since it was from Amsterdam that, years later, Menasseh ben Israel would come to England on his mission.

At an early age, Menasseh became rabbi in Amsterdam and was famous for his writings which attracted the attention not only of Jewish but also of Gentile readers who gained from them knowledge of Jewish concerns and attitudes such as had not been available before in the Gentile world. Like nearly all of the Amsterdam community, Menasseh was an ardent Lurianic Cabalist[3] looking for the coming of the Messiah and the deliverance of Israel from its sufferings. He believed that the hour of that coming was not far off. The mystical element entered into the enterprise for which Menasseh is chiefly famous, his attempt, made in the time of Oliver Cromwell, to arrange for the settlement of the Jews in England.

As a Puritan, Cromwell shared in that sympathy with the Jews and their history which is such a striking feature of English Puritanism, nourished on devotion to the Old Testament. Contacts between English Puritans and the Amsterdam community had been possible. Some English Puritans took their convictions to a logical conclusion by emigrating to Amsterdam and adopting Judaism as their religion.[4] More common than this extreme attitude was the Puritan hope that a Christianity such as theirs, absolutely purified from Papist abuses, would be congenial to the Jews and would bring about their conversion, an event which would be the signal for the arrival of the millennium. In order to effect their conversion it was necessary to bring them to England so that they could see for themselves the workings of the pure religion. On the Jewish side, it was believed by Menasseh and other enthusiasts that it was foretold in prophecy that the Messiah would not come until the Jews had been scattered to the ends of the earth. England was a remote corner or angle of the world in which the Jews were not yet established. Hence to settle them in that island would hasten the appearance of the Messiah.[5] Menasseh's strange messianic views, which were connected with rumours about the Lost Tribes of Israel, were expounded in his influential book, *The Hope of Israel*,[6] a work which reminds one curiously at times of Francis Bacon's Hebraic mysticism in the *New Atlantis*.[7]

It was in 1655 that Menasseh came to England, invited by Cromwell to explore the possibility of a settlement of the Jews in England. His visit aroused very great interest and excitement; the project was favoured by the liberal and the learned, for example by Ralph Cudworth, the Cambridge Platonist. On the other hand, antisemitism was aroused and detrimental legends circulated, for example a rumour that the Jews intended to convert St Paul's Church into a synagogue. Oliver Cromwell gave up the project because of this popular opposition. (Did Queen Elizabeth I also abandon some gesture towards the Jews because of Marlowe's antisemitism?)

At the Restoration, it was expected that the reception of the Jews would be abandoned, like other Puritan interests and policies, but this did not happen. Charles II allowed the settlement of the Jews, and that they were to be permitted to practise their religion. No grand pronouncements about toleration were made, but in unobtrusive and practical ways the settlement was made possible and controversy avoided. Thus Anglo-Jewry in its modern form began in the reign of Charles II, like the Royal Society.

The probable interactions between the English Puritan movement, culminating in the Revolution and the Protectorate, and the contemporary Amsterdam Jewish community, with its intense religious and cultural life and its earnest Lurianic Cabalism in expectation of the Messiah, is a phase of religious history which has not yet been examined. Both Jews and Puritans lived in excited expectation of a coming divine event. The Puritans expected the Second Coming and the Christian millennium. It has recently been argued that Puritan cultivation of science had as a motive the bringing-in of the millennium working to make the world worthy of it, which would hasten its advent.[8] Jewish Lurianic Cabalists worked with intensive meditation and prayer towards making possible the advent of the Messiah. The two movements may have interacted upon one another in more ways than we know.[9]

And the Messiah came, or was believed to have come. The extraordinary story of Sabbatai Sevi[10] was the culmination in the Jewish world of the intense messianic expectation resulting, ultimately, from the agony of the Expulsion and its aftermath, and fostered by the intense spiritual efforts of the Cabalists. Sabbatai Sevi, born in Smyrna in 1625, became known as a significant and prophetic personality whose disciples began to see in him the promised Messiah. Gradually, he came to see himself in this role and in 1665 he revealed himself as the Messiah. Immense excitement overtook all Jewish communities in both east and west and a mass movement of enthusiasm was set in motion. In a sense, this was the culmination of the Cabalist movements intensified by the Expulsion of 1492 which had exerted such profound influence in both the Christian and the Jewish worlds and which now, after nearly two centuries, reached a term. For the movement took a disastrous turn, profoundly disappointing its supporters, when in 1666 Sabbatai Sevi apostatised to Islam.

The extraordinary possibility has been suggested that there may have been English Puritan influence on Sabbatai Sevi. His father was agent in Smyrna for English Puritan merchants. Contacts between Puritan millennarianism and Jewish messianism were thus possible, and might account for the curious Christian influences on Sabbatai Sevi, though this problem is far from being solved.[11] Nor has the possible influence of these movements on the great poet of Puritanism ever (I believe) been suggested. Milton's *Paradise Regained* (published in 1671), with its sensitive exploration of the stages through which Jesus accepted his Messianic role, might possibly have been influenced, even unconsciously, by contemporary messianism, perhaps through Christian Cabala drawing close to the Jews.

The profound excitements, apocalyptic hopes, and deep

spiritual disturbances of the seventeenth century reached an extraordinary climax with the collapse of the Sabbatian movement. Neither the millennium nor the Messiah had come, but the great tide of spiritual effort left something on the shores of time when it receded. In 1660 the Royal Society was founded, tangible evidence of the arrival of Science.

In conclusion, I ask the reader to gaze at an etching by Rembrandt (Plate 16) (undated, probably 1651–3). The artist who lived near the Jews of Amsterdam and studied them so deeply shows here a figure who has been immersed in profound studies, as shown by the globe and other evidences of deep involvement in science. The melancholy and thoughtful student turns in surprise to see a vision, rays of light passing through a circular combination of letters, the central circle marked with the letters INRI, the monogram of Christ.

One of the earliest and most persistent interpretations of this impressive composition is that it represents Faust and is depicting a profound search for forbidden knowledge. This interpretation is now generally abandoned; it does not fit with the dignity and religious intensity of the subject. Further, the discovery was made by H. van de Waal that the outermost ring of the diagram, when read in reverse, contains the letters AGLA,[12] a formula referring to the Eighteen Benedictions, recited thrice daily in Jewish liturgy. The letters AGLA refer to the first words of the Second of the Eighteen Benedictions, *Attah gibbor le-dam Adonai*. The vision is therefore now seen as profoundly religious in content, both Christian and Jewish. The vague forms glimpsed outside the window are interpreted as half-seen angels, reflecting the supernal light into the diagram.

I would suggest that this etching is related to the subject of inspired melancholy, as studied in this book, the student being a Christian Cabalist to whom in the dark night of his melancholy labours the Divine Name is revealed.

EPILOGUE

This book suffers from the fact that the history of Christian Cabala has not yet been adequately attempted. On the Jewish Cabala there are many books, above all the fundamental works of Scholem, which have placed the whole subject on a solid basis of critical-historical enquiry. A work of corresponding importance on Christian Cabala has not yet appeared. François Secret's labours have provided, and are providing, materials for such a work, but he himself does not attempt any synthesis or defini- tion of the ideas of the Christian Cabalists. What seems to be particularly lacking is any sustained attempt, from any quarter, to define Christian Cabala in relation to genuine, or Jewish, Cabala. As one tries to think about this problem, one is faced with a void. It requires specialised training by Hebrew experts to tackle such a theme, and the book, or books, by such experts have not yet appeared.

The subject is of immense importance, nothing less than the new approach to the Judeo–Christian tradition made in the enthusiastic revival of Hebrew studies at the Renaissance. In its profoundly religious approach, Christian Cabala almost repeats the original situation from which Christianity derived. The early Christians appropriated a Christianised form of the Jewish religion. Similarly, the Christian Cabalists of the Renaissance appropriated Jewish mysticism or Cabala and used it for their own religious ends.

There is a wealth of spiritual experience waiting to be gathered from the great surge of interest in Jewish mysticism spread by the wandering exiles from Spain and Portugal. The emergence of Christian Cabala out of these waves of spiritual effort is a subject worthy of intense study and research; it is a neglected way into the spiritual history of Europe at one of its momentous turning-points.

Believing that this subject is of fundamental importance for the understanding of 'the occult philosophy of the Elizabethan age', I have tried in the first part of this book to give a provisional account of it, an outline which awaits the better, deeper, more expert treatment by those who are coming after, and who will explain to us the many things which we need to know. What was the effect on Christian Cabala of the fact that the Christian Cabalist was not expecting a Messiah to come, but a second coming of the Messiah who had already come, as Cabala had proved, so the Christian Cabalist believed? This certainly basically differentiated Christian from Jewish Cabala, but how did the difference work out in practice? What was the effect of the yoking together of Cabala and Hermeticism, of Hermes Trismegistus and Moses, by Pico della Mirandola through which Christian Cabala was again quite differentiated from Jewish Cabala, an entirely different movement, one would say, and yet one closely reflecting the Jewish original? Allied to this question is the problem raised in connection with Bodin as to whether objections to Christian Cabala could have had anything to do with the witch craze.

These are very large questions, and the point at which to begin study of them is at the source, namely in the work of Pico della Mirandola, the founder of Renaissance Christian Cabala. Awaiting such a fundamental study, the present book tries to give some general accounts of a few Renaissance Christian Cabalists, only a few and these very superficially treated. The inclusion of Agrippa as a Christian Cabalist underlies the importance of magic in the movement.

The work of Francesco Giorgi helps greatly towards distinguishing the Cabalist ingredients in the outlook from the other strands with which it is interwoven, Hermetic, Pythagorean, Neoplatonic. If the French translation of Giorgi's *De harmonia mundi* could be made more easily accessible to students, perhaps in the form of a facsimile reprint with commentary, this would do much towards providing enquirers with a fundamental key to a basic Renaissance movement. The Giorgi volume, if made more accessible, would help students towards placing the subjects of which it treats within recognisable categories of history of ideas.

In the meantime, on the insufficient foundation of my own studies in the first part of this book, I have moved into the Elizabethan age from the new angles which such studies suggest.

The argument, in over-simplified form, is that 'the occult philosophy of the Elizabethan age' was a Christian Cabalist philosophy, with its peculiar Rosicrucian blend of magic and science. This approach has been based on two main lines of enquiry. First, on the history of Christian Cabala leading up to its expression in the philosophy of John Dee. Second, on the iconographical approach, that is to say on the study of the imagery of this movement in its Elizabethan and Jacobean form.

I have attempted to apply here two sides of my own work. First, history of the Renaissance Hermetic–Cabalist movement which I attempted in *Giordano Bruno and the Hermetic Tradition*, and which I continued in relation to John Dee and Robert Fludd in *Theatre of the World*. This history I have expanded in the first part of the present book, with emphasis on Christian Cabala as formed in this movement. Second, I use the iconographical approach as adumbrated, with reference to the iconography of Tudor reform, in *Astraea. The Imperial Theme in the Sixteenth Century*. Further historical applications of this iconography were studied in *The Rosicrucian Enlightenment*, and, in relation to Shakespeare, in *Shakespeare's Last Plays*.

It is the combination of the history of Renaissance Hermetic–Cabalist thought, as it reached the Elizabethan age, and of its embodiment in an imagery expressive of pure religion, which I have used in the present book. The argument raises enormous questions, not the least of which is the possible connection between 'Cabalistic' types of meditation and great poetry.

On the purely religious and English-poetic side the movement described in this book would seem to belong to the tremendous theme of 'Jerusalem and Albion'. The Elizabethan Renaissance absorbs into the Hermetic–Cabalist tradition the Arthurian associations of Albion. This, I believe, is the root of Spenser, and I see Shakespeare as also, in his way, a Spenserian. The wedding together of Jerusalem and Albion as fundamental for the imaginative life of English poetry was already begun in the Elizabethan age.

The ultimate meaning of the esoteric imagery of darkness and light is the search for God.

> If I say, Peradventure the darkness shall cover me: then shall my night be turned to day.
>
> Yea, the darkness is no darkness with thee, but the night is as clear as the day: the darkness and light to thee are both alike.

NOTES

I MEDIEVAL CHRISTIAN CABALA: THE ART OF RAMON LULL

1 Engraved illustration to R. Lull, *Liber de gentili et tribus sapientibus* in R. Lull, *Opera omnia*, Mainz, 1721–42; reproduced in Yates, 'The Art of Ramon Lull', *Journal of the Warburg and Courtauld Institutes*, XVII (1954), pl. 17 (b).

The engraving is based on an illustration in a fourteenth-century manuscript, the *Electorium Remundi* (Paris, Lat. 15450) compiled by Lull's disciple Thomas Le Myesier. See 'The Art of Ramon Lull', p. 154, note; J. N. Hillgarth, *Ramon Lull and Lullism in Fourteenth-century France*, Oxford, 1971, p. 244.

2 The following résumé is based on my article 'The Art of Ramon Lull'. See also my book, *The Art of Memory*, London, 1966, ch. VIII.

3 See below, p. 18.

4 See my article, 'Ramon Lull and John Scotus Erigena', *Journal of the Warburg and Courtauld Institutes*, XXIII (1960), pp. 1–44.

5 The fundamental study is G. Scholem, *Major Trends in Jewish Mysticism*, Jerusalem, 1941, and many subsequent editions. References are to the 1946 edition of the English translation.

6 *Major Trends*, p. 92.

7 *Ibid.*, pp. 120–45.

8 Lull scholars in recent years have tended to emphasise more and more the connections of Lullism with Cabala. From the side of Hebrew scholarship there is a statement to the same effect in the article by Charles Singer in *The Legacy of Israel*, ed. E. Bevan and C. Singer, Oxford, 1927, p. 274: 'Lull was under strong Neoplatonic influence, and into Neoplatonic thought he was able to fit Cabalist developments. . . the later Christian Cabalists have been regarded as the spiritual descendants of Raymond Lull.'

9 'The Art of Ramon Lull', pp. 144 ff.

10 Lull's *Book of the Order of Chivalry* gives the rules of chivalry in the context of the Art. It is a branch of the Art for the use of knights; see 'The Art of Ramon Lull', p. 141. Published in English translation by William Caxton, it strongly influenced Elizabethan chivalry; see Yates, *Astraea. The Imperial Theme in the Sixteenth Century*, London, 1975, pp. 106–8.

II THE OCCULT PHILOSOPHY IN THE ITALIAN RENAISSANCE: PICO DELLA MIRANDOLA

1 See D. P. Walker, *Spiritual and Demonic Magic from Ficino to Campanella*, London (Warburg Institute), 1958, and *The Ancient Theology*, London, 1972; Yates, *Giordano Bruno and the Hermetic Tradition*, London, 1964, ch. I–IV.

2 The problem of Pico della Mirandola and Cabala still awaits expert treatment by Hebrew specialists. The present chapter, which it was necessary to include owing to the basic importance of Pico for the history of Christian Cabala, does little more than resume the attempts which I made in *Bruno*, ch. V, 'Pico della Mirandola and Cabalist Magic', though with an eye to the theme of the present book which is devoted more specifically to the religious aspect. Hence the emphasis of the chapter is on Pico as a *Christian* Cabalist.

3 See François Secret, *Les Kabbalistes Chrétiens de la Renaissance*, Paris, 1964, pp. 24–43.

4 Pico, *Apologia*, in *Opera omnia*, Bâle, 1572, pp. 180–1; quoted *Bruno*, p. 96.

5 *Opera omnia*, pp. 107–11; see *Bruno*, pp. 94 ff.

6 See Chaim Wirszubski's introduction to his edition of Flavius Mithridates, *Sermo de passione Dei*, Jerusalem, 1963.

7 See Chaim Wirszubski, 'Giovanni Pico's Companion to Kabbalistic Symbolism', in *Studies in Mysticism and Religion*, presented to G. G. Scholem, Jerusalem, 1967, pp. 353–62.

8 Fourteenth Cabalist Conclusion, Pico, *Opera*, pp. 108–9; cf. *Bruno*, p. 105.

9 For the traces of Christian Cabala in Jerome and in Nicholas of Cusa, see Brian P. Copenhaver, 'Lefèvre d'Etaples, Symphorien Champier, and the Secret Names of God', *Journal of the Warburg and Courtauld Institutes*, XL (1977), pp. 198–202.

10 Pico, *Apologia* in *Opera omnia*, pp. 180–1; cf. *Bruno*, p. 96.

11 Eleventh Cabalist Conclusion; *Opera*, pp. 108–9; cf. *Bruno*, p. 99.

12 Forty-eighth Cabalist Conclusion; *Opera*, p. 111; cf. *Bruno*, p. 100.

13 Fifteenth Magical Conclusion; *Opera*, p. 105; cf. *Bruno*, p. 91.

14 G. Scholem, article 'Kabbalah' in *Encyclopaedia Judaica*.

15 G. Scholem, *Sabbatai Sevi: The Mystical Messiah*, Princeton, 1973.

III THE OCCULT PHILOSOPHY IN THE REFORMATION: JOHANNES REUCHLIN

1 On Reuchlin, see Lewis W. Spitz, *The Religious Renaissance of the German Humanists*, Cambridge, Mass., 1963, pp. 61–80; François Secret, *Les Kabbalistes Chrétiens de la Renaissance*, Paris, 1964, pp. 44–70; and the very important article by Charles Zika, 'Reuchlin's *De verbo mirifico* and the Magic Debate of the late Fifteenth Century', *Journal of the Warburg and Courtauld Institutes*, XXX (1976), pp. 104–38.

A facsimile reprint of the *De verbo mirifico* and the *De arte cabalistica* was published in 1964 (Stuttgart–Bad Cannstadt).

2 *De verbo mirifico*, sig. b 2 recto (p. 23); cf. Secret, *Kabbalistes Chrétiens*, p. 44.

3 Brian P. Copenhaver, 'Lefèvre d'Etaples, Symphorien Champier, and the Secret Names of God', *Journal of the Warburg and Courtauld Institutes*, XL (1977), pp. 195 ff.

4 *De verbo mirifico*, Book III; cf. Secret, *Kabbalistes Chrétiens*, p. 49; Zika, *art. cit.*, pp. 115 ff.

5 See above, p. 20, and Yates, *Giordano Bruno and the Hermetic Tradition*, London, 1964, pp. 98 ff.

6 Secret, *Kabbalistes Chrétiens*, pp. 52–3.

7 Pico, *Opera*, p. 101; cf. *Bruno*, p. 148.

8 G. Scholem, *Major Trends in Jewish Mysticism*, Jerusalem, 1941; 1946 edn, p. 135.

9 See Spitz's essay on Reuchlin, 'Pythagoras Reborn' in *Religious Renaissance of the German Humanists*, pp. 61 ff.

10 See *Epistolae obscurorum virorum*, Latin text and English translation by F. Griffin Stokes, London, 1909.

11 *Epistolae obscurorum virorum*, pp. 535–6.

12 It has been said that the attack on Reuchlin laid down the lines that the Council of Trent would follow. See Martin Fleischer, *Radical Reform and Political Persuasion in the Life and Writings of Thomas More*, Geneva, 1973, pp. 73 ff.

IV THE CABALIST FRIAR OF VENICE: FRANCESCO GIORGI

1 On Giorgi, see D. P. Walker, *Spiritual and Demonic Magic from Ficino to Campanella*, London (Warburg Institute), 1958, pp. 112–19; Yates, *The French Academies of the Sixteenth Century*, London (Warburg Institute), 1947, pp. 43, 88, 91–2, 126, 243–4, 254, and Yates, *Giordano Bruno, and the Hermetic Tradition*, London, 1964, p. 151; François Secret, *Les Kabbalistes Chrétiens de la Renaissance*, Paris, 1964, pp. 126–40; Cesare Vasoli, *Profezia e ragione*, Naples, 1974, pp. 131–403.

2 *De harmonia mundi*, Venice, 1525 and Paris, 1545; French translation by Guy Le Fèvre de la Boderie, *L'Harmonie du monde*, Paris, 1578.

   The book is divided into Canticles, which are subdivided into Tones, which are again subdivided into Chapters. References to the work in the footnotes will follow these divisions.

3 *De harm. mun.*, I, 5, xvii. Since the letters of the Hebrew alphabet all have numerical values, number enters into these mystical calculations.

4 III, I, i (and assumed *passim*).

5 The Solomonic connections are implied throughout, an idea not peculiar to Giorgi but very generally assumed in the Renaissance; see René Taylot, 'Architecture and Magic', *Essays in the History of Architecture* presented to Rudolf Wittkower, London, Phaidon Press, 1967, pp. 131–403.

6 See Secret, *Kabbalistes Chrétiens*, pp. 106–21; J. O'Malley, *Gilles de Viterbe on Church and Reform*, Leiden, 1968.

7 Rudolf Wittkower, *Architectural Principles in the Age of Humanism*, London (Warburg Institute), 1949, pp. 90 ff.

8 On Giorgi and the divorce, see J. F. Maillard, 'Henry VIII et Georges de Venise: Documents sur l'affaire du divorce', *Revue de l'Histoire des religions*, 181 (1972), pp. 157–86; Vasoli, *Profezia*, pp. 181–202. The main documents are printed in *Letters and Papers of the Reign of Henry VIII*, ed. J. S. Brewer, London, 1876. The divorce is discussed by J. J. Scarisbrick, *Henry VIII*, London, 1968, though without mention of Giorgi.

9 Leviticus, 18: 16.

10 Deuteronomy, 25: 5–6.

11 Cecil Roth (History of the Jews in England, Oxford, 1941) regards the affair as of real importance in Jewish history, because, together with the contemporary Reuchlin–Pfefferkorn controversy, it began to rehabilitate Hebrew literature from the discredit which it had suffered in Europe since the rise of Christianity.

12 French Academies, pp. 43–4; see below, pp. 65–7.

13 Guy Le Fèvre de la Boderie, dedication of L'Harmonie du monde.

14 Nicholas Le Fèvre de la Boderie, 'Discours fort utile' prefixed to L'Harmonie du monde.

15 It is found in the Hermetic Liber XXIV philosophorum, whence Cusanus quoted it; see Bruno, p. 247, note 2.

16 Vasoli, Profezia, p. 233. For Giorgi on the Monas see particularly De harm. mun., I, 1, vi and I, 3, i, but the theme recurs throughout.

17 De harm. mun., I, 3, i.

18 See De harm. mun., I, 4, i–xiii.

19 De harm. mun., I, 4, iv–v. On the 'revaluation of Saturn' in the Renaissance, see further below, pp. 51 ff.

20 See De harm. mun., I, 3 and 4.

21 De harm. mun., II, 6, vii.

22 He was the author of a long, unpublished, poem.

23 Walker, Spiritual and Demonic Magic, pp. 42, 132 etc.

24 De harm. mun., I, 1, ii.

25 Vasoli, Profezia, pp. 401–3.

26 See P. J. Amman, 'The musical theory and philosophy of Robert Fludd', Journal of the Warburg and Courtauld Institutes, XXX (1967), pp. 220 ff.

V THE OCCULT PHILOSOPHY AND MAGIC: HENRY CORNELIUS AGRIPPA

1 See Yates, Giordano Bruno and the Hermetic Tradition, London, 1964, ch. VIII. On Agrippa, see particularly D. P. Walker, Spiritual and Demonic Magic from Ficino to Campanella, London (Warburg Institute), 1958, pp. 90–9.

2 Charles G. Nauert, Agrippa and the Crisis of Renaissance Thought, Urbana, University of Illinois Press, 1965.

3 For titles, see below, notes 5, 8.

4 De occ. phil, Lib. III, Cap. XII. The Name of Jesus, says Agrippa, contains the power of the Tetragrammaton, and no operations can now be

done without it. Agrippa, however, does not here give the Cabalistic proof that Jesus is the name of the Messiah.

5 For Agrippa and Erasmus, see the important article by Paola Zambelli, 'Cornelio Agrippa, Erasmo e la teologia umanistica', *Rinascimento*, XX (1969), pp. 1–59; also her introduction to her edition of Agrippa's unpublished works: *Cornelio Agrippa: scritti inediti e dispersi*, ed. P. Zambelli, *Rinascimento*, XVI (2nd series), 1965.

6 Nauert, *Agrippa*, pp. 9–11.

7 Nauert, *Agrippa*, pp. 17–19.

8 Zambelli, 'Umanesimo magico-astrologico e raggrupamenti segreti nei platonici della preriforma', Centro Internazionale di Studi Umanistici, Padua, 1960.

9 Nauert, *Agrippa*, p. 26.

10 Nauert, *Agrippa*, p. 30.

11 Würzburg, Universitätsbibliothek, MS. M. ch. q. 30. This early manuscript version is reproduced in facsimile as one of the appendices to Karl Anton Nowotny's edition of the *De occulta philosophia*, Graz, 1967. It differs considerably from the printed version of 1533. See further below, pp. 62 ff.

12 Nauert, *Agrippa*, p. 31.

13 *Ibid.*

14 *Ibid.* According to Pearl Hogrefe *(The Sir Thomas More Circle*, Urbana, University of Illinois Press, 1959, p. 224), whilst working with Colet, Agrippa published *An Oration . . on the Excellence of God's Word*, a plea for simple biblical Christianity. I have not been able to find this work which might confirm what other indications have suggested, that Agrippa was an evangelical, and that the whole vast apparatus of the Occult Philosophy was attached to 'a simple Biblical Christianity'.

15 Nauert, *Agrippa*, pp. 35 ff.

16 *Ibid.*, pp. 42 ff.

17 The contact was rather indirect. A friend of Agrippa's reported that he had seen Giorgi and had spoken of Agrippa to him; Nauert, *Agrippa*, p. 53.

18 Nauert, *Agrippa*, p. 56.

19 *Ibid.*, p. 73.

20 *Ibid.*, pp. 88 ff.

21 *Tiers Livre*, ch. XXV.

22 Nauert, *Agrippa*, p. 108.

23 *Ibid.* See also *Letters and Papers, Foreign and Domestic, Henry VIII*, V, 204–5.

24 Nauert, *Agrippa*, p. 110. Erasmus's letters to Agrippa are in the *Opus epistolarum Erasmi*, ed. P. S. Allen and H. W. Garrod, Oxford, 1906–11, X, 203, 209–11.

25 See Charles Zika's important article, 'Reuchlin and Erasmus: Humanism and the Occult Philosophy', *Journal of Religious History* (Sydney), IX (1977), pp. 223–46.

26 *De incertitudine et vanitate omnium scientiarum et artium*, 1526; many subsequent editions.

27 The *Asclepius*. Cf. *Bruno*, pp. 35 ff.

28 I Corinthians 2 : 2.

29 Apuleius, *The Golden Ass*, trans. W. Adlington. Cf. *Bruno*, pp. 173–4.

30 Erasmus, *Praise of Folly*, trans. T. Chaloner, Early English Text Society, 1965.

31 Philip Sidney, *A Defence of Poetry*, ed. J. A. Van Dorsten, Oxford, 1966, pp. 49–50.

32 The best modern edition is the facsimile of the 1533 edition edited by Nowotny, see above, note 11.

33 *Bruno*, pp. 130–43; Yates, *Theatre of the World*, London, 1969, pp. 23–4; Yates, *Shakespeare's Last Plays*, London, 1975, pp. 94–5.

34 Walker, *Spiritual and Demonic Magic*, pp. 36 ff.

35 See above, note 4.

VI THE OCCULT PHILOSOPHY AND MELANCHOLY:
DÜRER AND AGRIPPA

1 Erwin Panofsky, *Albrecht Dürer*, Princeton, 1945, I, pp. 242 ff.; Fritz Saxl, 'Dürer and the Reformation', in *Lectures*, London (Warburg Institute), 1957, I, p. 269.

2 Panofsky, *Dürer*, I, pp. 198 ff.; Saxl, *Lectures*, I, pp. 272 ff.

3 Quoted Saxl, *Lectures*, I, p. 273.

4 Raymond Klibansky, Erwin Panofsky, and Fritz Saxl, *Saturn and Melancholy*, London, 1964.

5 *Saturn and Melancholy*, pp. 286 ff.

6 *Ibid.*, pp. 15 ff. (English translation of the Pseudo-Aristotelian *Problemata physica*, in Aristotle, *Works translated into English*, ed. W. D. Ross, Oxford, 1930, vol. VII).

7 *Saturn and Melancholy*, pp. 255 ff.

8 *Ibid.*, pp. 351–2.

9 Quoted *ibid.*, pp. 355–7. A possible source for the idea of the 'degrees' of prophecy is Maimonides, *Guide of the Perplexed*, II, 45.

10 *Saturn and Melancholy*, p. 344.

11 *Ibid.*, pp. 352 ff.

12 Panofsky, *Dürer*, I, p. 168; *Saturn and Melancholy*, I, pp. 317–21.

13 In *Spiritual and Demonic Magic from Ficino to Campanella*, London (Warburg Institute), 1958. Though *Saturn and Melancholy* was not published until 1964, most of it had been written much earlier.

14 *Saturn and Melancholy*, p. 352.

15 Zika states that 'Reuchlin's influence is far more obvious and pronounced in the original 1510 manuscript version of Agrippa's work than it is in the printed edition published in 1555' (Zika, 'Reuchlin and the Magic Debate', *Journal of the Warburg and Courtauld Institutes*, XXXIX (1976), p. 138 note).

    Zika emphasises that Agrippa proclaims a Christian Magus, whose powers depend on Jesus Christ.

16 Natalis Comes, *Mythologiae*, Lib. IV. Cap. xxiv.

17 Thomas Walkington, *Opticke Glass of Humours*, 1607.

18 Panofsky, *Dürer*, p. 156.

19 *Ibid.*, p. 155.

20 The picture is reproduced in *Saturn and Melancholy*, together with two other pictures by Cranach on the same theme, and discussed on pp. 382–4. The discussion emphasises that Cranach is echoing Dürer's images but the full force of the comparison is not brought out owing to the failure to understand that the Dürer figure is in a trance of melancholy inspiration which is being compared to the evil trance of the witch.

VII REACTIONS AGAINST THE OCCULT PHILOSOPHY: THE WITCH CRAZE

1 See J. O'Malley, *Gilles de Viterbe on Church and Reform*, Leiden, 1968, p. 76.

2 On this see Cesare Vasoli, *Profezia e ragione*, Naples, 1974, pp. 224 ff; and above all A. Rotondo, 'La censura ecclesiastica a la cultura' in *Storia d'Italia*, V, *I documenti*, Turin, 1973, pp. 1436 ff.

3 Vasoli, *Profezia*, pp. 229–30.

4 Press Mark 7 b. 3.

5 See Yates, *Giordano Bruno and the Hermetic Tradition*, London, 1964, pp. 181–4; Rotondo, 'La censura ecclesiastica', pp. 1454–5.

6 Bruno had been encouraged by Patrizzi's initial success, which was soon reversed by the reaction. See *Bruno*, pp. 345–6.

7 M. A. Del Rio, *Disquisitionum magicarum libri sex* (1st ed., Louvain, 1599–1600), ed. of Cologne, 1679, pp. 164, 283, 339–40; cf. Charles G. Nauert, *Agrippa and the Crisis of Renaissance Thought*, Urbana, University of Illinois Press, 1965, p. 328, note 19.

8 Nauert, *Agrippa*, pp. 330–1. Del Rio had coupled Agrippa with the historical Faust. See below, p. 116.

9 Yates, *The French Academies of the Sixteenth Century*, London (Warburg Institute), 1947 (Kraus Reprint, 1967), pp. 43, 88, 91–2, 126, 132, 140, 288–9.

10 *Ibid.*, p. 88.

11 On La *Galliade*, see *French Academies*, pp. 43–4. On La Boderie's work for the Polyglot Bible, see B. Rekers, *Benito Arias Montano*, London (Warburg Institute), 1972, pp. 45, 47 ff.

12 See above, pp. 32–3.

13 See Pico della Mirandola, *De hominis dignitate: Heptaplus; De ente et uno*, ed. E. Garin, Florence, 1942, introduction by Garin, pp. 27–34.

14 'Monsieur Després'; see Wallace Kirsopp, *The Family of Love in France*, Sydney University Press, VI, 1964–5, p. 112.

15 On Postel and Cabala, see William J. Bouwsma, *The Career and Thought of Guillaume Postel*, Harvard, 1957.

16 The most recent study, which gives references to the literature, is that by Christopher Baxter, 'Jean Bodin's *De la démonomanie des sorciers*', in *The Damned Art, Essays in the Literature of Witchcraft*, ed. S. Anglo, London, 1977, pp. 76–105.

17 D. P. Walker, *Spiritual and Demonic Magic from Ficino to Campanella*, London (Warburg Institute), 1958, pp. 173–5. See also, Baxter, 'Jean Bodin', p. 89.

18 Bodin, *Démonomanie*, I, 3. For Pico on marrying earth and heaven and on the magical power of the Hymns of Orpheus compared to the magical power of the Psalms in Cabala, see *Bruno*, pp. 90, 104.

19 The attacks on Agrippa are mainly in *Démonomanie*, I, 3 and 5; II, 2. Bodin also attacks Reuchlin and Galatinus. In fact, his polemic is against Christian Cabalists whose wrong use of Cabala has infected the world with bad magic.

20 See H. Trevor-Roper, *Religion, the Reformation and Social Change*, London, 1967, pp. 146 ff.; Christopher Baxter, 'Johann Weyer's *De praestigiis daemonum*', in Anglo (ed.), *The Damned Art*, pp. 53–75. Baxter points out that Weyer, though lenient and liberal about witches, is still very severe against sorcery.

21 Nauert, *Agrippa*, pp. 59–61.

22 See *French Academies*, pp. 239 ff.; and my book *The Valois Tapestries*, 2nd ed., London, 1975, pp. 82 ff.

23 *French Academies*, pp. 261–2.

24 See the introduction by Kenneth Douglas McRae to Bodin's *The Six Bookes of a Commonweale* (English translation of his *République*), Harvard, 1962, pp. A10–A12.

25 Bruno used magic images and incantations which he found in the *De occulta philosophia*; see *Bruno*, pp. 196, 200 ff., 239 ff., 250 ff., 261 ff., etc.

26 *Bruno*, pp. 200–1.

27 Keith Thomas, *Religion and the Decline of Magic*, London, 1971, pp. 227 ff.

VIII JOHN DEE: CHRISTIAN CABALIST

1 On Dee, see my *Theatre of the World*, London, 1969; Peter French, *John Dee: The World of an Elizabethan Magus*, London, 1972.

2 On Dee's library, see *Theatre of the World*, pp. 8 ff.; French, *Dee*, pp. 40 ff.

3 John Dee, *The Mathematicall Praeface to the Elements of Geometry of Euclid of Megara* (1570), with an introduction by Allen G. Debus, New York, Science History Publications, 1975.

4 See *Theatre of the World*, pp. 20 ff.

5 Preface, sig. ciiii *recto*; see *Theatre of the World*, pp. 23–4, 191.

6 Yates, *Giordano Bruno and the Hermetic Traditions*, London, 1964, pp. 148–9; French, *Dee*, pp. 113 ff.

7 Charles Nauert, *Agrippa and the Crisis of Renaissance Thought*, Urbana, University of Illinois Press, 1965, pp. 24–5.

8 See C. H. Josten, 'A Translation of John Dee's "Monas Hieroglyphica"', *Ambix*, XII (1964), pp. 155–65.

9 *Ibid.*, pp. 127–55.

10 *Propaedeumata Aphoristica*, London, 1558.

11 Giorgi, *De harmonia mundi*, I, 3, i.

12 Written below Dee's *monas* symbol is a text from the Bible: *De rore caeli, et pinguedine terrae det tibi Deus*, (Genesis 27); 'God give thee of the dew of heaven, and of the fatness of the earth.' It is Isaac's blessing on Esau. This is a favourite text of Giorgi's which he quotes twice in the *De harmonia mundi*. In one of these passages the meaning assigned to dew is the usual one, that it refers to divine grace (*De harm. mun.*, II, 7, iv). In the other passage, the Hebrew word for dew is given and the meaning is said to be that dew is a symbol for the four-lettered Name of God, with references to Hebrew authorities (*De harm. mun.*, II, 7, xviii).

13 See Yates, *Astraea. The Imperial Theme in the Sixteenth Century*, London, 1975, p. 50.

14 See French, *Dee*, pl. 14.

15 The title-page of John Case's *Lapis philosphicus*, 1599, illustrates the pseudo-Aristotelian theory of the Saturnian inspired melancholy in an elaborate diagram which probably reflects some of Dee's ideas. The title-page is reproduced in S. K. Heninger, *Touches of Sweet Harmony*, San Marino, 1974, p. 218.

16 On the second period, see Yates, *The Rosicrucian Enlightenment*, London, 1972, pp. 37 ff.; R. J. W. Evans, *Rudolf II and his World*, Oxford, 1973, pp. 218–28.

17 *A True and Faithful Relation of what passed for many years between John Dee and . . and Some Spirits*, ed. Meric Casaubon, 1659.

18 Quoted by Evans, *Rudolf*, p. 224.

19 *Bruno, passim*. In Bruno's reforming movement, the Hermetic or 'Egyptian' element would seem to be dominant, but the Cabalist element is certainly there; see *Bruno*, ch. XIV, 'Giordano Bruno and the Cabala'. Bruno made constant use of Agrippa's *De occulta philosophia*, for magic images and incantations.

20 *Rudolf*, p. 275.

21 See *Rosicrucian Enlightenment*, pp. 45–7. There is a copy of the rare second Rosicrucian Manifesto, which contains the version of Dee's *Monas hieroglyphica*, in the British Library, catalogued as Philip a Gabella, *Secretioris philosophiae consideratio brevis*, Press Mark 1033. h. 6 (4). It should be consulted by all students of Dee's *Monas hieroglyphica*.

22 On Dee's third period, see Charlotte Fell Smith, *John Dee*, London, 1909, pp. 222 ff. The basic source for it is John Dee, *Diary for the years 1595–1601*, ed. John Bailey, 1880.

23 John Dee, *A Letter, Containing a . . . Discourse Apologeticall*, in *Autobiographical Tracts*, ed. James Crossley, Manchester, 1851, p. 72. The *Letter* was published in 1604. Dee says that he showed a draft of it to the Queen in 1592, and wrote it at Mortlake in 1595.

24 *Diary*, ed. Bailey, p. 23.

25 *Ibid.*, p. 45.

26 James VI and I, *Daemonologie*, Edinburgh, 1597; two London editions in 1603. See Stuart Clark, 'King James's *Daemonologie*', in *The Damned Art*, ed. S. Anglo, London, 1977, pp. 156–81. The book was one of the first defences of continental beliefs about witchcraft in English.

27 James VI and I, *Daemonologie*, p. 10.

28 John Dee, *To the King's Most excellent Majestie*, London, 1604. See French, *Dee*, p. 10.

IX SPENSER'S NEOPLATONISM AND THE OCCULT PHILOSOPHY: JOHN DEE AND *THE FAERIE QUEENE*

1 Alastair Fowler, *Spenser and the Numbers of Time*, London, 1964.
2 Angus Fletcher, *The Prophetic Moment: An Essay on Spenser*, Chicago and London, 1971, pp. 157, 275.
3 The 1580 edition of the *Letters* is printed at the end of Spenser's *Poetical Works*, Oxford University Press, 1912, and many subsequent editions, pp. 633 ff.
4 *Poetical Works*, Oxford ed., pp. 585 ff.
5 Particularly in Canticles II and III.
6 See above, p. 38.
7 Fowler, *Numbers of Time*, pp. 260 ff.
8 *Ibid.*, pp. 63 ff.
9 Spenser's plan for the poem is described in his Letter to Raleigh, printed with the first instalment of *The Faerie Queene* in 1590. It was not reprinted in the 1596 edition of the poem. The Letter to Raleigh has been endlessly discussed; see for example, Josephine Waters Bennett, *The Evolution of The Faerie Queene*, Chicago, 1942, pp. 24 ff.
10 A useful plan of planetary-angelic-Sephirotic schemes, set out as a memory system, is to be found in Giulio Camillo, *L'Idea del Theatro*, 1550; see Yates, *The Art of Memory*, London, 1966, pp. 129 ff., and the plan of the Theatre (facing p. 144). Camillo's *Theatre* was in Dee's library; see Yates, *Theatre of the World*, London, 1969, p. 11.

   The correlation of Sephiroth, angelic hierarchies, and planetary spheres is basic for the philosophy of Robert Fludd and can be seen set out in his diagrams. One of these, from a book published in 1626, is reproduced in my *Giordano Bruno, and the Hermetic Tradition*, London, 1964, pl. 7 (a).
11 The main material on virtues-planets-angels is to be found in the *De harmonia mundi*, I, 3 and 4. See above pp. 39–40.
12 *De harm. mun.*, I, 4, x.
13 *Ibid.*, I, 4, viii–ix.
14 *Ibid.*, I, 4, xiii.
15 *Ibid.*, I, 4, xii.
16 *Ibid.*, I, 4, iv–v.
17 *Ibid.*, 1, 4, xi.

18 *Ibid.*, I, 4, ii.

19 *Ibid.*, II, 7, xiii.

20 *Ibid.*, II, 7, xii.

21 Cf. Fowler, *Numbers of Time*, p. 52; Fowler notes that there was a tradition for numbering the virtues in Aristotle's *Ethics* as twelve.

22 *De harm. mun.*, I, 2, xiii.

23 Giorgi, when speaking of the *furor* which carries man beyond reason, refers to Aristotle in the *Problemata (De harm. mun.*, III, 4, iv). In many other passages where the *Problemata* is not explicitly mentioned, as here, it lies behind Giorgi's inclusion of Aristotle with the Neoplatonists.

24 *De harm. mun.*, I, 2, xiii.

25 Elizabethan Aristotelianism as a whole, awaits careful study. One of its most noted representatives, John Case (author of the *Sphaera civitatis*, 1588, on which see Yates, *Astraea. The Imperial Theme in the Sixteenth Century*, London, 1975, pp. 64–5 and pl. 9 (c)) is, I believe, a follower of the Pseudo-Aristotle of the *Problemata* who leads him in directions of a Pseudo-Aristotelian melancholy not incompatible with Dee's outlook. Since he was a protégé of the Earl of Leicester, Case and his work may well have been known to Spenser.

26 John Dee, *The Mathematical Preface* (1570), facsimile reprint, ed. Allen Debus, New York, Science History Publications, 1951, sig. a. i. *verso*. Cf. Aristotle, *Ethics*, Bk V, ch. 7.

27 See *Astraea*, pp. 69 ff.

28 *De harm. mun.*, III, 5, i–iii.

29 On Spenser and Dee's project for the reform of the calendar, see Spenser, *Works*, Variorum edition, II, pp. 243–4. It has been pointed out to me that a numerological interpretation of this poem, using Giorgi, has been worked out by Maren-Sofie Røstvig, 'The "Shepheardes Calendar" – A Structural Analysis', *Renaissance and Modern Studies*, XIII (1969), pp. 49–75.

30 *Bruno*, pp. 288–90, 392–4; *Astraea*, pp. 84–6, 108, 110, 119, 213–14.

31 *Bruno*, pp. 313–15; Yates, *The Rosicrucian Enlightenment*, London, 1972, pp. 16–17; R. J. W. Evans, *Rudolf II and his World*, Oxford, 1973, pp. 228–31.

32 *Bruno*, pp. 258 ff. Nauert confirms that Agrippa's works were probably the main source of Bruno's knowledge of Cabala (Charles G. Nauert, *Agrippa and the Crisis of Renaissance Thought*, Urbana, University of Illinois Press, 1965, p. 324).

33 *Bruno*, pp. 218 ff.; *Art of Memory*, pp. 314–19.

34 *Rosicrucian Enlightenment*, pp. 38–9, 46–7, 50–2, 58, 61, 65, 69, 83, etc.

35 *Ibid.*, pp. 32, 66–7.

X ELIZABETHAN ENGLAND AND THE JEWS

1 The study by R. J. Zwi Werblowsky, *Joseph Karo: Lawyer and Mystic*, Oxford, 1962, illuminates the Cabalist mysticism of a sixteenth-century authority on orthodox rabbinism. This aspect of Karo was formerly omitted or minimised.

2 Studied in G. Scholem's epoch-making, *Sabbatai Sevi: The Mystical Messiah*, Princeton, 1973.

3 The best study is that by Cecil Roth, *A History of the Marranos*, Philadelphia, revised edition of 1941, the main authority used in this chapter. But see also R. D. Barnett, *The Sephardic Heritage*, Jerusalem, 1971; J. B. Yerushalmi, *From Spanish Court to Italian Ghetto*, Columbia University Press, 1971; Raymond Renard, *Sepharad*, Mons, 1968; Leon Poliakov, *History of Anti-Semitism*, I, trans. R. Howard, London, 1974.

4 Moritz Brosch, 'The Height of the Ottoman Power', in *Cambridge Modern History*, Vol. III, 1934 ed., p. 105.

5 Roth, *Marranos*, pp. 203–4; and see also Roth, *History of the Jews in England*, Oxford, 1941, p. 141.

6 Roth, *Marranos*, pp. 222 ff.

7 See Lucien Wolf, 'Jews in Tudor England', in his *Essays in Jewish History*, 1934, pp. 73–90; and Roth, *Jews in England*.

8 Roth, *Jews in England*, p. 138, note I.

9 Cf. R. J. W. Evans, *Rudolf II and his World*, Oxford, 1973, p. 237.

10 Giorgi's work was criticised as too close to the ideas of marranos and Judaisers; see Cesare Vasoli, *Profezia e ragione*, Naples, 1974, p. 225.

11 Roth, *Jews in England*, p. 140.

12 *Ibid.*, pp. 143–4.

13 Roth, *Marranos*, pp. 239–40; Roth, *Jews in England*, p. 142. The legend is recorded by Daniel Levi De Barrios, *Casa de Jacob*, Amsterdam, *c.* 1683, pp. 5–6; see Roth, *Jews in England*, p. 279. For further information on Maria Nuñez and the whole episode, see Cecil Roth, *Life of Menasseh ben Israel*, New York, 1975, pp. 16 ff.

14 This is the date given in the De Barrios source, but a later date, 1597, has been suggested; see Roth, *Menasseh ben Israel*, p. 311.

15 Roth, *Marranos*, p. 240.

16 In his *Life of Menasseh ben Israel*. See further, below, pp. 214 ff.

XI THE REACTION: CHRISTOPHER MARLOWE ON CONJURORS, IMPERIALISTS, AND JEWS

1 John Bakeless, *Christopher Marlowe*, Cambridge, Mass., 1942, II, pp. 298–90.
2 See above, pp. 80–81, 84.
3 See Frank Baron, *Doctor Faustus: From History to Legend*, Munich, 1978.
4 See above, p. 76.
5 *Faustus*, I, i, 30–90.
6 *Ibid.*, 133–45. 'Shadows' probably means 'magic images', as in Bruno's *De umbris idearum*. See Yates, *Giordano Bruno and the Hermetic Tradition*, London, 1964, p. 197.
7 *Faustus*, I, i, 97–104.
8 *Ibid.*, 159.
9 *Faustus*, I, ii, 213–14.
10 *Faustus*, I, iii, 253–4.
11 *Faustus*, V, ii, 1939.
12 See above, p. 95.
13 Yates, *The Rosicrucian Enlightenment*, London, 1972, p. 244.
14 Bakeless, *Christopher Marlowe*, I, pp. 190 ff.
15 *Tamburlaine*, Part I, I, i, 13.
16 *Tamburlaine*, Part I, I, v, 50 ff.
17 *Tamburlaine*, Part I, V, i.
18 *Tamburlaine*, Part I, II, vii, 21–9.
19 See Yates, *Astraea. The Imperial Theme in the Sixteenth Century*, London, 1975, pp. 20 ff.
20 *Ibid.*, pp. 123–4.
21 One wonders whether the fact that the Elizabethan government had made treaties with the Turks enters into Marlowe's association of oriental cruelty with the idea of Empire. See J. B. Black, *Reign of Elizabeth*, Oxford, 1959, pp. 241 ff. on Elizabethan contacts with Turkey.
22 Bakeless, *Christopher Marlowe*, I, pp. 328 ff.
23 *Jews of Malta*, I, i, 38.
24 *Ibid.*, 121–8.
25 Bakeless, *Christopher Marlowe*, I, p. 365.
26 *Ibid.*, pp. 366 ff.
27 The three plays here considered do not, of course, constitute the whole of Marlowe's dramatic work. Considered as a trilogy, as here, and without discussion of other works which will need to be taken into account in a full new assessment, the three plays appear to be continuing on a

sophisticated level the type of propaganda against Leicester for employing Jews, sorcerers, poisoners, and so on, put out in *Leycesters Commonwealth*, 1584, attributed on not altogether certain grounds to Robert Parsons, the Jesuit. This propaganda was regarded as subversive of the queen's government (see Eleanor Rosenberg, *Leicester, Patron of Letters*, New York, 1955, pp. 289 ff.). Marlowe's continuation of it was also subversive. A close contemporary parallel is the propaganda of the Catholic League against Henri III in France (see above, p. 82).

XII SHAKESPEARE AND CHRISTIAN CABALA:
FRANCESCO GIORGI AND *THE MERCHANT OF VENICE*

1 Edition used, *The Merchant of Venice*, ed. John Russell Brown (Arden edition). On dating, see introduction to this edition, pp. xxi–xxvii.

2 *Ibid.*, pp. xxxviii–xxxi.

3 On the sources, *ibid.*, pp. xxvii–xxxii.

4 *Merchant of Venice*, IV, i, 180–96.

5 Arden Introduction, pp. l–lxxi, summarising the arguments of Nevill Coghill.

6 Daniel Banes, *The Provocative Merchant of Venice*, Malcolm House Publications, Silver Springs and Chicago, 1975. An *Addendum* was published by the same publisher, paged continuously with *The Provocative Merchant*, but with a separate title-page, dated 1976.

7 It is not necessary to suppose that Shakespeare knew Giorgi's work only through the French translation. He could have known of it as diffused in the Dee circle.

8 Banes, *The Provocative Merchant*, pp. 102–3, 106; *Addendum*, pp. 115–16. Banes notes the long discussion in Giorgi's *De harmonia mundi*, I, 7, xviii of dew and rain as signifying the mercies of God. Giorgi here quotes the text from Genesis, 27:28 on dew: *de rore caeli et pinguedine terrae det tibi Deas*. This text was used by Dee as the motto on his *Monas hieroglyphica*. See above, ch. VIII, note 12.

9 The name Jessica is probably derived from Iscah (more accurately translated as 'Yiskeh'), mentioned in Genesis, II:29, but it presents problems to Hebrew scholars; see J. L. Cardoso, *The Contemporary Jew in Elizabethan Drama*, Amsterdam, 1925, pp. 224–5.

10 *Merchant of Venice*, V, I, 58–65.

11 *Merchant of Venice*, III, 2, 114 ff.

12 Banes, *The Provocative Merchant*, p. 108.

13 V, I, 1–22.

XIII AGRIPPA AND ELIZABETHAN MELANCHOLY:
GEORGE CHAPMAN'S *SHADOW OF NIGHT*

1 George Chapman, *Poems*, ed. Phyllis Bartlett, New York-London, 1941, p. 19.
2 Robert Burton, *Anatomy of Melancholy*, ed. A. R. Shilleto, London, 1926–7, I, p. 451. Cf. Lawrence Babb, *The Elizabethan Malady: A Study of Melancholia in English Literature*, Michigan State College Press, 1951, p. 77.
3 See above, pp. 95–6.
4 *Hymnus in Noctem*, 8–15 (*Poems*, ed. Bartlett, p. 20).
5 *Ibid.*, 370–7 (*Poems*, ed. Bartlett, p. 28).
6 See above, pp. 62–6.
7 *Hymnus in Noctem*, 225–8 (*Poems*, ed. Bartlett, p. 25).
8 Raymond Klibansky, Erwin Panofsky and Fritz Saxl, *Saturn and Melancholy*, London, 1964, p. 381: the picture is reproduced on plate 14 of this book.
9 *Hymnus in Noctem*, 201–18 (*Poems*, ed. Bartlett, p. 24).
10 *Ibid.*, 249 (*Poems*, ed. Bartlett, p. 25).
11 *Hymnus in Noctem*, 255–68 (*Poems*, ed. Bartlett, p. 25).
12 The authors of *Saturn and Melancholy* (p. 381) interpret the figures in the sky as Luna and Mars, and between them a cherub.
13 *Ibid.*, pp. 351–65; see above, pp. 62–4.
14 Cf. Babb, *Elizabethan Malady*, pp. 73 ff.
15 See below, pp. 180–1.
16 *Hymnus in Noctem*, 395, 401 (*Poems*, ed. Bartlett, p. 28).
17 And as heauens Geniall parts were cut away
   By Saturnes hands, with a adamantine Harpey . . .
   So since that adamantine powre is giuen
   To thy chast hands, to cut of all desire
   Of fleshly sports, and quench to Cupids fire
       Hymnus in Cynthiam, 21–8 (*Poems*, ed. Bartlett, p. 31).
18 Natalis Comes, *Mythologia*, Lib. IV, cap. XXIV; cf. Roy Battenhouse, 'Chapman's *The Shadow of Night*: An Interpretation', *Studies in Mythology*, 1941, pp. 584 ff.; Douglas Bush, *Mythology and the Renaissance Tradition*, ed. New York, 1963, pp. 208 ff.
19 *Hymnus in Cynthiam*, 116–19 (*Poems*, ed. Bartlett, p. 33).
20 *Ibid.*, 187–9 (*Poems*, ed. Bartlett, p. 35); cf. Yates, *Astraea. The Imperial Theme in the Sixteenth Century*, London, 1975, p. 77. On the political allegory in the Hymns, see R. B. Waddington, *The Mind's Empire*, Baltimore, 1974, pp. 81 ff.

21 *Hymnus in Cynthiam*, 515–16 (*Poems*, ed. Bartlett, p. 142).

22 *Banquet of Sense*, 102 ff. (*Poems*, ed. Bartlett, pp. 78 ff.).

23 See below, pp. 210–11.

24 Chapman's completion of Marlowe's poem, *Hero and Leander*, has been seen as a reply to Marlowe's theme of the unchastity-before-marriage of the lovers. Chapman's continuation of the poem is an elaborately mythological defence of Chastity, with significant reference to chaste Ceremony – possibly a veiled defence of an Elizabethan reformed church.

25 Arthur Acheson, *Shakespeare and the Rival Poet*, London, 1903; Yates, *A Study of 'Love's Labour's Lost'*, Cambridge, 1936; M. C. Bradbrook, *The School of Night*, Cambridge, 1936.

26 In the well-known portrait of Raleigh in the National Portrait Gallery he appears in an elaborate black-and-white costume; his doublet is silver; his cloak is black, decorated with silver rays. The object of this black-and-white cult is the Moon, shown in the top left-hand corner. The combination of Saturnian chastity with Lunar chastity, expressed in *The Shadow of Night*, may well be a clue to the black-and-white liveries used by adorers of the Virgin Queen. Elizabeth's own colours were black and white.

27 P. M. Rattansi, 'Alchemy and Natural Magic in Raleigh's *History of the World*', *Ambix*, XIII (1966), pp. 122–38.

28 Walter Oakeshott, *Sir Walter Raleigh's Library*, London (The Bibliographical Society), 1968, pp. 300, 302.

29 R. J. W. Evans, *Rudolf II and his World*, Oxford, 1973, pp. 90 ff.

XIV SHAKESPEAREAN FAIRIES, WITCHES, MELANCHOLY:
KING LEAR AND THE DEMONS

1 *The Phoenix Nest*, London, 1593; ed. W. E. Rollins, Cambridge, Mass., 1931, 1969.

2 See above, p. 113.

3 See Yates, *Astraea. The Imperial Theme in the Sixteenth Century*, London, 1975, p. 97.

4 *Midsummer Night's Dream*, II, i.

5 *Astraea*, pp. 114–18.

6 *Ibid.*, pp. 112–14.

7 *Love's Labour's Lost*, IV, iii, 251–2.

8 The 'School of Night' theory was first put forward by Arthur Acheson, *Shakespeare and the Rival Poet*, London, 1903. See my *A Study of Love's*

Labour's Lost, Cambridge, 1936: M. C. Bradbrook, *The School of Night*, Cambridge, 1936.

9 *Love's Labour's Lost*, IV, iii, 226–54.

10 *Ibid.*, 339–42.

11 *Ibid.*, 361–2.

12 See Raymond Klibansky, Erwin Panofsky and Fritz Saxl, *Saturn and Melancholy*, London, 1964, pp. 16–18.

13 *As You Like It*, II, vii, 110.

14 *Ibid.*, 58–60.

15 *Hamlet*, I, iv, 40–1.

16 *Hamlet*, I, v, 40.

17 *Hamlet*, II, ii, 627–32.

18 See above, p. 91.

19 See above, p. 92.

20 In the *Daemonologie* (1597), James classes 'the Fayrie' as bad spirits (p. 57). Later he claims that witches see fairies. 'Sundry Witches have gone to death with the confession, that they have been transported with the Phairie to a hill, which opening they went in', and there saw a fairie Queene, who gave them a stone' (p. 74).

21 In 1596, James took offence at passages in Spenser's poem which he believed alluded unfavourably to his mother, and demanded of Elizabeth that Spenser should be tried and punished; see D. H. Wilson, *King James VI and I*, London, 1956 (paperback ed. 1966), p. 139.

22 *Macbeth*, I, vii, 22.

23 *Faerie Queene*, II, X, 27–32.

24 See Yates, *Shakespeare's Last Plays*, London, 1965, pp. 17 ff.

25 As he was later to do in *Cymbeline*; see *Shakespeare's Last Plays*, pp. 41 ff.

26 *King Lear*, II, iii; III, iv, 45 ff.; IV, i.

27 That Shakespeare made a detailed use of Harsnett's work has been proved by Kenneth Muir in his edition of *King Lear* (Arden edition, Introduction, pp. xvii, and Appendix 7, pp. 230–42). See also Kenneth Muir, *The Sources of Shakespeare's Plays*, London, 1977, pp. 202 ff.

Samuel Harsnett was an Anglican clergyman, at one time Archbishop of York. The Anglican church did not use the rite of exorcism, and it was one of the features of the Jesuit mission to England to emphasise this omission by multiplying cases of demonic possession, claiming that Jesuit priests had successfully exorcised the cases. Harsnett collected and published evidence of false exorcisms; see Keith Thomas, *Religion and the Decline of Magic*, London, 1971, pp. 438–90. Thomas relates Harsnett's book to contemporary controversy with the

Jesuits. Harsnett's exposure of Jesuit exorcisms was an important stage in the controversy. Thereafter it became common to print hostile accounts of Jesuit exorcisms on the continent; the Jesuit mission in England continued to claim successful exorcisms.

XV PROSPERO: THE SHAKESPEAREAN MAGUS

1 Yates, *Shakespeare's Last Plays; A New Approach*, London, 1975; another edition, *Majesty and Magic in Shakespeare's Last Plays: A New Approach to* Cymbeline, Henry VIII, *and* The Tempest, Boulder, 1978.

2 *Shakespeare's Last Plays*, pp. 116 ff.

3 *Ibid.*, pp. 22 ff.

4 *Ibid.*, pp. 32 ff.

5 *Ibid.*, pp. 93 ff.

6 *Ibid.*, p. 126, note 43.

7 Furio Jesi; see *Shakespeare's Last Plays*, pp. 113, 117–18.

8 *Ibid.*, pp. 113 ff.

9 See Yates, *Theatre of the World*, London, 1969, pp. 86–90; *Shakespeare's Last Plays*, pp. 121 ff.

10 Ben Jonson, *Timber or Discoveries, Works*, ed. C. H. Herford and Perg Simpson, Oxford, 1937, VIII, p. 587.

XVI CHRISTIAN CABALA AND ROSICRUCIANISM

1 See above, p. 36; and P. J. Amman, 'The Musical Theory and Philosophy of Robert Fludd', *Journal of the Warburg and Courtauld Institutes*, XXX (1967), pp. 198–227.

2 Yates, *The Rosicrucian Enlightenment*, London, 1972, *passim*.

3 *Ibid.*, pp. 206 ff.

4 See above, pp. 33–4.

5 *Rosicrucian Enlightenment*, pp. 30–1, 64–7.

6 *Ibid.*, pp. 30 ff.

7 See above, p. 42.

8 Yates, *Shakespeare's Last Plays*, London, 1975, pp. 17 ff.

9 The Rosicrucian manifestos were in circulation several years before the printed editions of 1614–15. A manuscript of the *Fama* was known in 1610 *(Rosicrucian Enlightenment*, p. 236).

10 On the Mersenne controversies, see Yates, *Giordano Bruno and the Hermetic Tradition*, London, 1964, pp. 432–40, 444–7.

11 Yates, 'The Hermetic Tradition in Renaissance Science', in *Art, Science,*

and History in the Renaissance, ed. Charles S. Singleton, Baltimore, 1967, pp. 255 ff.

12 *Rosicrucian Enlightenment*, pp. 103 ff.

13 *Ibid.*, pp. 118 ff.

14 Francis Bacon, *New Atlantis* (*Advancement of Learning and New Atlantis*), World's Classics, Oxford, 1906 (and many later reprints), pp. 283–4.

XVII THE OCCULT PHILOSOPHY AND PURITANISM: JOHN MILTON

1 See Yates, *Shakespeare's Last Plays*, London, 1975, *passim*.

2 See Christopher Hill, *Milton and the English Revolution*, London, 1977, ch. 22, 'The Millennium and the Chosen Nation'.

3 See Helen Darbishire, *Early Lives of Milton*, London, 1932, pp. 91, 285, etc.; Hill, *Milton*, pp. 59–61.

4 See R. J. Zwi Werblowsky, 'Milton and the *Conjectura Cabbalistica*', *Journal of the Warburg Courtauld Institutes*, XVIII (1955), pp. 104 ff. etc.; Hill, *Milton*, pp. 110 ff. etc.

5 Quoted in Yates, *Giordano Bruno and the Hermetic Tradition*, London, 1964, p. 439.

6 D. Saurat, *Milton: Man and Thinker*, London, 1944. See the discussion by Werblowsky, 'Milton', pp. 90 ff.

7 Werblowsky, 'Milton', p. 110.

8 Harold Fisch, *Jerusalem and Albion*, London, 1964, p. 125. But cf. Hill, 'Milton, pp. 279–80.

9 See above, pp. 159–61.

10 See above, pp. 64 ff.

11 Yates, *The Rosicrucian Enlightenment*, London, 1972, p. 185.

12 *Ibid.*, p. 186.

XVIII THE RETURN OF THE JEWS TO ENGLAND

1 See above, pp. 129–31.

2 This account, like my earlier references to the Amsterdam community (see above, pp. 111–13) is based on Cecil Roth, *A Life of Menasseh ben Israel*, New York, 1975 (reprint of the 1934 edition). See also Cecil Roth, *A History of the Marranos*, Philadelphia, 1941, and other works mentioned at ch. X, note 13 above.

For an easily accessible and still valuable account, see *The Legacy of Israel*, ed. Charles Singer, Oxford, 1927, pp. 365–6. Benedict Spinoza was a Sephardic Jew of Amsterdam, educated in the Jewish school of the city where Menasseh ben Israel was one of his teachers. Lives of Spinoza usually contain some reference to Menasseh.

3 Roth, *Marranos*, pp. 249–50. The extent to which Lurianic Cabala and the expectation of a Messiah was ingrained in the marrano outlook was revealed in 1665–6 when the Messianic frenzy aroused by Sabbatai Sevi was found to have as strong a hold on the highly educated Amsterdam community as it had on the communities of the Levant.

4 For example, Joanna Cartwright and her son Ebenezer. In 1649, Joanna and Ebenezer, described as English Puritans converted to Judaism and residing in Amsterdam, presented a petition to the English government urging the recall of the Jews to England. See Roth, *Marranos*, pp. 259–60.

5 Roth, *Menasseh*, p. 207. The text cited was Deuteronomy 28: 64: 'And the Lord shall scatter them among all peoples, from one end of the earth even unto the other.'

6 Menasseh's *Spes Israelis* was published at Amsterdam in 1650 with a dedication to the English government. In the same year an English translation was published, and a Spanish translation, dedicated to the Amsterdam community (Roth, *Marranos*, pp. 186 ff.).

7 See above, pp. 204–5.

8 See Charles Webster, *The Great Instauration*, London, 1975, ch. I–III.

9 As I have suggested in my review of Webster's book in the *New York Review of Books*, 27 May 1976, pp. 27–9.

10 See the remarkable book by G. Scholem, *Sabbatai Sevi: The Mystical Messiah*, Princeton, 1973.

11 For discussion of Sabbatai Sevi and English Puritanism, see Scholem, *Sabbatai Sevi*, pp. 101 ff., 107, 153 ff. Scholem is not in favour of Puritan influence on the Messiah. Yet the possible contacts were there in the presence of English Puritan merchants in Smyrna, and the curious similarities in atmosphere between Puritan millennarianism and the Jewish Messianism – both movements flourishing at about the same time – is surely strange and impressive.

12 See H. van de Waal, 'Rembrandt's Faust Etching, a Socinian Document, and the Iconography of the Inspired Scholar', *Oud-Holland*, 79 (1964), pp. 7–48. Rembrandt had close connections with Menasseh ben Israel and the Amsterdam Jews. (I am indebted to Dr David Goldstein for the quotation from the Eighteen Benedictions.)

INDEX

Routledge Classics
Get inside a great mind

The Rosicrucian Enlightenment
Frances Yates

'brilliant analysis of events, movements, relationships and consequences . . . compulsive reading.'
Asa Briggs

In a remarkable piece of detective work, the renowned historian Frances Yates reveals the truth behind the mysterious 'Fraternity of the Rose Cross', detailing the Rosicrucian impact on European political and cultural history. On the way, she utterly transforms our understanding of the origins of modern science, placing key figures such as Descartes, Bacon, Keppler and Newton firmly in the context of an occult tradition. This is a rare and startling work of scholarship that no reader can afford to ignore.

Pb: 0–415–26769–2

Medicine, Magic and Religion
W. H. R. Rivers

'The restraint, power and fineness of Rivers' mind make it impossible to be patient with critics who feel uncomfortable in the presence of his greatness.'
Robert Graves

Immortalized as the hero of Pat Barker's award-winning *Regeneration* trilogy, Rivers was the clinician who, in the First World War, cared for the poet Siegfried Sassoon and other infantry officers injured on the Western Front. He became a prominent member of the British intelligentsia of the time. *Medicine, Magic and Religion* is a prime example of his intellect, mixed with a very real interest in his fellow man. A social institution, it is one of Rivers' finest works, introducing the then revolutionary idea that indigenous practices are indeed rational, when viewed in terms of religious beliefs.

Pb: 0–415–25403–5

For these and other classic titles from Routledge, visit
www.routledgeclassics.com

Routledge Classics
Get inside a great mind

Totem and Taboo
Some Points of Agreement between the Mental Lives of Savages and Neurotics
Sigmund Freud

'With *Totem and Taboo* Freud invented evolutionary psychology.'
Oliver James

Widely acknowledged to be one of Freud's greatest cultural works, when *Totem and Taboo* was first published in 1913, it caused outrage. Thorough and thought-provoking, *Totem and Taboo* remains the fullest exploration of Freud's most famous themes. Family, society, religion are all put on the couch here. Freud's theories have influenced every facet of modern life, from film and literature to medicine and art.

Pb: 0–415–25387–X

A General Theory of Magic
Marcel Mauss

'It is enough to recall that Mauss' influence is not limited to ethnographers, none of whom could claim to have escaped it, but extends also to linguists, psychologists, historians of religion and or religion and orientalists.'
Claude Lévi-Strauss

As a study of magic in 'primitive' societies and its survival today in our thoughts and social actions, *A General Theory of Magic* represents what Claude Lévi-Strauss called the astonishing modernity of the mind of one of the century's greatest thinkers. At a period when art, magic and science appear to be crossing paths once again, *A General Theory of Magic* presents itself as a classic for our times.

Hb: 0–415–25550–3   Pb: 0–415–25396–9

For these and other classic titles from Routledge, visit
www.routledgeclassics.com

Routledge Classics
Get inside a great mind

Sex and Repression in Savage Society
Bronislaw Malinowski

'No writer of our times has done more than Bronislaw Malinowski to bring together in single comprehension the warm reality of human living and the cool abstractions of science.'
Robert Redfield

In *Sex and Repression in Savage Society* Malinowski, one of the founders of modern anthropology, applied his experiences on the Trobriand Islands to the study of sexuality, and the attendant issues of eroticism, obscenity, incest, oppression, power and parenthood. In so doing, he both utilised and challenged the psychoanalytical methods being popularised at the time in Europe by Freud and others. The result is a unique and brilliant book that, though revolutionary when first published, has since become a standard work on the psychology of sex.

Pb: 0—415—25554—6

Romantic Image
with a new epilogue by the author
Frank Kermode

'In this extremely important book of speculative and scholarly criticism Mr Kermode is setting out to redefine the notion of the Romantic tradition, especially in relation to English poetry and criticism ... a rich, packed, suggestive book.'
Times Literary Supplement

One of our most brilliant and accomplished critics, Frank Kermode here redefines our conception of the Romantic movement, questioning both society's harsh perception of the artist as well as poking fun at the artist's occasionally inflated self-image. Written with characteristic wit and style, this ingeniously argued and hugely enjoyable book is a classic of its kind.

Hb: 0—415—26186—4   Pb: 0—415—26817—2

For these and other classic titles from Routledge, visit
www.routledgeclassics.com

Routledge Classics
Get inside a great mind

Modern Man in Search of a Soul
Carl Gustav Jung

'He was more than a psychological or scientific phenomenon; he was to my mind one of the greatest religious phenomena the world has ever experienced.'
Laurens van der Post

Modern Man in Search of a Soul is the perfect introduction to the theories and concepts of one of the most original and influential religious thinkers of the twentieth century. Lively and insightful, it covers all his most significant themes, including man's need for a God and the mechanics of dream analysis. One of his most famous books, it perfectly captures the feelings of confusion that many sense today.

Hb: 0–415–25544–9   Pb: 0–415–25390–X

Science of Mythology
C. G. Jung and Carl Kerényi

'Jung was probably the most significant original thinker of the century.'
Kathleen Raine

This book investigates the authors' contention that an appreciation of mythology is crucial to an understanding of the human mind. It argues that ancient myths were built up from primordial images carried within our unconscious reflecting ancestral experiences common to us all. Myths surround us today as much as they did in classical times, making this the perfect guide for those who want to unearth their significance and gain an insight into their own predicament.

Hb: 0–415–26743–9   Pb: 0–415–26742–0

For these and other classic titles from Routledge, visit
www.routledgeclassics.com